Russian Religious Thought

Russian Religious Thought

Edited by
Judith Deutsch Kornblatt
and
Richard F. Gustafson

THE UNIVERSITY OF WISCONSIN PRESS

The University of Wisconsin Press
114 Murray Street
Madison, Wisconsin 53715

3 Henrietta Street
London WS2E 8LU, England

Library of Congress Cataloging-in-Publication Data
Russian religious thought / edited by Judith Deutsch Kornblatt
   and Richard F. Gustafson.
      276 p.   cm.
      This volume is based on, but not limited to, essays presented at a conference in 1993.
      Includes bibliographical references and index.
      ISBN 0-299-15130-1 (cloth: alk. paper).
      ISBN 0-299-15134-4 (pbk.: alk. paper).
         1. Christianity—Russia—History—Congresses.   2. Russkai͡a pravoslavnai͡a
   t͡serkov'—History—Congresses.   3. Orthodox Eastern Church—Russia—History—
   Congresses.   4. Religion—Philosophy—History—Congresses.   5. Russia—Church
   history—Congresses.   6. Russia—Civilization—Congresses.
      I. Kornblatt, Judith Deutsch.   II. Gustafson, Richard F.
      BR932.R87   1996
      274.7'08—dc20   96-15084

Dedicated to
Father John Meyendorff
in memoriam

Contents

Acknowledgments

We wish to thank the National Endowment for the Humanities, an independent federal agency, for their generous support of this book in the form of a grant for the Conference on Russian Religious Thought (Madison, 1993) out of which this project grew, and for editorial assistance in the preparation of the volume. We would also like to thank the Kemper K. Knapp Bequest Committee at the University of Wisconsin–Madison, as well as the Office of International Studies and Programs, the Center for Russia, East Europe, and Central Asia, and the Department of Slavic Languages and Literatures, all of which offered financial and logistical support.

This volume could not have been written without the input of all participants at the Conference on Russian Religious Thought, whose papers, commentary, and discussion greatly enriched the introduction and articles collected here. We would like to thank every one of the invited participants listed at the end of the introduction, as well as the registrants who contributed to the lively atmosphere of intellectual exchange. Of the latter, we would like to single out two for special thanks: Boris Jakim and Charles Ford. Their comments, corrections, and additions at the conference furthered the study of Russian religious thought.

Neither the conference nor the volume would have been possible without the contributions of two senior scholars who have devoted much of their careers to the study of Russian thought: Emeritus Professor Marc Raeff delivered the keynote speech at the conference, providing much material for the introduction; and Emeritus Professor James Scanlan delivered a paper on Fedorov (not represented here), read through and commented on the completed volume, and provided an afterword.

Peyton Engel assisted throughout, with preparation and oversight at the conference, in the background introductions to each section of the volume, and by providing general editing assistance. Neither the conference nor the book could have happened without him.

The outside readers of the manuscript helped enormously, through both their generous support of the project and their specific suggestions for improvement. Allen N. Fitchen, Director of the University of Wisconsin Press, the members of the Press board, Susan Tarcov, Raphael Kadushin, and all of the Press personnel deserve special mention for their professionalism, their enthusiasm, their respect, and their technical skill.

Judith would like to thank her earlier mentors in the study of Russian religious thought: the late Father John Meyendorff of St. Vladimir's Seminary, and two professors who have gone on to become colleagues, friends, and now collaborators, Richard Gustafson and Paul Valliere. George Kline has also extended valuable advice and support. For his acute editorial assistance, unlimited confidence, and hours of child care, Marc Kornblatt deserves exceptional thanks for this volume, as well as for Judith's career as a whole.

Richard would like to thank Jaroslav Pelikan, Sterling Professor of History and Religious Studies at Yale University, as teacher, scholar, and friend. In addition, he expresses special thanks to Judith Kornblatt, Paul Valliere, and George Kline for their continued support and friendship.

Russian Religious Thought

Introduction

Judith Deutsch Kornblatt and Richard F. Gustafson

Modern Russian religious thought took root in the days of Tolstoy and Dostoevsky, watered by the ideas and metaphors of the earlier Slavophiles, whose study of German idealism had turned them toward a recovery of their own ecclesiastic tradition. It flourished at the height of Russian Modernism, and came to fruition in the diaspora following the Russian Revolution. Today, in order to find direction in the confusion of post-Soviet society almost a hundred years after the death of Vladimir Soloviev, believers and nonbelievers in Russia are returning to the words of the pre-Revolutionary and emigré religious philosophers who once gave contemporary philosophical expression to the ideals of the culture of Russian Orthodoxy. As students of Russian culture, we, too, cannot ignore their legacy. Indeed, the great Russian novelists, artists, musicians, and historians whom we revere were acquainted with at least their central writings and often worked in response to their main ideas. Yet in the Soviet period these seminal thinkers were cast into the realm of "idealism" and, thus, of silence, many literally exiled from their native shores and deprived of the opportunity to publish in their homeland. Two generations of philosophers remained unreprinted and banished to library vaults.

Soviet scholarship, which for ideological reasons minimized the role of religion in the development of Russian society and culture, created a canon of heroes and thinkers, writers and ideas, that glorified the triumphant "radical materialists," ignoring the shared Russian Orthodox culture of the "radicals" and the "idealists." Western and especially American scholars of Russian culture in the central decades of this century, themselves under the influence of a liberal academic tradition skeptical of religion, ironically fell under the sway of the Soviet model on a number of points. The result is that, with the demise of the Soviet Union, the Russians have entered into a period of rapid reassessment of their religious roots with insufficient scholarship and materials to buttress their new faith, and Western scholars have been confronted with embarrassingly large gaps in their knowledge. This volume attempts to fill a few of those gaps by focusing on some of the main thinkers and ideas from that silenced realm of Russian culture.

The current retrieval of "Holy Rus' " and the "native" Russian philosophical tradition within Russia is sometimes driven by nationalist yearnings for an ahistoric "Russian Idea," as Russians now try to rediscover national values distorted over the past seventy years. This volume has a less political goal: to highlight the central concerns of this era within their historical, philosophical, and theological contexts. The contributors do not profess to proclaim a ruling "idea," but rather aim to analyze how, why, and in what terms the major representatives of modern Russian religious thought in the last part of the nineteenth and first part of the twentieth century grappled with, constructed, or posed anew basic questions of being and knowing.

A scholarly retrieval of Russian religious thought will prove valuable for more than a contextualized understanding of the Russians, whether of Dostoevsky's period or today. It will also expand our understanding of "Western" thought by including in it a tradition that plays with and against the philosophy and theology of the great Western thinkers who have formed our own worldview. Modern Russian religious thought is one of the few Western movements of *religious* philosophy since the secularization of thought that followed the Renaissance and Reformation. Furthermore, it is the only postmedieval movement of religious philosophy to give expression, mainly in the language of Western philosophy, to the specifically Eastern Christian worldview. In this body of writing we see in philosophical form doctrines of sin and salvation, of God and grace, of humanity, history, and culture, that arise from a Christian experience markedly different in its values and piety from both Roman Catholicism and Protestantism. Here we have Christianity as the Other. In this mirroring otherness, contemporary Western religious thinkers are finding new ways of viewing their own traditions and Western scholars can find new keys to unravel the alterity of Russian culture.

This volume contains essays on four seminal thinkers from the modern Russian tradition: Vladimir Soloviev, Pavel Florensky, Sergei Bulgakov, and Semën Frank. The NEH-sponsored conference that provided the initial impetus for the present collection (see below) also included papers on the iconoclastic thinker Nikolai Fedorov, who, like Soloviev, gave expression in the late nineteenth century to the views that inspired the work of the other three. As the volume took shape, however, we chose to focus on the other four since there is a coherence among their central ideas and since, despite the vital importance of the Eastern Orthodox ground from which they spoke, they tended to use an idiom familiar to Western ears. A number of major thinkers—Lev Shestov, Nikolai Berdiaev, Vasily Rozanov, among others—have also been excluded or, rather, reserved for later research either because they are already better known to the Western audience, or because their views do not flow as consistently from those of their nineteenth-century mentor, Soloviev. The field of Russian religious thought in America is in the making, and we leave room for much work in the future.

In their cultural attitudes and their styles of philosophy the four thinkers here included range from a decided Western orientation toward systematic philosophical thinking, as in Soloviev and Frank, to the more Russian-centered dogmatic theology of Bulgakov and the aestheticized Orthodoxy of Florensky. Despite their various approaches they all share the predominant dual focus of most Russian religious thought on the doctrines of Incarnation and Deification, and the attendant stress on moral and social issues, the philosophy of history, and the relation of religion and culture. It is the dual focus on Incarnation and Deification that is characteristic of Eastern Christian medieval thought, and which, especially in the ramifications that such a focus has on the theologies of human nature and salvation, provides the greatest contrast with Western Christianity. The work of these four thinkers represents the best of the modern Russian rereading of that medieval tradition, and it is around its themes that the essays of this volume cluster.

The volume is interdisciplinary; contributors include theologians, historians, scholars of philosophy, religion, and Russian literature. By examining the works of these seminal thinkers with the tools of a variety of disciplines, we hope to correct assessments of their thought that may have solidified over the decades when creative research was forbidden (in the Soviet Union), or largely ignored (in American scholarship). For readers whose exposure to Russian religious thought has been principally through the reinterpretation of symbolist poets and critics, many essays in this volume will indeed seem "revisionist," forcing us to rethink assumptions heretofore considered axiomatic. We will see that the symbolist reading of Soloviev is not the only available one; we may also discover symbolist tendencies in others we might not have noticed. We will be reminded of the importance of patristics for modern Russian thought, and we will learn a new vocabulary used to speak of the world and of God. Some of the essays included in this volume show how like the West is Russia; many others show how it is different. All contribute to the creation of a new interdisciplinary and contextualized study of Russian religious thought.

Background: Orthodoxy, Slavophiles, and the Russian Religious Renaissance

The logic of Russian history is decidedly different from that of the West. Russia entered the stream of Western experience, we could say, with the adoption of Christianity in 988 C.E. The Christianity Russia adopted, however, was not the Latin Christianity that was to become the dominant molding force of the modern Western world, but the Byzantine and Greek Christianity that shaped an empire destined to decline and fall. The intellectual and philosophical consequences of this choice cannot be overemphasized. The Byzantine tradition prided itself on its efforts to reach out to all in their native tongues, unlike the Latins who compelled their followers to master the language of the center. The early mission of Saints Cyril and Methodius to the Slavs brought the Good News already translated into Slavonic. The later Kievan culture that grew from Byzantine roots was thus doubly alienated from the Latin West, destined to encourage learning in the native Slavonic and based on Slavonic translations from the Byzantine Greek. Thus medieval Russian intellectual culture grew up in isolation from the whole Latin tradition and to a great extent from the classical Greek heritage as well. Aristotle, Augustine, and Aquinas remained unknown. And whereas in the West medieval Christian culture is marked by a flourishing of philosophy and theology in the various schools of scholasticism, medieval Russian culture developed its "theology in colors," not verbal treatises of an abstract order, but the liturgically centered tapestries painted on wood we call icons. For medieval Russia, philosophy and theology as we think of it were available through the translations of such Church Fathers as Saint Athanasius, Saint Basil, Saint Gregory of Nazianzus, and Maximus the Confessor, as well as the important Neoplatonic thinker Pseudo-Dionysius and the very popular ascetical and mystical writings of various lesser Fathers, which were the "how-to" books of their day. It is this translated tradition that modern Russian religious thought will revisit and revise.

In the West, the revision of medieval thought begins with what we call the Renaissance and the Reformation, the simultaneous rediscovery of the pre-Christian classical tradition and the reformulation of the Christian vision associated with the formation of Protestantism. The Eastern Christian world did not experience this intellectual revolution. Muscovite Russia knew virtually nothing of the heady secularizing speculation spawned by this turn of events. Western and modern influence was seen in the seventeenth-century reform of the liturgical books, the reaction to which caused a schism in the Russian Church and the creation of splinter groups of "Old Believers," determined to preserve the purity of their religious practice. But no significant body of philosophical or theological speculation on either side grew out of this schism. When at the beginning of the eighteenth century Peter the Great positioned Russia on a new, modern, secular, and Western course, the stage was set for an opening-up to the central concerns of modern Western thought, which to be sure had already been seeping into seventeenth-century Russia through the ecclesiastical academies founded under Jesuit influence. In Russia, therefore, the Enlightenment did not grow out of the Renaissance and Reformation, but invaded a foreign and medieval realm. This invasion was welcomed in the eighteenth century by some, but spurred a counterattack from others, and nineteenth-century Russian thought is characterized by a solidified opposition between the so-called Westernizers and Slavophiles. Modern Russian religious thought springs from the tradition of the Slavophile thinkers of the nineteenth century, not untouched, however, by "Western" ideas, for the Slavophiles would have had few critical or historical genres with which to enter the philosophical arena were it not for the German Idealists.

The Slavophiles were attempting to respond to the dilemma of Russian culture noted by Pëtr Chaadaev in his famous First Philosophical Letter published in 1836: "We have nothing that is ours on which to base our thinking. . . . We are, as it were, strangers to ourselves . . . , a culture based wholly on borrowing and imitation" (Edie 1:111–12). To remedy this crisis of imitation of the West, the Slavophile Ivan Kireevsky proposed in 1856 a "new principle in philosophy": "I believe that German philosophy, in combination with the development which it received in Schelling's last system, could serve us as the most convenient point of departure on our way from borrowed systems to an independent philosophy corresponding to the basic principles of ancient Russian culture," where he maintained there were "lofty examples of religious thought in the ancient Holy Fathers" (Edie 1:213). For Kireevsky and his fellow Slavophile thinkers the basic problem with

Western thought was its unbounded rationalism; they derived Hegelian panlogism from Aristotle, whose system, Kireevsky asserted, "broke the wholeness of man's intellectual self-consciousness and transferred the root of man's inner convictions from the moral and aesthetic sphere into the abstract consciousness of deliberative reason," thereby destroying "all motivations capable of elevating man above his personal interests" (Edie 1:185–87). In the Church Fathers, Kireevsky believed he found the foundations for an epistemology of "elevated reason" where man strives "to gather into one indivisible whole all his separate forces": "abstract logical capacity," "enraptured feeling," "aesthetic sense," and "love of the heart" are to be brought together, and man "should constantly seek in the depth of his soul that inner root of understanding where all the separate forces merge into one living and whole vision of the mind" (Edie 1:198–99). Kireevsky's response became paradigmatic for Russian religious thought: Western traditions of thought were simultaneously revered and rejected; issues stemming from the contemporary concerns of Western thought were reacted to usually in Western terms, but corrected by a Russian view associated in some way with the Orthodox tradition; the unexpressed intention is the urge to give verbal form to a "native," Russian, Orthodox worldview.

The tension between a Westernizing intellectual elite and a traditionalist popular culture grew out of the complexities of Russian culture stemming from the reforms of Peter the Great. Historical grounding was provided for all contributors to this volume by the words of Professor Marc Raeff, who reminded us that, whereas the usual view sees the Slavophile reaction and the later development of Russian religious thought as unique moments in Russian history, it would be more appropriate to see the eighteenth and nineteenth centuries as a time of expanding religious awareness of the elite and a growing convergence of the elite and popular cultures, especially in the second half of the nineteenth century. The eighteenth century saw the renewed interest in individual spiritual experience we associate with such figures as Novikov, Shvarts, and even Skovoroda. The century also witnessed Paissy Velichkovsky's highly successful attempt to renew the Hesychast strain in the Russian religious tradition, which resulted in the flowering of modern monasticism in the next century. The reign of Alexander I and especially the War of 1812 marked a "return to religion on the part of many who had become Voltairians in the 18th century," in Raeff's words. Clerical education was reformed, and the government and the Church both supported translations of Scripture and literature of piety. In the nineteenth century Metropolitan Filaret of Moscow "consciously tried to create as many ties to society as was possible," encouraging the clergy to become aware of Western scholarship and fostering a renewed interest in Church history and patristic studies. In 1863 he sponsored the foundation of the Society for the Lovers of Spiritual Enlightenment, whose publications joined those of the various dioceses and ecclesiastical academies, not to mention journals of the more popular press, such as *Christian Readings (Khristianskie chteniia)* and *The Orthodox Interlocutor (Pravoslavnyi sobesednik)*. This "interpenetration between the clerical and lay communities of scholarship" was accompanied by a growing interest in popular culture; the Imperial Geographic Society, founded in the reign of Nicholas I, "was one of the important agencies that carried out what we would call fieldwork studies of Old Believer communities and practices," and later the workshops at Abramtsevo and Talashkino trained several generations of Russian artists in the folk traditions. The preservation and renewal of the religious tradition among the Westernizing elite and the growing convergence of the elite and popular cultures reinforced each other and helped to prepare the ground for the development of modern Russian religious thought (Raeff, keynote speech). These interests coexisted, sometimes benignly, sometimes antagonistically, with the atheistic tradition of Vissarion Belinsky and the later radical critics, as well as with a general decline in ecclesiastic order and authority. At the expense of an understanding of a unique concentration of religious and secular thought, only the latter phenomena contributed to the standard Soviet picture of nineteenth-century Russian history and was extensively researched over the past seventy-five years. It is the former that this interdisciplinary, contextually based volume hopes to retrieve.

The beginning of the twentieth century witnessed the results of this long period of historical preparation. The turn of the century already knew well the work of Vladimir Soloviev, who died in 1900. Soloviev grounded his work on Kireevsky's "new principle in philosophy"; he would write "to justify the faith of our fathers" in the language of Western philosophy. It was Soloviev's volumes, together with important contributions of the older Slavophiles and the strange but compelling vision of Soloviev's older contemporary, Nikolai Fedorov, that inspired the younger generation of Russian thinkers and thus gave rise to the remarkable growth of religious thought in early-twentieth-century Russia. Many of that younger generation had first been influenced by the various strains of positivist thought that were popular in the later decades of the nineteenth century, and some began their careers as Marxist philosophers. The intellectual and practical limitations of positivism, especially when accompanied by a radical political action that seemed to threaten the very security of the country, led many of these thinkers to reconsider their positions. Philosophical societies with an interest in religion were formed, and groundbreaking meetings between members of the newly educated clergy and the more secular oriented intellectuals were arranged. This was the era of symbolism, when poets sang the praises of Soloviev's mystical Sophia, and various idealist and occult philosophies were in vogue (see Carlson; Rosenthal). In 1909 there appeared a remarkable volume, *Signposts (Vekhi)*, in which some of the most respected of the younger Western-oriented and Marxist philosophers announced their disenchantment with positivism and entertained some form of return to the "faith of our fathers." Among these were a philosopher who became well-known in the West, Nikolai Berdiaev, and two thinkers represented in this volume, Sergei Bulgakov and Semën Frank. Bulgakov eventually became a priest, as did Pavel Florensky who, as a poet, mathematician, physicist, linguist, and art historian with an especial interest in the icon most dramatically represents this heady moment of Russian culture known as the Silver Age. This period has also been called the "Russian religious renaissance" (see Zernov), and the period of theological liberalism in Russian Orthodoxy (see Valliere, this volume).

The Bolshevik Revolution and following civil war changed the intellectual, aesthetic, and theological climate, and, in 1922, some hundred scholars and philosophers were exiled from the Soviet Union. The work of the modern Orthodox revival had to be continued abroad; of those in this volume only Pavel Florensky remained, finally to be executed in 1937. The diaspora community founded universities, theological academies, and publishing houses, and many of the philosophers and theologians, Bulgakov and Frank among them, published their major works in exile. With the collapse of the Soviet Union in the so-called "period of reprint," this religious tradition has returned to Russia.

Modern Russian Religious Thought

Vladimir Soloviev, the first systematic Russian religious thinker, had a lifelong desire to reconcile what were seemingly opposed points of view: East and West, Orthodoxy and Roman Catholicism, religion and secular learning, theological speculation and philosophical analysis. All his work, we could say, is built on a desire to transcend the fundamental opposition of intuition and intellect, stemming from his three mystical visions of Sophia, God's idea of Creation known as His Divine Wisdom. Sophia was an image common in Russian iconography, as well as in a number of mystical, esoteric, or occult systems, and Soloviev attempted to embody it in a series of poems that later inspired the

Russian symbolists, and to use it as a foundational building block of his philosophical system known as Godmanhood (*bogochelovechestvo*; see below on terminology). His various theoretical works, which are all grounded in the related metaphysical idea of "total unity" (*vseedinstvo*) and epistemological orientation he called "integral knowledge" (*tsel'noe znanie*), demonstrate this reconciliation by their weaving together of religious, dogmatic, or patristic assumptions and philosophical demonstration in the manner of Hegel and Schelling, not without borrowings from the empiricists, the rationalists, and the Neoplatonists. Believing that the dogma of the Trinity is a revelation of the metaphysical structure of all reality, Soloviev constructs his philosophical and theological treatises around a series of triads which are meant to reflect that trinitarian structure and effect his reconciliations. Godmanhood (*bogochelovechestvo*) is made of God, man, and matter; humanity consists of spirit, mind, and soul (an important patristic triad); epistemology combines intuitivism, rationalism, and empiricism; the Divine embodies the ideals of Goodness, Truth, and Beauty. Much is enigmatic in Soloviev's personality and his writings, and this has led to varying estimates of his meaning and accomplishments. Indeed, the three other thinkers included in this volume responded to Soloviev, often using his terms, but each took something different from his mentor.

In order to demonstrate the richness of his thought, as well the foundation he built for twentieth-century Russian religious thought, the three chapters on Soloviev in this volume represent three quite different approaches to his writings, as they touch on three different areas of his work. Richard F. Gustafson traces one theological theme throughout Soloviev's oeuvre. Characteristic of his piece is the attempt to relate Soloviev to the canonical literature of the Eastern Christian tradition. Unaware of the unique foci of Eastern Orthodoxy, and often ungrounded in patristics, many scholars have unknowingly applied "Western" modes to Soloviev, not to speak of Tolstoy, Dostoevsky, and a legion of lesser-known Russian thinkers. In Soloviev, according to Gustafson, we see the process of rereading the medieval patristic tradition and the first surfacing of the central ideas of Incarnation and Deification. The Church Fathers saw these two ideas as mutually interconnected. As Beatrice de Bary, a specialist on the Eastern Christian tradition, reminds us,

in Orthodox doctrine there is a sense in which humanity's rootedness in God already exists "logically prior" to the individual's particular journey to deification. This gift of deification is already implied, at least according to the Eastern Fathers, in the gift of similitude which the Creator bestows on humanity at creation. According to these Eastern Fathers, the gift of createdness "in the image and after the likeness of God" is a necessary foundation of deification, just as it is a necessary foundation of the hypostatic union in Christ.

At the same time, de Bary argues,

the gift of deification is "given" to humanity through the miracle of the Incarnation. A certain ontological reformation or regeneration of *human nature* was *already* accomplished in Christ, since human nature was given back its essential character of being in the image of God, i.e. of being in communion with God. It is not sacramental life in the Church nor an individual's ascetical effort that determines the rootedness of human nature in God; it is Christ's hypostatic union that has determined and made that rootedness available to humanity. Deification, in this sense, has already been planted in human soil and makes it possible for the ascetic to take *free* advantage of that rootedness in God. (Conference proceedings)

Gustafson's chapter demonstrates how these two interrelated doctrines lie at the heart of Soloviev's doctrine of salvation, even as it shows the Russian philosopher's creative reworking of the medieval vision.

Maria Carlson confronts some of the major issues raised by Soloviev's concept of Sophia, a subject examined by two chapters on Bulgakov as well. It is most appropriate that she approaches this subject by exploring Soloviev's relationship to gnosticism, a system of thought in which Sophia plays a significant role; her treatment of the similarities and differences between Soloviev and the Valentinian gnosis is the most detailed one now available. There is no question that Soloviev was acquainted with and fascinated by these teachings. His nephew Sergei Soloviev, himself a minor symbolist poet, wrote extensively of this gnostic leaning in his biography of his uncle, and Carlson relies heavily on his assessment, as well as the recently published early manuscript entitled "Sophie." Indeed, this fascination with the poetic worldview of gnosticism was one of the major attractions Soloviev had for the symbolists, for whom the obscure and the occult were positive values. But since so much of our assessment of Soloviev has been shaped by the symbolist reception of him, the issue for us is how to assess critically Soloviev's relationship to gnostic teaching. We might recall the words of the Jesuit theologian Hans Urs von Balthasar, written in 1962:

[Soloviev] follows through the history of Western sophiology from Valentinus by way of the Kabbala to its baroque representatives—Boehme, Gichtel, Pordage, Rosenroth, Arnold—to Swedenborg and to Franz von Baader. But because in reading all these and many others he fully appropriates them for himself, the muddy stream runs through him as if through a purifying agent and is distilled in crystal-clear, disinfected waters, answering the needs of his own philosophical spirit, which (in contrast to that of so many of his speculative compatriots) can live and breathe only in an atmosphere of unqualified transparency and intelligibility. (3:291–92)

Carlson makes clear for us the basic elements of the ancient gnostic vision with which Soloviev acquainted himself, probably in an attempt to understand or find some context for his own visions of Sophia. It should be added that he also grounded his versions of Sophia in the more traditional Wisdom texts from the Book of Proverbs (esp. chaps. 8–9) and in the mystical tradition of Jewish Kabbalah. Soloviev failed, however, to make a dogmatically acceptable description of Sophia's relationship to the Trinity, a problem that he passed on to the other sophiologists in this volume, Bulgakov and Florensky.

Judith Deutsch Kornblatt confronts another central issue inherited from the symbolist reception of Soloviev. The period from the end of the nineteenth century right through the Revolution was marked by a sense of impending catastrophe, and the idea of the Apocalypse surfaced in the works of many writers and artists. Soloviev himself was not untouched by this sense of foreboding, and in some of his poems even alludes to visions of the devil. Certainly, the last years of his life were darker in spirit than those when he optimistically prophesied the Universal Church, and in the final months he had a sense of his imminent death. In the very last piece he wrote, he claimed that "the historical drama has been played out and there remains only the epilogue, which however, as with Ibsen, could last for five acts" (Solov'ev 10:225–26). All this led those who knew him to read his remarkable late work *Three Conversations*, with its embedded story of the Antichrist, as a public rejection of his earlier hopeful visions of salvation. Most major studies of Soloviev take this view as axiomatic. Yet a careful reading of all of Soloviev's work of the late period, including both philosophical works and his poetry, does not in fact reveal this pessimism. In 1898, for instance, in his study of Auguste Comte, he strongly reasserts his teaching about Sophia and the metaphysics that follows from it. His unfinished "Theoretical Philosophy," while in its present form somewhat ambiguous, can certainly be and has been read as a restatement of his general philosophical vision. In her article Kornblatt shows that the darker reading of Soloviev's "Short Story of the Antichrist" relies too heavily on surface content, and results from a failure to pay attention to the context and genre of the work. Soloviev was a master of different voices and loved mystification and humor, and Kornblatt demonstrates that with attention to these issues the "Short Story of the Antichrist" turns out to be another document demonstrating the consistency, if not always logical rationality, of Soloviev's conception of Godmanhood (*bogochelovechestvo*).

Father Pavel Florensky is the major theologian of the symbolist period. At the center of his work is the issue of reason raised by the Slavophiles, but unlike Soloviev he did not stress the role of intuition in the epistemological event. For Florensky, himself a mathematician and logician, the central flaw in Western logical procedures is that this logic is a logic of things, of isolated entities with no inherent inner connection. He wanted a logic adequate for the trinitarian conception of consubstantiality, where the three persons share one nature, a view he considered appropriate for all human knowledge and love. At the heart of his revision of logic he placed the idea of antinomy, the simultaneous affirmation of opposites, of A and non-A. All truth is antinomian, and all antinomian truths are but aspects of the one Truth. This law of knowledge is also the law of love, where the other (*drugoi*) is the friend (*drug*), and only in the presence of this other is my "I" affirmed in the world as "he." All others are friends, and all are affirmed in the presence of the one Other and Friend. (Florensky's communal dialogue has been fruitfully examined in light of similar grapplings by his philosophical contemporaries, Mikhail Bakhtin and Martin Buber.)

Florensky's worldview is further complicated by another metaphysical assumption with which he works: he replaces the Western understanding of a particular thing as an enclosed entity always equal unto itself with the patristic and especially Hesychast assumption that a particular thing is composed, as it were, of both an "essence" (*ousia*) and its outward moving "operations" or "energies" (*energeia*). The "energy" is understood to be both equal and not equal to the "essence," and all entities can interrelate and even interpenetrate through their "energies" even as their "essences" remain as it were intact. This understanding of particular things grounds Florensky's conception of total unity: "All things are interrelated. . . . The energy of things impinges upon other things, each lives in all and all in each" (Zenkovsky 2:878–79). These two major characteristics of his way of thinking are often consciously employed to argue particular points and always assumed.

The two chapters on Florensky in this volume reflect these basic metaphysical assumptions. Steven Cassedy demonstrates the complexity of Florensky's view of the material world. He rightly stresses the significance of the doctrine of the Incarnation and appropriately recalls Saint John of Damascus' words: "I honor [matter], not as God, but as something filled with divine energy and grace." The material world for Florensky, Cassedy argues, has a privileged status as a realm where transition, mediation, or revelation of the divine is possible. As Florensky said, "everything has a. . . . *dual existence* and another, metaempirical essence. . . . The doors of the beyond are flung open to the gaze of all"

(Zenkovsky 2:879). Cassedy focuses on objects and experiences that are "ontically transitional" between the two realms, most particularly on icons and words, the very two aspects of human creation to which Florensky devoted so much attention. The iconostasis, understood as a "sancturial barrier," stands as a most dramatic symbol of such an ontically transitional realm. In both icons and words, Cassedy finds the paradox of separation and contact that this ontic ambiguity entails, and he alludes to both the antinomian logic and the essence/energy metaphysics that mark Florenskys' way of thinking. It should be added, as Frank Poulin has done, that Florensky, a priest, always thought in terms of what is called "ecclesiality" (*tserkovnost'*): "the purpose of such ontically transitional objects is not only to allow men and women a form of limited contact with the divinity, but also to further ecclesiastical participation and wholeness [*sobornost'*]. It is this second point which may represent the most significant aspect of Florensky's world vision" (conference proceedings).

David Bethea also focuses on the notion of the "sanctuarial barrier," the "*limen* without which the philosopher cannot imagine his crossover zone." He notes that Florensky, as a symbolist theologian, understands the symbol as a "crossover zone between the phenomenal and noumenal," and he quotes Florensky's definition: "A metaphysical symbol is that essence whose energy bears within itself the energy of another, higher essence, and is dissolved in it; its joining with it and through it manifestly reveals that higher essence. A symbol is a window to another, not immediately given essence." In his chapter, Bethea argues that Florensky's way of antinomial and symbolist thinking is markedly different from Western modes of thought, which allow for some middle ground of "agreement" and compromise between the axiological extremes. He demonstrates this by analyzing Florensky's reading of Dante. Bethea's startling conclusion is that while Dante is "even in the early fourteenth century deeply humanist," Florensky turns out to be even in the twentieth century "rather anti- (or perhaps better, 'otherly'?) humanist," by which Bethea means that he rejects many of the assumptions of the Western Renaissance and hearkens back to a medieval Christian worldview, albeit an Eastern Christian one. This conclusion can be substantiated by the biases against renaissance art in favor of the icon Florensky reveals in his writings on icons. Bethea also claims that, unlike Dante, Florensky's "pious love never attached to, never *desired*, any one actual person," and that this too is revelatory of his antihumanist stance. Whether this judgment is correct or not we cannot say, but perhaps it is best again to recall that Florensky always speaks from the vantage point of ecclesiality. As Stephen Baehr commented, "instead of stressing Florensky's 'apparent absence of *love for the concrete other*,' a more useful comparison might be between Dante's and Florensky's theology, . . . since despite important differences both revolve around the central Christian idea that the ultimate path to God is through love" (conference proceedings).

Sergei Bulgakov is the most important Russian sophiologist; he used Soloviev's conception of Sophia to shape a whole system of dogmatic theology. Whereas for Soloviev Sophia was imagined in connection with the Logos and thus retained its traditional connection with Christ, Bulgakov in his mature dogmatic theology boldly relocated Sophia at the heart of the trinitarian Godhead. He argued that the three "persons" of the Divinity were defined in the creed by their modes of coming to be—unbegotten, born of, and proceeded from—but that the one "nature" remained unidentified or uncharacterized. It is this "nature" that he associates with Sophia, understood as both wisdom and glory: "God has, or possesses, or is characterized by Glory and Wisdom, which cannot be separated from him since they represent his dynamic self-revelation in creative action and also in his own life" (Bulgakov 53). Sophia, as the self-revelation to itself and *ad extra* to the world, is an "eternal reality in God" and also "provides the foundation for the existence of the world of creatures" (Bulgakov 109). Unlike Soloviev, Bulgakov explores the trinitarian character of Sophia, even though his later critics considered him somewhat heretical in this. Bulgakov also redirects the doctrine of creation *ex nihilo* and even asserts the "fundamentally divine character of the world," because Sophia "united God with the world as the one common principle, the divine ground of creaturely existence" (Bulgakov 109, 113). He insists that "it is of first importance for us to grasp both the unity and the 'otherness' in this unique relation of the creation to its Creator" (Bulgakov 113). Sophia thus has both a heavenly and a creaturely mode of existence, and Bulgakov imagines the world process as the story of the creaturely Sophia's approximation to the likeness of the divine Sophia. Thus his whole vision reworks the doctrine of deification.

Father Michael Meerson approaches sophiology when he suggestively explores Bulgakov's philosophical anthropology. Meerson traces the development of Bulgakov's thinking by showing its connections to the German idealist tradition, to the central issues of trinitarian theology, and to modern Russian religious thought, beginning with the Slavophiles and culminating for Bulgakov in Florensky. Philosophically and theologically oriented, Meerson's study reveals the subtle differences in the assumptions about both divine and human nature that exist in the Western and Eastern traditions of Christian thought.

Put most simply, it can be said that in the West each entity is assumed circumscribed, self-enclosed, and equal to itself, while in the East the entity is open to and in relation to what is other than itself. The philosopher Nikolai Lossky, who worked in the Leibnizian tradition of monadology, liked to insist that his monads were all open windows and doors. This conception of a being as "being for" Meerson rightly connects with Bakhtin's notion of "unfinalizability." That Bulgakov and Bakhtin are working within a tradition that has deep roots in the Eastern Christian world can be demonstrated by pointing not only to patristic parallels, but also to the work of their older compatriot Leo Tolstoy, whose metaphysical views, hidden in his diaries, included a definition of self as an "eternally growing soul:" and a conception of the God toward which it grows as "being for someone" (Gustafson 98). Personalism, although variously conceived, is at the heart of Russian religious thought.

Bernice Glatzer Rosenthal discusses the development of Bulgakov's concept of Sophia specifically, from the moment of his discovery of Soloviev's work in 1902 to the inception of his systematic studies of dogmatic theology written in exile. She places the significant moments in Bulgakov's thinking within their historical context, thereby illuminating the various shades of his meaning. Rosenthal stresses three aspects of Bulgakov's sophiology: his understanding of an Orthodox "economy" and eschatology, his interest in the sanctification of "the world," and the identification and exaltation of femininity in Sophia. These interrelated themes were inherited from Soloviev but given new focus by Bulgakov. Rosenthal shows how Bulgakov grounded the sanctification of the world in biblical theology, but her references to his tribute to Mother Earth, recalling the Russian folkoric Mother Moist Earth, should not be overlooked. Bulgakov often made more than verbal play of the phrases Mother of God (*Bogomater'*) and matter of God (*Bogomateriia*). As Rosenthal suggests, Bulgakov was by no means a feminist in the terms of the 1990s, but in his own context he condemned Picasso's dismembered female figures as blasphemy against the soul of the world and against all flesh. It is Sophia who connects earth and the eternal.

Paul Valliere confronts Bulgakov's sophiology from an entirely different angle. Like Rosenthal he, too, is interested in the historical context, but for Valliere the context is specifically theological. Valliere places sophiology directly in the tradition of Soloviev's Godmanhood (*bogochelovechestvo*), but he retranslates this phrase into what he believes is not only better English, but also a more accurate rendering of Soloviev's intention, the "humanity of God." Why, Valliere asks, did sophiology and the theology of the humanity of God surface precisely at this time in Russian history? His answer to this question gives him the hermeneutical key to Bulgakov's texts: sophiology is a reworking of Eastern Christian theological thought designed to deal with the reality of modern secularizing and Westernizing Russian culture. Sophiology thus was to fill the theological void left by the peculiar structure of Russian historical experience. Valliere gives special stress to the role of human creativity, or "economy," that Bulgakov's sophiological views bring into focus. Sophia is the "ground of the unity of the cultural process," without which human agents "would be incapable of undertaking creative work." Valliere's contribution is to show how this view of cosmic creation is both similar to and different from the traditional doctrine of deification.

Semën Frank has produced what the historian of Russian philosophy V. V. Zenkovsky calls the "most significant and profound system in the history of Russian philosophy" (Zenkovsky 2:871). He follows in the tradition of Soloviev's total unity (*vseedinstvo*) and Godmanhood (*bogochelovechestvo*), but nonetheless attempts in his philosophy to work free of theological assumptions, even while he hopes to produce a system in accord with basic dogmatic teachings. In this way he is even more difficult than the other thinkers examined in this volume, for, although he might seem most comprehensible in the terms of Western secularizing thought, his basic assumptions are often very different. Like the sophiologists, Frank stresses the "inner connection of the 'mystery' of man with the cosmos," although more than most he "lacks a clear distinction between the Absolute and the world" (Zenkovsky 2:872). Zenkovsky may well be correct in his claim that Frank's "originality is not in the metaphysics of total-unity," but in his epistemology, or, more accurately, in the epistemological "*foundation* which he developed for this metaphysics" (Zenkovsky 2:871).

Father Robert Slesinski treats directly this main theme of Frank's work, the relationship of the epistemological event to the doctrine of total unity (*vseedinstvo*, which he translates as "pan-unity"). Frank works from one central thesis: "the known content 'A' is delineated . . . on its dark background, but it is not detached from it. On the contrary, it is known precisely on this background, on this basis, as something inseparably belonging to it." This thesis implies a kind of *metalogical* unity between "A" and "non-A." Thus, Frank's work turns on an original formulation of Florensky's notion of antinomies. Indeed, Frank's whole mode of philosophy, Slesinski reminds us, results from an attitude toward the Russian dilemma regarding reason; for Frank philosophy is "the rational transcendence of the limitations of rational thought." Slesinski's chapter gives an exceptionally lucid summary of Frank's phenomenological analysis of the epistemological event, without sidestepping the complexities and contradictions it entails.

George Kline, who was one of the first and remains one of the few trained philosophers in America to undertake the study of Russian religious thought, explores the relationship of Frank's moral and social philosophy to Hegel, and provides an important balance with which to approach the end of this volume. Although not denying the important similarities between Frank and the other Russian philosophers of total unity (*vseedinstvo*) and what Kline translates as "organic religious togetherness" (*sobornost'*), he also sees the clear mark of Hegel in Frank's account of the "spiritual foundations of society" (the title of one of Frank's major works). Kline first establishes a link to Hegel through Frank's central terminology, and then goes on to examine issues of law, right, ethics, and civil society in both philosophers. Frank's turn toward Western philosophy is not a turn away from Orthodox and "Russian" modes of thought, Kline suggests, but rather an acknowledgment that Hegel is "no less firmly grounded in religious values and theological principles." This latter fact was obscured in Russia by the "radical" thinkers of the nineteenth century and the Russian Revolution, who distorted Hegel through Marx's dialectical materialism, and eventually banished "idealist" philosophy from Soviet Russia. As we recover the work of Soloviev, Florensky, Bulgakov, and Frank in the post-Soviet era, Kline's chapter reminds us that we must look for what is familiar as well as what is exotic in these thinkers.

Finally, Philip Swoboda confronts the question of Frank's relation to traditional Orthodox teaching head-on, leaving aside questions of the "orthodox" and/or "Orthodox" nature of modern Russian Orthodoxy in general. He sees Frank's work in its historical development and stresses the continuity of conceptions, even after there is a more obvious turn toward Christian ideas or at least vocabulary. The central paradox for Swoboda is that Frank imagines the human self as by "nature" rooted in the divine and yet called toward some sort of deification. He feels that Frank loses sight "of the fact that the term 'deification' (*theosis*, *theopoiesis*) is a verbal noun, and hence descriptive of a process, or, at the very least, of the result of a process, but not of an eternal *relationship*." For Swoboda, this insistence on relationship over process conflicts with the tenor of patristic thought, although it might be added that in the doctrine of creation in the image of and likeness to God, most Eastern Fathers considered that the divine image remained intact, perhaps a bit sullied after the Fall, and that deification was the process of bringing the likeness into accord with the clarified image. In much of Russian religious thought, what *is* is in the process of *becoming* what it is. And we should recall de Bary's observations on the interrelationship between the doctrines of Incarnation and Deification in patristic thought. Still, Swoboda demonstrates a significant shift of emphasis between the Fathers'

Deification and Frank's Godmanhood, and one which reminds us of the
tension between (rational) philosophy and ("mystical") theology that
runs, to differing degrees, throughout all the thinkers of the Russian religious renaissance. It is also an excellent piece on which to conclude this
interdisciplinary survey of Russian religious thought; it demonstrates
the broad angles from which to approach the works of the thinkers represented here. As Slesinski tells us, Frank's *The Object of Knowledge* is both
reminiscent of Soloviev's *Critique of Abstract Principles* and a forerunner
of sorts to Heidegger's *Being and Time*. Russian religious thought indeed
must be examined within a tradition of its own *and* as an important
expression of modern intellectual and spiritual thought as a whole.

Terminology

By way of conclusion, we must attend to problems of terminology and
translation. Modern Russian religious thought draws its vocabulary
from several different traditions, often translating and adding subtleties
to terms which, in the original, were already laden with ambiguity. Paul
and the New Testament, the Church Fathers, Kant, Hegel, and Schelling
all contribute terminology that the Russian thinkers then "make their
own." Further ambiguity arises when those terms are translated into
English, especially because Russian word formation is much more flexible than English, and allows the conjoining of nouns to form new
compound nouns and adjectives on the one hand, and the creation
of abstract nouns with the addition of a variety of suffixes on the
other. *Vseedinstvo* is a combination of "all" and an abstract form of
"one"; *bogochelovechestvo* is a compound formed from "God" or the
prefix for "divine," and "humanity" or "manhood," as it is usually
although awkwardly translated in this combination phrase; *tsel'nost'*
and the adjective *tsel'noe* derive from the root for "whole," but are
also related to a root for health, and even kiss. Perhaps most difficult
of all is the term *sobornost'*, created by the addition of an abstracting
suffix to the multivalent term for council, synod, cathedral, and as-
sembly or other gathering. Developed in the works of the Slavophiles,
and on through Soloviev to the twentieth century, *sobornost'* implies
a whole comprising interparticipatory, independent, but organically
interrelated parts. Sometimes translated by the phrase "multiplicity-
in-unity," the term is similar to general romantic notions of the relationship of unity in multeity (see Abrams 220), although the Russian
emphasis is somewhat different, for it retains its ecclesial root in a way
that Wordsworth, for example, would not accept. Equally confusing is
the multitude of available terms for being or essence (*sut'*, *sushchnost'*,

sushchestvo, sushchee, sushchestvovanie, bytie, bytnost', etc.), sometimes related to each other by their varying degrees of abstraction, sometimes contrasting with each other as Creator to created, sometimes direct synonyms, and sometimes not. And how should one translate *tserkovnost'* (Church-ness?), or *mnogoedinstvo* (multiple-unity?), or *dvuedinstvo* (dual-unity?), or *lichnost'* (person-ness—sometimes personality, sometimes individual)?

In this volume, we have accorded authors the flexibility to translate terms as they think best, adding explanations where necessary, and including the original in parentheses as often as possible to retain the complexity of the term often lost in translation. By juxtaposing several translations, we hope to begin a general reassessment of previous translations that many feel are inadequate, and to normalize the translation of other terms to be used repeatedly as the study of Russian religious thought grows in America.

Transliteration follows the Library of Congress system, with some modifications for Russian names in the text and explanatory notes.

Contributors

The impetus for this volume was an NEH-sponsored Conference on Russian Religious Thought, held at the University of Wisconsin in Madison on June 4–6, 1993. The essays here selected for inclusion (about two-thirds) all benefited from the scholarly interaction afforded by the conference setting, and from extensive communication between participants and with the editors following the meeting. We therefore consider as contributors to the final collection of essays all who participated in the initial conference: speakers, invited commentators, and also registrants, some of whom greatly enriched the discussions following each panel. All comments were recorded and transcribed in the proceedings, and many have been incorporated into this introduction and helped the revisions that the papers underwent after the conference. Below is a list of all invited participants, including their discipline and institution at the time of the conference (current affiliation in brackets):

Papers

David M. Bethea, Vilas Research Professor of Slavic Languages, University of Wisconsin–Madison. Paper on Florensky.

Maria Carlson, Associate Professor of Slavic Languages, University of Kansas. Paper on Soloviev.

Steven Cassedy, Professor of Slavic and Comparative Literature, University of California–San Diego. Paper on Florensky.

Richard F. Gustafson (conference co-organizer), Olin Professor of Russian, Barnard College, Columbia University. Paper on Soloviev.

George L. Kline, Nahm Professor of Philosophy, Emeritus, Bryn Mawr College. Paper on Frank.

Judith Deutsch Kornblatt (conference co-organizer), Associate Professor of Slavic Languages, University of Wisconsin–Madison. Paper on Soloviev.

Irene Masing-Delic, Professor of Slavic Languages, Ohio State University. Paper on Fedorov (read in absentia).

Father Michael A. Meerson, Rector of Christ the Savior Orthodox Church, NYC, Ph.D. in Theology, Fordham University. Paper on Bulgakov.

Marc Raeff (keynote speaker), Bakhmeteff Professor of Russian Studies, Emeritus, Columbia University. Speech on historical background to Russian religious renaissance.

Evgenii Borisovich Rashkovskii, Senior Research Fellow, Institute of World Economy and International Relations, Academy of Sciences of Russia; editor (with N. V. Kotrelev) of a major two-volume collection of Soloviev's works. Paper on Soloviev.

Bernice Glatzer Rosenthal, Professor of History, Fordham University. Paper on Bulgakov.

James P. Scanlan, Professor of Philosophy, Emeritus, Ohio State University. Paper on Fedorov.

Svetlana Semenova, Senior Research Associate, Gorky World Literature Institute, Academy of Sciences of Russia; editor of 1982 Moscow edition of Fedorov. Paper and commentary on Fedorov.

Father Robert Slesinski, Rector, Sts. Peter and Paul Byzantine Catholic Church, Bethlehem, Pennsylvania. Paper on Frank.

Philip J. Swoboda, Assistant Professor of History, Lafayette College. Paper on Frank.

Paul Valliere, McGregor Professor in the Humanities, Butler University. Paper on Bulgakov.

George Young, independent scholar, Ph.D. in Slavic Languages and Literature, Yale University. Paper on Fedorov.

Vladimir Zielinsky, Professor, Università Cattolica del Sacro Cuore, Brescia, Italy. Paper on Frank.

Discussants

Stephen Baehr, Professor of Russian, Virginia Polytechnic Institute and State University. Commentary on Florensky panel.

Beatrice De Bary, Ph.D. candidate in Religion, Columbia University. Commentary on Frank panel.

Caryl Emerson, A. Watson Armour III Professor of Slavic Languages and Literatures and of Comparative Literature, Princeton University. Commentary on Frank panel.

Peyton Engel, Ph.D. candidate in Slavic Languages and Literatures, University of Wisconsin–Madison. Commentary on Fedorov panel.

Hilary Fink, Ph.D. in Slavic Languages and Literatures, Columbia University [Assistant Professor of Russian, Yale University]. Commentary on Fedorov panel.

Gregory A. Gaut, Visiting Assistant Professor, Moorhead State University, Minnesota [Assistant Professor of History, St. Mary's University, Minnesota]. Commentary on Soloviev panel.

Margaret J. Gillespie, Ph.D. candidate, Harvard Divinity School. Commentary on Bulgakov panel.

Vladimir Golstein, Assistant Professor of Russian, Oberlin College [Assistant Professor of Russian, Yale University]. Commentary on Frank panel.

David Maclaren McDonald, Associate Professor of History, University of Wisconsin–Madison. Commentary on Bulgakov panel.

Alexandar Mihailovic, Assistant Professor of Russian, Hofstra University. Commentary on Bulgakov panel.

Francis Poulin, Ph.D. in Slavic Languages and Literatures, University of Wisconsin–Madison. Commentary on Florensky panel.

Leonard J. Stanton, Associate Professor of Russian, Louisiana State University. Commentary on Fedorov panel.

Theofanis G. Stavrou, Professor of History, University of Minnesota. Commentary on Soloviev panel; unable to attend because of illness.

I. Christina Weinberg, Ph.D. in Slavic Languages and Literatures, Columbia University. Commentary on Soloviev panel.

Works Cited

Abrams, M. H. *The Mirror and the Lamp: Romantic Theory and the Critical Tradition.* London, Oxford, New York: Oxford University Press, 1953.

Balthasar, Hans Urs von. *The Glory of the Lord: A Theological Aesthetics,* vol. 3: *Studies in Theological Lay Styles.* Edinburgh: T. & T. Clark, 1986. Trans. of German *Herrlichkeit,* 1962, 1969.

Bulgakov, Sergei. *The Wisdom of God: A Brief Summary of Sophiology.* London: Williams & Norgate; New York: Paisley Press, 1937.

Carlson, Maria. *"No Religion Higher Than Truth": A History of the Theosophical Movement in Russia, 1875–1922.* Princeton: Princeton University Press, 1993.

Conference proceedings. Conference on Russian Religious Thought, Madison, Wisconsin, June 4–6, 1993. Unpublished transcript.

Edie, J. M., J. P. Scanlan, Mary-Barbara Zeldin, eds., with the collaboration of George L. Kline. *Russian Philosophy*. 3 vols. Chicago: Quadrangle Books, 1965; Knoxville: University of Tennessee Press, 1965, 1976.

Gustafson, Richard F. *Leo Tolstoy, Resident and Stranger*. Princeton: Princeton University Press, 1986.

Raeff, Marc. Keynote speech, Conference on Russian Religious Thought, Madison, Wisconsin, June 5, 1993. Unpublished transcript.

Rosenthal, Bernice Glatzer, ed. *The Occult in Modern Russian and Soviet Culture*. Ithaca: Cornell University Press, forthcoming, 1997.

Solov'ev, Vladimir. *Sobranie sochinenii*. Ed. S. M. Solov'ev and E. L. Radlov. 2d. ed. 10 vols. St. Petersburg: Prosveshchenie, 1911–14. Reprinted with 2 additional volumes, Brussels: Zhizn' s Bogom, 1966–70.

Zenkovsky, V. V. [Zen'kovskii]. *A History of Russian Philosophy*. Trans. George L. Kline. 2 vols. London: Routledge & Kegan Paul, 1953.

Zernov, Nicolas. *The Russian Religious Renaissance of the Twentieth Century*. London: Darton, Longman & Todd, 1963.

SOLOVIEV

Background

Vladimir Sergeevich Soloviev (1853–1900) is the central figure in the Russian religious renaissance, and certainly one of the greatest Russian thinkers of all time. His interests ranged from systematic philosophy to literary criticism, poetry, and theology, and his work is an expression of mystical experience as much as of a desire to deal with religious faith in more rigorous philosophical terms.

Soloviev was born into a large, comfortable family, prominent on the Moscow cultural scene. His father, Sergei Mikhailovich Soloviev, was rector of Moscow University and author of the highly acclaimed *History of Russia from Ancient Times (Istoriia Rossii s drevneishikh vremen)*. Sergei Soloviev ensured an excellent secular education for his son, who nonetheless still felt a bond to religious ritual and doctrine through his paternal grandfather, Mikhail Vasil'evich, an Orthodox priest. Further ties to tradition were promoted by his mother, Poliksena Vladimirovna, a distant relative of the eighteenth-century Ukrainian religious thinker and poet Grigorii Skovoroda. At the age of nine, while attending a church service, Soloviev claims he had the first of three visions of the divine Sophia, and we can understand his subsequent life's work as an attempt to reconcile the mystical with the rational, the modern secular with the traditional and sacred.

After a brief period during which he declared himself an atheist and devoted himself to the sciences, Soloviev returned to religion and, upon his graduation in history and philology from Moscow University in 1873, spent a year at the Moscow Theological Academy. In 1874, he defended his master's thesis, *The Crisis of Western Philosophy. Against the Positivists (Krizis zapadnoi filosofii. Protiv pozitivistov)*, and began to teach at Moscow University. He went to England the following year in order to study occult and mystical teachings, and there, in the British Museum, Soloviev had his second vision of Sophia, wherein he was instructed to seek her further in Egypt. His third and final vision appeared in the desert outside Cairo. Although several early poems describe a mystical *tsaritsa*, he was not to write specifically about his own visions until 1898.

Soloviev returned to Moscow via Europe in 1876, but resigned his teaching position over political issues within the university, and moved to St. Petersburg in 1877, where he secured a new position. Over the next few years (1877–1880) Soloviev delivered perhaps his most famous series of lectures, entitled *Lectures on Godmanhood (Chteniia o bogochelovechestve)*, and in 1880 he defended his doctoral dissertation, *A Critique of Abstract Principles (Kritika otvlechennykh nachal)*. Also during these years, Soloviev intensified his friendship with the much older Dostoevsky, whom he had met even before he left for England. In a public lecture in 1881, after Alexander II's assassination, Soloviev implored Alexander III to spare his father's killers. This effectively put an end to his academic career. Although Soloviev withdrew from university life, he continued publishing, now more and more in the Russian liberal press and occasionally abroad when censorship precluded publication at home. He wrote repeatedly of the "Universal Church" and reconciliation of East and West, causing many of his conservative friends to accuse him of betrayal of Russian Orthodoxy in favor of Catholicism, although he indicted both Eastern and Western Christians for un-Christian behavior. In the 1890s, increasingly disillusioned with Western liberalism as well as with Russian nationalism, Soloviev turned his attention to aesthetics and ethics, publishing *The Justification of the Good (Opravdanie dobra*, 1897), and returned to theoretical philosophy. He continued to write and travel until his death, apparently from exhaustion; he visited Zagreb and Paris in 1887 and even returned to Egypt in 1899.

Soloviev's legacy is enormous: his work inspired a generation of sophiologists and was one of the major influences on the symbolist movement, and its rediscovery today is one of the leading factors in the post-Soviet revival of the tradition of Russian religious thought.

—Peyton Engel

Bibliography

Major Works

Krizis zapadnoi filosofii. Protiv pozitivistov, 1874.
Filosofskie nachala tsel'nogo znaniia, 1877.
Kritika otvlechennykh nachal, 1877–80.
Chteniia o bogochelovechestve, 1877–81.
Tri rechi v pamiat' Dostoevskogo, 1881–83.
Dukhovnye osnovy zhizni, 1882–84.
Natsional'nyi vopros v Rossii, I/II, 1883–88/1888–91.
Istoriia i budushchnost' teokratii, 1885–87.
La Russie et l'Église Universelle, 1889.
Smysl liubvi, 1892–94.
Opravdanie dobra, 1897 (revised and expanded 1899).
Teoreticheskaia filosofiia, 1897–99 (unfinished).
Tri razgovora, 1899–1900.

English Translations

The Antichrist. Trans. W. J. Barnes and H. H. Haynes. Edinburgh: Floris Books, 1982, 1990. *Tale of the Anti-Christ.* Edmonds, Wash.: Holmes Publishing Group, 1989.
The Crisis of Western Philosophy (Against the Positivists). Trans. and ed. Boris Jakim. Hudson, N.Y.: Lindisfarne Press, 1996.
Foundations of Theoretical Philosophy (excerpts). Trans. Vlada Tolley and James P. Scanlan. In *Russian Philosophy,* vol. 3: *Pre-Revolutionary Philosophy and Theology—Philosophers in Exile—Marxists and Communists,* ed. J. M. Edie, J. P. Scanlan, and Mary-Barbara Zeldin, with the collaboration of George L. Kline. Knoxville: University of Tennessee Press, 1965, 1976. 97–134.
God, Man and Church: The Spiritual Foundations of Life. Trans. Donald Attwater. London: J. Clarke, 1938.
The Justification of the Good; An Essay on Moral Philosophy. Trans. Nathalie A. Duddington. London: Constable, 1918.
Lectures on Divine Humanity. Trans. Peter Zouboff. Rev. trans. and ed. Boris Jakim. Hudson, N.Y.: Lindisfarne Press, 1995.
The Meaning of Love. Trans. Jane Marshall. Rev. trans. Thomas R. Beyer. Introd. Owen Barfield. Stockbridge, Mass.: 1985, 1992.
Plato. Trans. Richard Gill. London: S. Nott, 1935.
Russia and the Universal Church. Trans. Herbert Rees. London: G. Bles, 1948.
A Solovyov Anthology. Arranged by S. L. Frank. Trans. Nathalie A. Duddington. New York: Scribner, 1950.
War, Progress, and the End of History. Trans. A. Bakshy. Ed. and rev. trans. Thomas R. Beyer. Introd. Czesław Miłosz. Hudson, N.Y.: Lindisfarne Press, 1990.

Secondary Sources in English, Selected

Allen, Paul M. *Vladimir Soloviev: Russian Mystic*. Blauvelt, N.Y.: Steinerbooks, 1978.

Cioran, Samuel D. *Vladimir Solov'ev and the Knighthood of the Divine Sophia*. Waterloo, Ontario: Wilfrid Laurier University Press, 1977.

Groberg, Kristi A. "The Eternal Feminine: Vladimir Solov'ev's Vision of Sophia." *Alexandria* 1 (1991): 76–95.

Kornblatt, Judith Deutsch. "Solov'ev's Androgynous Sophia and the Jewish Kabbalah." *Slavic Review* 50, no. 3 (1991): 487–96.

Lopatin, L. M. "The Philosophy of V. Soloviev." Trans. A. Bakshy. *Mind* 25 (1916): 425–60.

Lossky, N. O. "The Philosophy of Vl. Solovyev." Trans. Natalie Duddington. *Slavonic Review* 2 (1923): 346–58.

Lossky, N. O. "Vladimir S. Solovyev." *History of Russian Philosophy*. New York: International Universitites Press, 1951. 81–133.

Munzer, Egbert. *Solov'ev: Prophet of Russian-Western Unity*. London: Hollis and Carter, 1956.

Stremooukhoff, D. *Vladimir Soloviev and His Messianic Work*. Ed. Philip Guilbeau and Heather Elise MacGregor. Trans. from the French by Elizabeth Meyendorff. Belmont, Mass.: Nordland, 1980.

Sutton, Jonathan. *The Religious Philosophy of Vladimir Solovyov: Towards a Reassessment*. New York: St. Martin's Press, 1988.

Zenkovsky, V. V. *A History of Russian Philosophy*. Trans. George L. Kline. 2 vols. London: Routledge & Kegan Paul, 1953. 2:469–531.

Zernov, Nicolas. *Three Russian Prophets: Khomiakov, Dostoevsky, Soloviev*. London: SCM Press, 1944.

Zernov, Nicolas. *The Russian Religious Renaissance of the Twentieth Century*. London: Darton, Longman & Todd, 1963. 290–93.

1

Soloviev's Doctrine of Salvation

Richard F. Gustafson

Vladimir Soloviev's religious thought is an elaboration of what he called in philosophical language "total unity" (*vseedinstvo*) and in theological language "Godmanhood" (*bogochelovechestvo*). He understood our life as fallen from these metaphysical ideals and our salvific task in life to reinstate them. In his writings, while often borrowing procedures from the Western philosophical tradition, he cast this basically religious worldview into an Eastern Christian mold, which thus shaped his understanding of the process, purpose, and meaning of salvation. In what follows I should like to place Soloviev's doctrine in its Western and Eastern theological contexts and to explore the moral, social, ecclesiological, and Christological implications of his understanding of salvation.

For Soloviev, Christianity is primarily a religion of salvation. The salvation he imagined always entailed in some form the overcoming of separation. "If Christianity is the religion of salvation," he stated explicitly in the third Dostoevsky speech, "if the Christian idea consists in recovery, in the internal unification of those principles whose separation is ruin, then the essence of the true Christian task is what in logical language is called *synthesis*, and in moral language, *reconciliation*" (1883, 3:214).[1] The first task the young student set for himself, not surprisingly then, was the overcoming of philosophical separatism. He undertook his heroic study of world religions and mythologies, Western philosophy, Greek and Latin patristics, and occult systems of various sorts in order to unite them; separate, they were one-sided and hence untrue, but together, if reconciled in an appropriate way, they could provide an adequate form for the contemporary expression of the "faith of our fathers" which he thought of as "the universal religion" (*"La Sophia,"* 1976, 3). The young idealistic scholar understood this universal religion as "not just the positive synthesis of all religions, but also as the synthesis of religion, philosophy, and science, and then after that of the spiritual or interior sphere with the exterior sphere, with political and social life" (*"La Sophia"* 5). In becoming universal, he believed, religion would cease to be an exclusive phenomenon, isolated from other spheres of human life, by including them in itself and thus becoming "more than religion."

The methodology of this all-encompassing universal religion reflects what will become Soloviev's basic procedure. He reworks the Hegelian "negative" dialectic into a "positive synthesis" of three unfolding realms, here science, philosophy, religion; elsewhere empiricism, idealism, mysticism (intuitivism), or body (soul/sensation), mind, will (spirit), or matter, man, God. These three realms are then also imagined hierarchically, with the lower realms subordinated to the higher ones on the basic assumption that "unification presupposes subordination" (1882–84, 3:404). This proper hierarchical ordering of any reality is what Soloviev means by "positive synthesis." It is this hierarchical ordering that constitutes the structure of salvation.

This structure of salvation, however, characterizes the world not only as it ought to be, but also as it truly is. In the *Lectures on Godmanhood* (*Chteniia o bogochelovechestve*, 1877) Soloviev details his description of absolute reality as a trinity in positive synthesis with a peculiar combination of Christian, gnostic, Hegelian, Schellingian, and Neoplatonic terms. However, he also pictures his trinitarian Absolute as the source from which our world, the world as it "ought not to be," originates. From the second hypostasis, the Father's self-expression called Christ, which is made from the union of Logos (the Father's energy) and Sophia (the world soul), Sophia emerges in search of her self, using her freedom to break the union and start out on her own. Creation, thus understood as an exercise of freedom, is the first separation. And Christ, understood as the original union of the Logos and Sophia, is what we might call the idea of Creation.

This idea of Creation is imagined as a harmonious realm, a unity of all particular things Soloviev calls "entities." He associates these entities with the notions of atom, idea, and monad, and he understands them as dynamic bundles of energy, unlike Leibniz's monads, reaching out and opening up to others in what we might call kenotic acts wherein they "make room for" (*davat' v sebe mesto*) each other and exist in a state of "mutual interaction" and "mutual penetration." The material world, which has its beginning with Sophia's separation from Logos, is arranged according to this idea of Creation but as its opposite, characterized by "impenetrability" and composed of a "chaos of disparate elements." With such a conception of Creation, salvation inevitably takes its ancient Christian form of restoration. Soloviev marks his early adherence to this idea by his repeated reference in the original Greek to Origen's famous version of it: "the restoration of all things" (*he apokatastasis ton panton*).

Origen, the first systematic Christian theologian and coiner of the term "Godman" (Quasten 2:80), created the first metaphysical theory of Creation and Redemption in the Christian tradition, a theory that served as a model for Soloviev in the *Lectures on Godmanhood*. Origen, whom Soloviev characterized as "one of the most original and richly endowed minds in all the literature of the Church" (*Pis'ma* 4:300), imagined that in the beginning God created all "rational beings" (*logikoi*) to live freely in harmony with Him. With time this harmony lost its appeal, and some of these rational beings exercised their freedom by rebellion. God cast these rebellious beings away from him, and the extent of their rebellion determined their new status: the least rebellious became angels, the most, demons, and those in between, souls. For these in-between beings God created the world of time, space, and matter and put the souls into bodies to live in it. The sufferings encountered in this world of matter are taken to be of pedagogic value, teaching the souls their way back to their original harmonious state where God will be all in all. Soloviev shares with Origen the belief in the preexistence of souls, the notion of a cosmic fall that precedes the Fall of Adam and Eve and accounts for the existence of the material world, and the conception of salvation as universal restoration of all things.

What Soloviev does, however, is to restate Origen's theory of Creation and Redemption in modified Neoplatonic terms he borrows from Schelling, who himself shares the "preoccupations and problems . . . of Neo-Platonic Christianity in Patristic writings" (Schelling lii). For Schelling, as for Soloviev, "the positive is always the whole or unity and that which is contrasted with it is division of the whole, discord. . . . The identical elements which existed in the unified whole are in the divided whole; the matter in both is the same . . . but the formal aspect of the two is totally different" (Schelling 46). For Schelling, as for Soloviev, salvation entails a restoration of unity, which he imagines as a dispelling of darkness by the light of reason. Soloviev rewrites Schelling's story of cosmic salvation in Christian terms and thereby restores the patristic tradition of the cosmic Christ.

Scripture says that Christ is "before all things, and in Him all things hold together" (Col. 1 :17). To the Greek Fathers of the fourth century this Christ was understood as the *Logos*, the reason, order, and meaning that come from God into the world. For Basil the Great, "He welded all the diverse parts of the cosmos by links of indissoluble attachment and established between them so perfect a fellowship and harmony that the most distant, in spite of their distance, appeared united in one universal sympathy" (Pelikan, *Jesus* 65). For Saint Athanasius the Great: "to keep the universe from disintegrating back into nonbeing, God made all things by the eternal Logos of God itself and endowed the creation with being. . . . God guides [the universe] by the Logos, so that by the direction, providence, and ordering of the Logos, the creation may be illumined and enabled to abide always securely" (Pelikan, *Jesus* 66).

Soloviev cast this conception of the ordering, salvific Logos into a modern scientific framework and into geological time: the "Logos *ad extra*," understood as an active force of unity, is "provoked by the negative action of disparate being to positive opposition, to the manifestation of its unifying force." This results in successive stages of unity, from gravity, to chemical composition, organic forms, and ultimately to the "perfect organism," the human being (1877, 3:145–48). In the world process the Logos *ad extra* "strives to be realized or incarnated in the chaos of disparate elements." Thus for Soloviev the history of Creation is at once a process of Incarnation and Salvation.

This direct association of Salvation with Incarnation and the disassociation of Salvation from the Fall of Man remove Soloviev's doctrine from the central concerns of most modern Western theories of redemption. In the beginning of the Christian era salvation had been imagined most often as Christ's victory over sin, death, and the devil. This work was accomplished by the whole of Christ's life, from the Incarnation to the Passion, Death, and Resurrection. Christ's work thus conceived effected both deliverance from sin, death, and the devil, and reconciliation between God and the world (Aulen 36–80). For some this victory was understood to be coupled with a redemption in the form of some ransom paid to the devil. This conception of salvation by Christ the Victor was common throughout the whole of early Christendom.

The dominant Western tradition was shaped in the early Middle Ages, especially by Saint Anselm and his highly influential *Cur Deus Homo?* Anselm changed the focus from Christ as Victor to Christ as Victim. Now the issues were cast within the traditional Latin concern (since Tertullian) for satisfaction, merit, and punishment and in the traditional Roman imagery of the law court and the bank. Salvation came to be understood as the Sacrifice of Christ, which was interpreted as man's satisfaction to God in the form of a just punishment and payment for sin.

Redemption was now paid to God, not the devil (Grensted 88–145). The central salvific event, formerly understood as Christ's whole life, death, and resurrection, now narrows to the Passion and Crucifixion. The work of salvation likewise changes its direction: the movement of the loving God toward man becomes man's movement toward the just God. Salvation becomes "objective" atonement, the change in God's attitude that results from the appeasement of His wrath. With Abelard this objective view of the atonement is redirected toward man whose "subjective" change of heart, inspired by the example of Christ, is now considered meritorious (Aulen 95–97).

The story of this doctrine in the West from the Middle Ages up into the nineteenth century revolves around these latter two conflicting views, the objective and subjective readings of atonement. Luther turned the discussion decidedly in the subjective direction with his focus on justification, and salvation became centered on righteousness, either "infused" or "imputed" (Pelikan, *Christian Tradition* 4:138–55). With Schleiermacher the modern stress on the psychological emerges in his characteristic assumption that salvation in the sense of a personal change in spiritual life must precede atonement in the sense of a reconciliation with God. This moved the doctrine of Salvation away from the Christ as Victim theory, which taught the opposite, and away from the Christ as Victor theory, which did not separate the notion of salvation and atonement (Aulen 136). Soloviev's doctrine of Salvation sidesteps this dominant Western tradition and reworks the early Christ as Victor theory in the light of the Eastern Christian Logos-Incarnation theology, which, as we shall see, he understands in both the Alexandrian tradition of logos-flesh and the Antiochian tradition of logos-man (Grillmeier 167–439).

Soloviev dismisses the Western tradition. "The Latin theologians of the Middle Ages," he asserts, "introduced into Christianity the juridical character of ancient Rome," when they created their "well-known legal theory of redemption as satisfaction through paying a fine for a divine law that has been broken" (3:163). This theory, which Soloviev understands was introduced mainly through Anselm and spread by Protestant theology, is rejected, even though he believes it is not without some "true meaning." In fact he later details his understanding of this true meaning, by focusing on the process of subjective atonement, which he calls "redemption." He casts this redemption, however, not into the mold of legal theory, but into the ancient Neoplatonic triad of purification, illumination/ascension, and perfection/union. And like Schleiermacher he understands this subjective atonement as the "passive" and preparatory work before the "active feat of salvation" (1885–87, 4:590, also 458–60, 583–84).

Soloviev rejects the Western legal theory of objective redemption, because he believes it has obscured the true meaning of the doctrine by assuming "crude and unworthy conceptions of the Divinity and its relationship to the world and man" (3:164). These crude conceptions, which Soloviev believes make any genuine incarnation and salvation impossible, are deism and pantheism. With deism, God is incorrectly imagined as a being separate from the world and man, and with pantheism, God is incorrectly imagined as the universal substance of the world. In their place Soloviev offers his doctrine of God as "transcendental *in himself* . . . but in *relation* to the world *manifesting himself* [*iavliaetsia*] as an active creative force" (3:165). In a fashion characteristic of his Logos-Incarnation theology, Soloviev insists that "it is not the transcendental God that is incarnated in Jesus . . . , but God the Logos." Furthermore, the "*personal* incarnation [of the Logos] in an individual man is but the last in a long series of other incarnations, physical and historical," so that the "appearance of God in human flesh is but a fuller, more perfect theophany in a series of other incomplete, preparatory, and transformative theophanies." Thus in Soloviev's cosmic vision "all nature is drawn and strives toward man, while the whole history of humankind is directed toward the Godman." In response to the dominant Western tradition, Soloviev can insist that "Christ's work is not a juridical fiction" or the outcome "of some impossible lawsuit," but a "real feat [*podvig*], a real struggle and victory over the evil principle . . . , a real salvation of humanity" (3:164), because he imagines this salvation within the cosmic scheme of his Logos-Incarnation theology. His doctrine of Christ and His work, however, is grounded in the central idea of godmanhood (*bogochelovechestvo*).

This central idea asserts that "man is a certain union of Divinity with material nature." The human being is assumed to be made of three constituent elements, the divine, the material, and the specifically human element called reason, which is the uniting "relationship of the other two" (3:166). In its original form this relationship entails the direct and immediate subordination of the material principle to the divine. In this form it is a "prototype of humanity," the "primordial man." This primordial man is thus a positive synthesis of three elements hierarchically ordered. When with the Fall this order is reversed and the actuality of man is centered in the material principle with the divine principle being "just a possibility," primordial man is replaced by "natural man."

This natural man's rejection of the subordination of the natural principle to the divine can be overcome only by the free subordination
of the former to the latter in a "spiritual man." However, this free
subordination can be accomplished, Soloviev insists, only through the
appearance of a "new spiritual man" who actually unites Divinity with
nature in one "person [*litso*]." This person who is both "God and an
actual natural man," Soloviev maintains with the Christology of the
fifth through seventh Councils consciously in mind, has "two natures,"
each with its own distinct "will" (3:166–67). The inner unity of the
two natures and wills of the Godman is achieved when the divine
principle "makes room in itself for" its humanity and by this "inner
self-limitation . . . liberates its humanity . . . to renounce itself in favor
of the divine principle." This restoration of the original hierarchical
order, which is accomplished by the Incarnation in the person of Christ,
is the initial moment of Christ's salvific work. When Soloviev asserts,
however, that the "primordial, immediate unity of the two principles
in man . . . , represented by Adam" in his paradisiacal innocence and
"destroyed by original sin," cannot be "simply restored" but must be
"attained" by a "free act" of both the divine and human natures, he sets
the stage for his original reading of Christ's work as a "double feat"
of salvation.

While Christ's work begins with the Incarnation, it is accomplished
throughout his life. The process begins with and rests on the kenotic act:
"Christ as God freely renounces the Divine glory and thereby as man receives the possibility of *attaining* that Divine glory" (3:169). This process
of attainment, however, is actually reduced to two specific events that
comprise Soloviev's unique conception of the double feat of salvation.
The "feat of the spirit" is represented in the three temptations of Christ,
which several years later Dostoevsky reworked into the famous Grand
Inquisitor section of *The Brothers Karamazov*. Soloviev reads the three
temptations as challenges to the hierarchical ordering, addressed by the
Satanic evil principle to the human principle in Christ. These challenges
take the form of temptations to an exclusive and one-sided domination
of any of the three elements, matter, mind, spirit. Once this tendency
to "self-affirmation" is subdued, the first part of Christ's double feat of
salvation is complete: "Christ subordinates and harmonizes his human
will with the divine will, divinizing [*obozhestvliat'*] his humanity after
His Divinity became man [*vochelovechenie*]" (3:170). This aspect of the
salvific work follows the schema of Antiochian logos-man theology.

This ultimate act in the drama of logos-man theology does not exhaust
Christ's double feat, however, because, being a complete human being,
Christ has both a rational will (the specifically human element) and

a body of flesh. Following the logic of the Alexandrian logos-flesh theology, Soloviev insists that the logos "became not only man [*voch-elovechilsia*] but also flesh [*voplotilsia*]." The feat of the spirit, therefore, must be completed by a "feat of the flesh," a subjugation of the material principle by another "process of self-denial—suffering and death" (3:171). The Passion, therefore, is not seen as a redemptive agony of blood, sweat, and death as in the typical Western *theologia crucis*. It is a struggle for power and control over the body, which, "cleansed by the death on the Cross," loses its material heaviness to become "a direct expression and instrument of the Divine spirit, a true *spiritual body*." The second feat, the feat of the flesh, thus culminates in the Resurrection, which is understood as "the inner reconciliation of matter and spirit" and demonstrates that the "final and distinctive truth of Christianity is the spiritualization and divinization [*obozhestvlenie*] of the flesh" (3:375). Thus from the initial kenotic act through the divinization of the will and the flesh, Soloviev's conception of Christ's work as a double feat of salvation, which begins with the Incarnation and ends with the Resurrection, is grounded in the great Eastern Christian idea of "deification."

Salvation as deification is the "chief idea . . . of all of . . . the theology" (Epifanovich 125) and the "very heart of religious life in the Christian East" (Popov 165). Long neglected by Western theologians and summarily dismissed as a materialistic conception by Harnack (Harnack 2:239ff.), the doctrine of deification "has an importance it would be hard to overestimate in the evolution of the Patristic tradition" (Turner 94). The central feature of this doctrine is its grounding in a "craving for physical renewal through contact with the divine nature" wherein the ideal of moral perfection is not understood as the cause or purpose, but the condition or result (Popov 167). Deification does not mean union with the Absolute or the attainment of absolute perfection, but the acquisition of immortality, bliss, and a superhuman fullness and intensity of life often coupled with a transfiguration of the natural cosmos itself.

Historically there were two major versions of this doctrine, a "realistic" reading based on the deified flesh of Christ, and an "idealistic" or mystical reading based on a Neoplatonic view of God (Popov 167–211). The realistic tendency (Iraeneus, Athanasius, and Cyril of Alexandria) equated salvation with the conquest of death and the attainment of "incorruptibility" (Gr. *aphtharsia*, Russ. *netlennost'*), grounded the doctrine in the Incarnation, and stressed the role of the Mother of God as the one who bore Life and hence could know no corruption. The idealistic tendency (Origen, the Cappadocians, Pseudo-Dionysius, and Maximus the Confessor) equated salvation with an intellectual and moral union with

God felt as an ecstasy of mind and love, grounded the doctrine in the Neoplatonic view of passive, disparate matter progressively penetrated by the unifying force of the divine, and stressed the role of the transfigured human mind in the contemplation of the incorporeal beauty of nature understood as a reflection of the divinity in the world. The two tendencies generally coexisted, and the "easy glide from the physical to the mystical" has made this doctrine difficult for the Western mind (Turner 95). The Russian Soloviev, however, made the Eastern Christian doctrine of deification, understood as both the idealistic and realistic overcoming of division and death, the cornerstone of his theology of Godmanhood.

But Soloviev shaped this theology both within the Eastern Christian tradition and against it. He certainly considered that his understanding of Christianity was "completely in accord with the teaching of the Holy Orthodox Church," which he believed to be found in "Scripture, the definitions of the seven ecumenical councils, and the works of the Holy Fathers, beginning with the Apostolic Fathers and ending with Maximus the Confessor . . . [and] John of Damascus" (*Pis'ma*, 1891, 3:204–5). Yet from his earliest days he felt the need to counter this tradition with an activist reading of the Christian message. Untroubled by the Western fear of the Pelagian heresy inherited from Augustine and bolstered by the implications of the undoing of monotheletism, Soloviev took as axiomatic that Christ's work is our work too: "by His death and resurrection He saved the world in principle, at its root and center, but the extension of that salvation to the whole sphere of human and world life and the realization of the principle of salvation in all our reality He could not accomplish alone, but only together with humanity itself, for by coercion and without his knowledge and consent no one can actually be saved" (1891, 6:386–87). The enemy of this activist approach Soloviev found in what he considered the monastic distortion of the faith, and he hoped for what he called "the decline of the medieval worldview" (6:381–93).

The doctrine of deification became the instrument Soloviev used to transform the monastic reading of Christianity so characteristic of patristic literature. In Christianity, he wrote, "humanity is obliged not to contemplate the divine, but itself to become divine" (1882–84, 3:376). This "new religion," he argued, is not based on "passive veneration [*theosebeia*] or worship of God [*theolatreia*]," but on an "active action of God [*theourgia*]" understood as a "cooperative action of Divinity and humanity for the re-creation of the latter from the fleshly or natural into the spiritual or divine . . . , not creation from nothing, but transubstantiation" (3:377). And he consistently separated this notion of re-creation from the monastic tradition of asceticism and its ideal of the "angelic life": "from a Christian point of view an angel . . . is lower than man in essence and destined purpose . . . , [and] those Eastern Fathers of the Church, who both praised and established the 'angelic order' of monasticism, considered the highest goal and destiny of man to be perfect union with God—not *angellosis*, but divinization or *deification*, *theosis*" (1898, 9:233). What distinguishes Soloviev's doctrine of salvation from the patristic tradition of Eastern Christianity is his application of the idea of deification not to the individual monk contemplating in the monastery but to all human beings living in the world community.

For all human beings the first and personal task of salvation, Soloviev argues in his pivotal work *The Spiritual Foundations of Life* (*Dukhovnye osnovy zhizni*, 1882–84), is the "combination" (*sochetat'*) of our life with divine life (3:301). This task entails a rebirth and sanctification of human nature, its will, mind, and body. The paradox of this pursuit of deification is that once we have accepted God and subordinated ourselves to God's will, we cannot sin unless we are tempted, but temptation is built into our nature. "Spiritual life is not something given once and for all," and "spiritual man is not a simple being, whole and complete," for in him there continue to exist "two living forces, the *originating principle* [*nachatok*] of the new life of grace and the *remnant* [*ostakok*] of the former life of sin" (3:332; emphasis in original). The purpose of this built-in temptation is to strengthen the former through struggle with the latter. As with Christ, but in reverse order, Satan's temptations are read as challenges to the hierarchy of will, mind, and body. Meeting these challenges is our work of salvation.

Temptations of the body come first to test the newly reborn of the spirit, lest they fall into the illusion that they are just spirit; they are challenged by our continual turning upward toward the divine in prayer, by which we yield our will to the one who "possesses the good and can convey the power of the good to us" (3:315). This first task, like all the work of salvation, is grounded in the Godhuman process: all good and all grace come from God, and in prayer we "*do not oppose*" that good but "agree with our will" to accept it (3:316). Temptations of the mind such as self-importance, vanity, and envy test the fact that "in truth there is no mine and theirs . . . and we are all in solidarity" (3:330). We are challenged by our sacrificial reaching outward to others with almsgiving, the "first, elementary, and simplest expression of a moral order based on mutual solidarity and unanimity" (3:345). This second task of salvation consists in "the extension to others of that grace which we ourselves receive from God in true prayer" (3:342). Temptations of the will such as deception, exploitation, violence, and murder test our power and authority and are challenged by fasting, the exercise of our will in its proper hierarchical ordering directed downward to our material nature. This third task of salvation consists in the extension of the "activity of divine grace to both our animal nature and to the whole world," for "just as the incarnated God saved humanity, so humanity reunited with God must save all of nature." "Each in his own body can collaborate [*sodeistvovat'*] with the redemption of the universal body" (3:345–46). These three tasks of salvation—prayer, almsgiving, and fasting—are the "three basic actions of religious life," and they are understood in Eastern Christian fashion as actions in collaboration, in "synergy" (Gr. *sunergeia*; Russ. *sodeistvie*) with God. But still "it is not in our personal power to unite *completely* with the Divinity, to save humanity, or regenerate nature," for the ultimate task of salvation is not personal, but universal.

For Soloviev the goal of salvation is "deified mankind." He assumes that the "historical phenomenon of Christ the Godman is inseparably united with the whole world process" (1896, 8:216). He believes that the "Godman, who is the union of Divinity with human nature in one individual person, is the *originating principle*, the necessary foundation and center, while the end and completion is Godmanhood or, more exactly, deified mankind" (1884, 4:158; emphasis in original). What Christ begins "singly" can be accomplished only when people strive to attain it "collectively" (*sobiratel'no*) (1884, 3:303). "When not only certain particular souls but all beings devote themselves to God" both in their hearts and in their lives, then will this "Kingdom of God be not only *above* all, which it already is, but also *in all*," and God will be *"all in all and all will be one in Him"* (3:318–19).

Deified mankind is thus equated with the idea of the Kingdom of God, and the attainment of it is a form of the Origenist restoration of all things. Salvation understood as the establishment of this Kingdom of God entails the reestablishment of the "true *organization* of everything that exists." In this organization "nothing harms another and nothing disappears," everything is "contained and preserved" in the one place that kenotically "makes room in itself for everything" and is the "only true place for everything," and everything shares a "complete *unity of mood . . .*, devoted to the will of God which wants *everything to be saved*" (1885–87, 4:599; emphasis in original). This true organization of everything, of course, is the shape of reality in Christ, which is the union of Logos and Sophia, the metaphysical principle of God's expression or other. Salvation understood as the deification of mankind is the incarnation of this Christ and thus the establishment of the Kingdom of God on earth.

Soloviev's notion of the Kingdom of God as deified mankind is the ground for his doctrine of the Church. "The Church is mankind deified by Christ, and, with faith in the Church, to believe in mankind means only to believe in its *capacity for deification*, to believe in the words of Saint Athanasius the Great, that in Christ God became man in order to make man God" (1882, 3:222; emphasis in original). The Church, as the goal of the Incarnation and Salvation, is what is to be realized on earth. "The Church, or the Kingdom of God, must not remain *only* above us or be *only* an object of our reverence or worship; it must also be in us ourselves as the ruling force and free life for all mankind" (1883, 4:50; emphasis in original). This conception of the Church as an active principle being incarnated in us and thus realized on earth is a natural extension of the vision of *logos* reordering creation that shapes Soloviev's whole worldview.

With this understanding of the Church Soloviev rewrites Khomiakov's doctrine of *sobornost'*: "The Church is not just a gathering together [*sobranie*] of people (believers), but mainly *that which gathers them together* [*sobiraet*], i.e., the essential form of union given to people from above by means of which they can participate [*byt' prichastny*] in Divinity" (1882–84, 3:384; emphasis in original). And Soloviev, in contrast to Khomiakov, conceives his doctrine of the Church universally and with a clear sense of gift and task. "The Church is not *just* the Godhuman foundation of salvation for *individual* people, but also the Godhuman economy [*oikonomia*] for the salvation of *this* world," which means that the "mystical union of human societies in Christ must be expressed in their clear brotherly union among themselves. The first is given from above and does not depend on us directly; the second must be our own task" (1883, 4:107; emphasis in original). The model of this task of universal salvation is the post-Chalcedonian, dyotheletic Christ's deifying subordination of his humanity.

In Christ His humanity—his rational will—was subordinated completely in everything to the Father's will, and through this feat of self-renunciation He subordinated His material nature, healing, transfiguring, and resurrecting it in a new spiritual form. Likewise in the Church the Divine Holiness, received by the will and reason of humanity, must be extended through a feat of self-renunciation by people and nations to all of mankind, to all its natural life, and through that to the life of the whole world for its recovery, transfiguration, and resurrection. (4:51)

On this doctrine of the Church as deified mankind to be attained universally in this world, and on this ecclesiology shaped by the metaphor of the Kingdom of God, Soloviev grounded his theology of Church reunion. This ecumenical theology he shaped according to his vision of theocracy. The ten years that Soloviev spent on the elaboration of this theory of ecclesiological reunion and in the pursuit of his ecumenical policy ended in failure, and Soloviev eventually had to change his temporal perspective on the coming of the Kingdom of God: "being the union of everything with God, the . . . universal Church can be realized in actuality only through universal history, in the whole life of all mankind, in the whole sum total of times and peoples" (1896, 7:315). This larger perspective allowed Soloviev, especially in the last decade of his life, to develop his doctrine of salvation by exploring the other major metaphor he employed for the Church, the "body of Christ."

As the metaphor of the Kingdom of God allowed Soloviev to detail relationships of authority between God and man and among men, nations, and separated Churches, the metaphor of the body of Christ serves him as a vehicle to clarify the relationship of humanity to the world of nature and matter. The body of Christ is the visible Church, which grows according to the divine form of the Church, the invisible Church, which is "perfect and unchanging in God." This divine form of the Church is Sophia in her pristine union with the Logos. Soloviev believes that this divine form is "originally given to us as a divine *seed*" (1882–84, 3:388–89) and "develops so that at the end of time it will embrace all of humanity and all of nature in one universal Godhuman organism" (3:380). This one universal Godhuman organism thus consists of three parts, "spirit" in the form of the "invisible Church," "soul" in the form of the "visible Church," and "body" in the form of "external, material nature" (3:378). Salvation is understood as the "reunification of these three parts of the world that are now separated." The resultant body of Christ will be a "reunified world, triune in all its makeup . . . , the true and full image and likeness of the triune God, His true kingdom, the expression of His power and glory." In this body of Christ, "everything feeble and fleshly will be absorbed in the resurrection of the spiritual body" so that "everything spiritual will be completely incarnated and everything material will be completely spiritualized" (3:381).

In the Church, as the body of Christ, this incarnation and trans-figuration is accomplished through the sacraments, which "embrace and sanctify not only the moral and spiritual life of man, but also his physical life and . . . reunite with the Divinity the originating principles of the material nature of the whole visible world" (3:399). Baptism "reunites the Spirit of God, which at the beginning of Creation had hovered over the waters . . . , with water, the original *element* of the material world"; chrismation and extreme unction sanctify "the *vegetable* element," and the Eucharist "nutrimental matter"; marriage purifies and gives meaning to the "generative function of *animal* life" (3:400;

emphasis in original). In this way the sacraments "restore the union of Divinity with the originating principles of the whole of creation . . . so that all of creation may become the true image of the Divinity" and be "transfigured into a living envelope and milieu of the highest spiritual and divine powers, the body of God" (3:425). Salvation understood as the full realization of the body of Christ thus entails cosmic transfiguration.

This cosmic transfiguration, originated in the Church through the sacraments, must be realized by all men in the world community through love. As Soloviev argued in his famous article *The Meaning of Love* (*Smysl liubvi*, 1892–94), the starting point for this salvific love is the relationship of the sexes, because the division of the human being into male and female is itself "a state of disintegration and the beginning of death" (7:33). "The task of love consists in *justifying in fact* the meaning of love given at first only in feeling; it demands that combination [*sochetanie*] of two given limited beings which would create from them one absolute, ideal personality" and would result in the "restoration of the human form in its wholeness" (7:24). This ideal, human being can be restored only by a positive synthesis of the animal, human, and divine elements within man: erotic love and family love, grounded in the animal and human instinct for survival, must be subordinated to the higher, divine principle within. This subordination is "natural for man in his wholeness" and "leads to immortality" (7:38). Salvation thus entails the conquest of death and a recovery of immortality. The resultant true, spiritual love is "not a weak imitation and intimation of death, but a victory over death, not a . . . denial of the flesh . . . , but its rebirth, salvation, and resurrection" (7:40).

This restored human being, male and female united in God, is not sufficient for salvation, however, because a "person can be really saved, i.e., can revive and perpetuate his individual life in true love only jointly or together with all" (7:50). This "all" Soloviev imagines, following Fedorov whose "Philosophy of the Common Task" with its doctrine of deification as the "realistic" conquest of death he here addresses, includes all people now living, the visible Church, and all our deceased "fathers," the invisible Church. Salvation must entail some form of overcoming the deathly replacement of generation by generation. Such a salvation begins with the "religion of ancestors, that foundation of all culture," and must encompass tradition, art, and the science of history" (7:56). But Soloviev proposes no fantastic task of universal resurrection.

Rather the salvation of all is to be accomplished through the expanding process of "combination" (*sochetanie*) that is now called by the Greek word for combination, *syzygy*, a relationship of "loving interaction" with the environment, social, political, and natural. The model is the combination of male and female in the creation of the true human being. Each environmental element is imagined as female ("and this is not just a metaphor"), a "real, living being with whom we find ourselves in the closest and fullest interaction, while never fusing into indifferentiation" (7:58). With such combinations established, the division between male and female, between nation and nation, between Church and Church, between man and nature, between the living and the dead, and ultimately between this world and the divine will be overcome in one grand transfiguration of reality. Salvation thus ultimately means the unique union of Creator and Creation understood as the total incarnation and hence realization of the cosmic Christ, that unique combination of divinity and humanity, "not separate and not confused," which is called Godmanhood.

Soloviev's first model of the doctrine of salvation, as expressed in his major works up through the *Lectures on Godmanhood*, was shaped after Origen's conception of creation as a fall and salvation as a restoration of all things. But as Soloviev turned his attention more to the details of the process of this salvation, in the moral and spiritual terms outlined in *The Spiritual Foundations of Life* (1882–84), in the biblical, theological, and ecclesiological terms explored in *The Great Controversy and Christian Politics* (1883) and *The History and Future of Theocracy* (1885–87), and in the aesthetic and cosmological terms detailed in "Beauty in Nature" (1889), "The General Meaning of Art" (1890), and "The Meaning of Love" (1892–94), his conception of the doctrine of salvation became in fact more "orthodox," which is to say more grounded in the Christology of Chalcedon as understood in the Eastern Christian tradition and especially as expressed by Maximus the Confessor, "after Origen the strongest philosophical mind in the Christian East" (1896, 12:598). According to the renowned theologian and scholar Hans Urs von Balthasar, "Soloviev's true starting point in the Christian past is Greek patristic thought before the Schism, especially in its definitive form in the work of Maximus the Confessor" (*Glory of the Lord* 287).

Maximus obviously had a great appeal for Soloviev (Garrigues 7–22). Maximus' general tendency to draw from and rework the whole past philosophical tradition, especially the "heretical" and "gnostic" Origen and the Neoplatonic and seemingly monophysite Pseudo-Dionysius, into a Chalcedonian orthodoxy resembles Soloviev's own approach to past thinkers and systems of thought. Furthermore, if Origen coined the noun "Godman," it was Maximus the Confessor who first used "Godhuman" as an adjective and general concept "frequently and freely" (Thunberg, *Man and the Cosmos* 71), thereby making it a central organizing principle of his thought, just as Soloviev did once again so many centuries later. And Maximus was the major intellectual force behind the resolution of the heresy of monothelitism. He shaped the central arguments for the two natures and the two wills—divine and human—in Christ, the Godman, which thereby preserved in the face of the divine the human freedom so important to Soloviev. Moreover it was Maximus' innovative conception of the relationship between the divine and the human in the Godman (Prestige 291–94), his notion of *perichoresis* (mutual permeation) which entails "reciprocity" and "double penetration" (Thunberg, *Microcosm and Mediator* 22–29), that seems to have provided Soloviev with his model for the mutual interaction and mutual penetration of all entities in Christ. And Maximus shared Soloviev's and Origen's tendency to equate Creation with the Fall (Balthasar, *Kosmische Liturgie* 184–85). But what is most significant for Soloviev in the present context is Maximus the Confessor's general vision of creation and salvation.

At the center of this vision is the Church, which as a unity of multiplicity is for Maximus an image of God and Creation. "When in the Church the created multiplicity assembles around Christ, who is the only *logos* of the totality—assembles without confusion, but also without separation between the divine and the human, as the Chalcedonian formula states—then the Church expresses . . . one and the same principle and one and the same power of unity on the level of creation," as does Christ on the level of divinity (Thunberg, *Man and the Cosmos* 117). For a unity there must be different elements to be unified, and Maximus imagines five fundamental "differences" (*diaphora*): (1) Creator and Creation; (2) intelligible and sensible or ideal and real; (3) heaven and earth; (4) paradise and inhabited realm; and (5) male and female. In the fallen world these ontological "differences" are rent asunder by moral "divisions" (*diairesis*), which Christ in his salvific work reconciles. Man is called to continue Christ's work, which in monastic fashion Maximus believes entails ascetic detachment and mystical contemplation, leading to a "syzygistic" union that overcomes all divisions, while retaining the differences. This conception of deification is a union shaped after the Chalcedonian Christ who is both God and man "without confusion and without separation" (Thunberg, *Microcosm and Mediator* 356). It is this vision of God and Creation as Church, grounded in the Chalcedonian doctrine of the Godman and built around a notion of syzygistic union of differences, that provided Soloviev the model for his own vision of Godmanhood.

To the extent that in the Church all is in accord with the absolute whole . . . , all *divisions* [*otdeleniia*] and disconnections fall away, but all *distinctions* [*razlichiia*] remain. . . . There are no divisions, but there remains the distinction between the invisible and visible Church . . . , there remains in the visible Church the distinction among the many tribes and peoples . . . , and there remains the distinction between the Church of those who teach and those who learn, between the clergy and the people, between the mind and the body of the Church. [There are no divisions, but the distinction remains, just as does] the distinction between husband and wife which is not an obstacle, but the foundation for their perfect union. (1894–96, 8:473–74; emphasis in original)

Soloviev reshapes the medieval and monastic elements of Maximus' Chalcedonian reworking of the Eastern Christian tradition from Origen and the Cappadocians through Pseudo-Dionysius into a nineteenth-century philosophical theology, expressed in the language not of Greek patristics but of German idealism, and addressed not to monks but to the intellectual elite and Church leaders of the divided inhabited world of Russia and the West. The great Eastern Christian doctrine of salvation as deification was thereby transformed from a monastic justification for the contemplative life into a grand moral, ecumenical, and cosmological scheme designed to restore the "faith of our fathers" to modern man.

Note

1.   All references to Soloviev will be from the Brussels reprint unless otherwise noted. Dates will be included where appropriate.

Works Cited

Aulen, Gustaf. *Christus Victor: An Historical Study of the Three Main Types of the Atonement*. New York: Macmillan, 1960.

Balthasar, Hans Urs von. *The Glory of the Lord*, vol. 3: *Studies in Theological Lay Styles*. Edinburgh, 1986. Trans. of German *Herrlichkeit*, 1969.

Balthasar, Hans Urs von. *Kosmische Liturgie. Maximos der Bekenner: Hoehe und Krise des greichischen Weltbildes*. Freiburg, 1961.

Epifanovich, S. L. *Prepodobnyi Maksim Ispovednik i vizantiiskoe bogoslovie*. Kiev, 1915.

Garrigues, Juan Miguel. *Maxime le Confesseur: La charité avenir divin de l'homme*. Paris, 1976.

Grensted, L. W. *A Short History of the Doctrine of the Atonement*. Manchester, Eng.: University of Manchester Press, 1920.

Grillmeier, Aloys. *Christ in Christian Tradition*. Vol. 1. Atlanta, 1975.

Harnack, Adolf von. *History of Dogma*. Rpt. 7 vols. New York, 1961.

Pelikan, Jaroslav. *The Christian Tradition*. 5 vols. Chicago: University of Chicago Press, 1971–86.

Pelikan, Jaroslav. *Jesus, through the Centuries*. New Haven: Yale University Press, 1985.

Popov, Ivan V. "Ideia obozheniia v drevne-vostochnoi tserkvi." *Voprosy filosofii i psikhologii* 97 (1909): 165–213.

Prestige, G. L. *God in Patristic Thought.* London: S.P.C.K., 1977.

Quasten, Johannes. *Patrology.* Rpt. 3 vols. Westminster, Md.: Christian Classics, 1984.

Schelling, F. W. J. *Of Human Freedom.* Trans. James Gutmann. Chicago: Open Court, 1936.

Schmemann, Alexander. *Ultimate Questions.* New York: Holt, Rinehart, Winston, 1965.

Solov'ev, Vladimir. *Sobranie sochinenii* (12 vols.) and *Pis'ma* (4 vols.). 3d ed. rpt. 16 vols. Brussels: Zhizn's Bogom, 1966–70.

Solov'ev, Vladimir. *"La Sophia" et les autres écrits français.* Ed. François Rouleau. Lausanne: La Cité, 1978.

Thunberg, Lars. *Man and the Cosmos: The Vision of St. Maximus the Confessor.* Crestwood, N.Y.: SVSP, 1985.

Thunberg, Lars. *Microcosm and Mediator: The Theological Anthropology of Maximus the Confessor.* Lund: C.W.K. Gleerup, 1965.

Turner, H. E. W. *The Patristic Doctrine of Redemption.* London: Mowbray, 1952.

2

Gnostic Elements in the Cosmogony of Vladimir Soloviev

Maria Carlson

Prayer of the Revelation of the Great Mystery
In the name of the Father and of the Son and of the Holy Spirit
Ain-Soph, Jah, Soph-Jah

In the name of the Unutterable, Awesome, and All-powerful, I
call upon gods, demons [daimons], men, and all living creatures.
Gather into one the rays of your power, block the path of the
source of your own desires, and become partakers of my prayer,
that we may capture the pure Dove of Zion and acquire the
priceless pearl of Ophir, that the roses may unite with the lilies
in the valley of Sharon. O most holy Divine Sophia, essential
image of the beauty and sweetness of the transcendent God, the
bright body of Eternity, the Soul of worlds and the one Queen of
all souls, by the inexpressible profundity and grace of thy first
Son and beloved, Jesus Christ, I implore thee: descend into the
prison of the soul, fill our darkness with thy radiance, melt away
the fetters that bind our spirit with the fire of thy love, grant us
light and freedom, appear to us in visible and substantial form,
incarnate thyself in us and in the world, restoring the fullness of
the Ages, so that the deep may be confined and that God may
be all in all.
—Vladimir Solov'ev, "Album I [MS]," 1875[1]

Vladimir Soloviev wrote the "Sophia Prayer" in London in 1875, where
he had been sent by the administration of Moscow University specifically "to study the monuments of Indian, gnostic, and medieval philosophy at the British Museum" (Sergei Solov'ev 113). The Sophia Prayer
is only one of several textual clues that provide justification for Dmitry
Merezhkovsky's observation in 1908 that "Vladimir Soloviev is a gnostic, possibly the last great gnostic of all Christianity" (Merezhkovskii

133). Merezhkovsky meant to imply by his comment not that Soloviev had become a heretic in the eyes of the Orthodox Church by embracing a mystical, heretical doctrine, but that he came to religion by meditation, intuition and spiritual cognition rather than by either faith or willed and pragmatic action (Merezhkovskii 132). A modern reader of Soloviev might add that behind Merezhkovsky's observation stood a highly specific, Neoplatonic worldview shared by both Soloviev and Merezhkovsky, as well as by other representatives of the God-seeking intelligentsia of the Russian religious renaissance.

Merezhkovsky's comment on Soloviev does not imply that Soloviev identified, adopted, and mechanically applied a specifically gnostic doctrine in his work, although he was without question familiar with the theological and historical contours of that doctrine and found certain aspects of it congenial to his own thought. Vladimir Soloviev, however, was by no means the first intellectual to be seduced by the poetry of the gnostic cosmogony, by the concept of the primacy of Sophia Wisdom over the Creation, or by the psychic power of gnostic imagery and mythology (which can be very powerful indeed). Being a profoundly creative man, Soloviev was creative in his appreciation of gnostic concepts, particularly of the gnostic Sophia.

Soloviev's work contains a certain base of assumptions and uses terminology so highly evocative of the gnostic tradition that the latter's influence cannot be lightly dismissed. An examination of this tradition can only serve to clarify Soloviev's choice of terminology and to focus certain concepts more precisely, although it is bootless to look for complete coincidence between Soloviev's sophiology and that of the various streams of Christian gnosticism. For the sake of limiting this potentially boundless discussion of gnostic influences on Soloviev's thought, I would like to address broadly one theme: the influence of gnostic cosmogony (i.e., the hypothesis of creation and evolution) on Soloviev's thought. The material presented on the following pages is by no means exhaustive; it serves only to initiate the discussion of Soloviev's gnostic tendencies by pointing out certain curious parallels between the best-known gnostic speculation, the Valentinian gnosis, and Soloviev's own sophiology. The ramifications of the discussion, however, are manifold, for the seed of gnostic sophiology, nurtured by Soloviev, would bear fruit in the theology of Sergei Bulgakov and other contemporary sophiologists, none of whom are entirely free of this heretical doctrine.

Many contemporary discussions of gnosticism (outside professional religious/philosophical contexts) reduce it to mere pantheistic dualism or to a simplistic cosmic struggle between Light and Darkness, Good and Evil, or between Spirit and Matter. Gnosticism is in fact a far more complex and sophisticated phenomenon, its arcane texts presenting a variety of both Christian and non-Christian formulations and dealing with many subjects in addition to the origin of things and the nature of God. A highly developed Christian gnosis frequently appears to have much in common with traditional Christianity, and Christian gnostics enthusiastically claimed Jesus Christ as their own. Jesus, after all, wrote down no doctrine himself; the Scriptures were written by others who lost, suggest the gnostics, the real meaning of his message.[2] Being highly syncretistic, however, gnosticism freely added Judaic, Buddhist, Egyptian, and Persian elements to the Christian mystery. The differences among the various systems of gnosis, such as Manicheanism, Mandeanism, and Barbelo-gnosticism, or Ophitic and Basilidean gnosticism (not to mention later incarnations, such as the Bogomil or Albigensian doctrines of the Middle Ages or the modern Theosophists), can be considerable, and tracing their specific influence is no simple task.

Tracing gnostic influence is further complicated by the dearth of concrete texts and reliable sources. Until the discovery of the Nag Hammadi "library" in Egypt in 1945, original sources were relatively few. Only a handful of purportedly gnostic manuscripts or contemporary works about gnosticism existed at the turn of the century. These included the Coptic fragments of the *Pistis Sophia* (discovered in the late eighteenth century and held in the British Museum, where Soloviev probably saw them), *The Two Books of Jeu* (also called *The Book of the Great Mysterious Logos*), parts of the *Corpus Hermeticum*, the Odes of Solomon, and the "Hymn of the Pearl," to mention the best known. Most of the information on gnosticism available to Soloviev would still have come from the works of the early heresiologists Irenaeus, Tertullian, Hippolytus, and Clement of Alexandria. These Fathers of the Church wrote extensively on the gnostics, and several of them (notably Irenaeus) had studied the Valentinian speculation in great detail, citing extensively from now-lost sources. Additional gnostic themes and elements are found in the writings of the mystical theologians most admired by Soloviev: Origen, Saint Maximus the Confessor, and Dionysius the Pseudo-Areopagite (whose works incorporated or discussed various Neoplatonic and gnostic elements and who placed special emphasis on the doctrine of *theosis*, or the deification of man). Soloviev, who studied at the Moscow Spiritual Academy as well as at Moscow University, would have been familiar with this body of literature.

Soloviev was also well versed in the literature of mysticism (oriental Buddhism, Hebrew Kabbalah, and various occidental streams) and theology (patristic and modern). His knowledge clearly extended to the literature of Neoplatonism. In the British Museum Soloviev additionally read the Renaissance "theosophists," such as Jakob Boehme (1573–1624), and very likely was familiar with Boehme's disciples John Pordage (1607–1681), Johann Georg Gichtel (1638–1710), and Gottfried Arnold (1666–1714), author of *Geheimnisse der göttlichen Sophia* (Leipzig, 1700). Finally, Vladimir Soloviev had read the works of his brother Vsevolod's eccentric acquaintance, Mme. Helena Petrovna Blavatsky (1831–1891), founder of the Theosophical Society and creative architect of a compelling modern gnostic gospel. Her first major work, *The Secret Doctrine* (1888), claimed to be just such a "synthesis of science, religion, and philosophy" as Soloviev's "grand synthesis" or "universal religion," which was to reorient all of human knowledge and redefine metaphysics based on a modern reading of secret ancient models. This striving to re-cognize and reunite the various elements of a lost tradition fragmented by the ravages of modern positivism and pragmatism, to discover the single and harmonious metaphysical Truth that underlies all material complexity, is a basic feature of gnostic systems, past and present; this same syncretic impulse is everywhere present in Soloviev.

Thus Soloviev's own philosophical thought, which appears to be as eclectic and syncretistic as gnosticism itself, was opened early in his life to the entire tradition of metaphysical speculation (he was a young and impressionable twenty-two when he went to London to work in the British Museum). The mature Merezhkovsky, no casual heretic himself, must have easily recognized the gnostic roots of the cosmogony Soloviev originally considered and then repeatedly refined, divesting it of its more sensational mythological elements and adding contents from other systems. Neither did Soloviev's younger contemporaries, the second generation of symbolists (the "philosophers"), view Soloviev's eclectic mix of gnostic, idealist, and mystic thought with esoteric Christianity as at all inconsistent. Andrei Belyi, one of Vladimir Soloviev's most devoted admirers, brightly observed that, after all, "Christian metaphysics is the result of the intersecting influences of hermeticism, gnosticism, and philosophy of the Neoplatonists" (Belyi 620).

With the limited exception of Samuel D. Cioran (17–20) and Paul M. Allen, explicators of Soloviev have avoided detailed discussion of gnostic elements in his philosophical writings. Many commentators perceived certain gnostic aspects in his worldview, but speedily labeled them "Neoplatonic" (possibly to avoid rough theological terrain or unwelcome ecclesiastical attention). In some cases they erroneously mistook Soloviev's elaborations of Christian gnostic terminology and conceptualization for an esoteric Christian paradigm. This would partially explain why Soloviev has not more often been discussed by secondary literature within a gnostic context, although his contemporaries certainly recognized that dimension of his work.

A second and more compelling reason for the avoidance of the discussion of Soloviev's gnostic dimension would be that the Church itself discouraged the explicit exploration of anyone's gnostic tendencies, let alone Soloviev's, who was revered by many members of the God-seeking intelligentsia as the greatest of all Russian Orthodox metaphysicians. Gnosticism had been declared a heresy almost from the first days of Christianity, and the first six centuries of the Christian era witnessed attacks on the doctrine by dedicated heresiologists and respected Fathers of the Church. In turn-of-the-century Russia, the Orthodox Church continued to persecute heretical sects, especially the *khlysty*, whose doctrine had a considerable gnostic dimension. Thus the less-marked term "theosophy" (lower-case *t*) or "Christian theosophy" was not infrequently used as a euphemism for gnostic tendencies; the term was certainly applied to Soloviev more than once.

Various historical, intellectual, and spiritual parallels between the time of the gnostics (most broadly the first century B.C. through the first six centuries A.D.) and the *fin-de-siècle* were not lost on contemporaries. They viewed both periods as times of "crisis of culture and consciousness," times that saw a confrontation between Eastern and Western cultures, times when new faiths were evolving out of old and discredited mystery religions. Gnosticism was a historically earlier expression of a similar human sense of existentialism, spiritual emptiness, and alienation from a decadent world that we associate with the end of the nineteenth century. That Soloviev and his generation (rejecting the prevailing scientific positivism and decadence of the period, coping with the weakening of traditional religion, and seeking a new religious worldview) should be interested in and conversant with gnosticism is not at all surprising. During their lifetime Soloviev's contemporaries not only saw the publication of many studies of gnosticism and the enthusiastic activity of archaeologists and historians of comparative religions, but also witnessed the creation of entire systems of modern gnosis, both pagan and Christian. Here one might mention that the neo-Buddhist Theosophy of Mme. Blavatsky, mentioned above, and the "Christian Theosophy" (upper-case *T*) of Dr. Rudolf Steiner (1861–1925), are both modern gnostic doctrines; Dr. Steiner would later speak in his lectures of Soloviev as a mediator between East and West and a true clairvoyant who anticipated Steiner's own vision of the coming of the Christ in the etheric world, while Western Anthroposophists would write books about Soloviev (Allen 341–43).[3]

How should we understand gnosticism, then, for the purpose of this discussion? Gnosticism is a religious-philosophical system that holds that the concept of *knowledge* is superior to the concept of *faith* (the foundation of traditional religion). Gnosticism is thus a religious *philosophy*, but not a religion; as such, it would have a certain appeal to thinkers of mystic inclinations who were raised in a historically positivistic age, as was Soloviev. The knowledge that gnosticism claims to have or to seek, moreover, is a total and systematic knowledge, including within itself all the natural and speculative sciences, cosmology, history, anthropology, mythology, philosophy, and theology / theogony. Gnosticism is both highly syncretic and synthetic, for all its unfamiliar and esoteric detail. But the Gnosis, being "knowledge of God," is not to be identified with mere *rational cognition*, since God is Unknowable and Ineffable; rather, gnostics claim, their system is a higher, more intuitive form of *spiritual cognition*, a *vision of truth*, or revelation, revealed to the elite few who are spiritually sophisticated enough to receive it.

The basic premise of gnostic thought is that the Godhead is utterly transcendent and alien to the material world in which mankind dwells. The undefined and undefinable Godhead dwells beyond all time, space, and understanding, in an Abyss of Profundity, whose "light is darkness to mortal eyes, because of the superabundance of its brilliancy" (Mead 311; this is also the *photismos* of the monks of Mount Athos, the "Light of Tabor" of the Hesychasts, the mystic or divine Light, the Invisible Fire, etc.). Yet for all its "beyondness" and incomprehensibility, the Godhead is the ultimate source of All, including the pneumatic, spiritual self in man. The gnosis teaches that the origin of the human pneumatic self is divine and that the material world that holds the pneumatic self prisoner is demonic. It is important to note that in gnostic systems, evil, matter, and the demonic are defined relatively, by their distance from the Goodness and Spirituality of the Godhead. Evil and matter are *less perfect*, hence more demonic, only because they are further in distance from the complete perfection of the Godhead. The point of existence is to release, through special knowledge (i.e., *gnosis*), the pneumatic self from the fetters of matter and to return it to its natural home in the realm of the light of pure Spirit. Thus all gnostic thought is dualistic; it is premised on the *perceived but illusionary* oppositions of Light and Darkness, Divine and Demonic, Spiritual and Material, noumenal and phenomenal. Gnosticism begins here, but it does not end here.

In all cases, gnostic doctrines are emanationist, eschatological, and soteriological. The redemption of spirit from matter, of light from darkness, and the restoration of a precosmic *status quo* are, in fact, *the* central principle of the gnosis. The world exists because divine substance, spirit, removed itself sufficiently from the Godhead to fall into matter. The story of the redemption of this divine substance *is* human history. The difference among gnostic systems lies precisely in their speculations about the nature of the precosmic fall of Spirit (divine element) into Matter and the precise agent and manner of redemption, but not in the fact of the fall itself.

The best known of the gnostic cosmogonies that describe the precosmic fall of Spirit into Matter is that of Valentinus, in which the key protagonists in the precosmic fall and the subsequent redemption are the Sophia, the Christos, and Jesus. Valentinus (2d cent., ca. A.D. 140), the most influential of the gnostic theologians, based his system on Ophitic texts (with some Platonic and Pythagorean matter). That Soloviev was well acquainted with the Valentinian speculation is clear not only from his article "Gnosticism" for the *Brokgauz-Efron Encyclopedia* (*Entsiklopedicheskii slovar' Brokgauza-Efrona*; "Gnostitsizm," in Solov'ev 10:323–28), but also from a second article in the same work, "Valentinus and the Valentinians" ("Valentin i Valentiniane," in Solov'ev 10:285–90). Valentinus was, according to Soloviev, "the most famous of the gnostic philosophers and one of the most brilliant thinkers of all time," the creator of a "rigorous, consistent, and poetically original system" ("Valentin," 10:285, 288). Defining gnosticism as a philosophy, Soloviev termed it a "theosophical" system whose purpose was to unite "the divine principle and the world, absolute and relative being, the infinite and the finite" ("Gnostitsizm," 324). The articles reveal Soloviev's detailed knowledge of gnosticism; they should, however, be approached cautiously by the reader. During the late nineteenth century, while the *Brokgauz-Efron Encyclopedia* was being published, Soloviev's articles would have been strictly overseen by the Church censorship (*dukhovnaia tsenzura*; Church censorship was lifted only in 1905). Since gnosticism was a heresy, Soloviev's encyclopedia entries would have had to reflect the Church's position; indeed Soloviev's article "Gnosticism" conforms strictly to Irenaeus' *Adversus omnes haereses* in the approved manner.

The Valentinian speculation represents the mainstream of gnostic thought; it received the greatest attention from the patristic heresiologists and was the best-known and most accessible tradition before the later discoveries of Nag Hammadi (1945). One of the more important implications of the Valentinian speculation for mystic thought is its assumption that matter is derived from an original spiritual source. Since matter is viewed negatively, this implies a divine "failure" on some level; it also implies that this failure, being divine in origin, can and will be redeemed. Materiality, for the Valentinians, was a devalued and derivative spirituality, less perfect and more "evil" for being the more distant from the source of all perfection; matter remained, however, an essentially spiritual (if devalued) condition. Immensely complex, the Valentinian cosmogony supporting this idea is given in simplified form below.

At the beginning of Valentinus' gnostic universe stands the All-Unity (Gk. *hen kai pan*; Soloviev's *Vseedinstvo*). It has also been called the Pure Light, the Unknowable, the Ineffable, the Unutterable, Bythos (Abyss of Profundity), the Divine Principle, the Absolute One, and many other names. This Principle, in order to make Itself known, autonomously emanates, producing a series of pairs, or syzygies, in a descending order of dignity; these are the Aeons, also called Eternities, of the Pleroma. The first emanation, or Aeon, is the feminine Silence (sometimes called Ennoia [Thought], or Grace). The syzygy of the Abyss and the Silence engenders the masculine Nous (Mind, Intelligence) and the feminine Aletheia (Truth); they in turn emanate the Logos (Word) and Zoi (Life), and they, in turn, produce Anthropos (Man) and Ecclesia (Church). This Ogdoad (the sum of the first eight emanations) engenders twenty-two further syzygies (the Decad and the Dodecad), the last being the feminine Aeon/Eternity Sophia (Wisdom; hence Soloviev's reference to Sophia as the "bright body of Eternity" in the Sophia Prayer).

The totality of thirty Aeons constitute the Fullness of Absolute Being: the nonmaterial, nonspatial, and nontemporal Perfection of the Pleroma. The fullness of the Pleroma is consolidated and encompassed by the Power of Limit (*horos*; sometimes called the Cross and associated with the Christos). Beyond the Pleroma is the Shadow (Darkness) and the Void; it will eventually become Cosmos, the realm of matter, space, and time.

Of all the Aeons, only Nous has been granted the possibility of understanding the One, but all of the other Aeons wonder about the One and wish to know It. Most curious of all was Sophia, who was farthest from the Ineffable One and who existed at the very edge of the Fullness and Perfection of the Pleroma. In her desire and passion to comprehend the One that cannot be comprehended, she gives way to her desire to imitate the One and emanates without syzygy (i.e., without a consort, as the One did). She produces only "formlessness" (the Abortion) and thereby "falls" (sins) into the Cosmic Darkness.[4]

Concerned about the repercussions of Sophia's fall into the darkness beyond the Pleroma, the Power of Limit returns the Fallen Sophia to the Fullness of the Pleroma, but pushes the "formlessness" she has produced out of the Pleroma. The One now emanates two additional Aeons, the Christos and the Holy Spirit (the Comforter). The Christos ensures that the Pleroma will remain untroubled by explaining the One to the Aeons (this explanation is the Gnosis). Christos also temporarily leaves the Pleroma to "enform" the formlessness as a lower Sophia, and then returns into his perfect pleromic state. All of the Aeons together then produce the unpaired Aeon Jesus, the "Common Fruit" of the Pleroma (the "fruit of the cross"), who will have an important role to play in the redemption of the enformed offspring of Sophia. Thus occurs the precosmic "Fall" of the Aeon Sophia that initiates human history.

The lower Sophia is granted awareness of her divine origin by Christos. She longs to return to the light of the Pleroma, but she is unable to penetrate the Limit. Alone in the Darkness of the Void, she suffers, and her sufferings become states of being, becoming eventually psychic and material substance, the *prima materia* of the world in which man lives. Thus in some variants the material world was created from the Grief, Fear, Bewilderment, and Ignorance experienced by the lower Sophia in the Void, while her "Turning Back Toward the Life-Giver" produced the psychic world, standing between matter and spirit (Jonas 187–88).[5] In other variants Laughter, the "luminous substance," is added to the passions that create the material world.[6] Certainly a lower Sophia with a sense of humor would have appealed to Soloviev, who was well-known for his satiric and humorous poems and plays on lofty subjects.

Eccentric as this cosmogony may seem to the modern reader, Soloviev presented a nearly identical cosmogony in an interesting manuscript, written in French in early 1876, while he was in Cairo and Sorrento. The manuscript, which Soloviev originally described as "a work of mystical, theosophical-philosophical-theurgical-political content" and finally titled "Sophie," was not published in his lifetime; provocatively, Soloviev's original title for it was "Principes de la religion universelle," implying that in mystical gnosticism he perceived some fundamental religious doctrine that underlies all others (Sergei Solov'ev 119, 129ff.; *Pis'ma* 2:23, 27). Although Soloviev himself chose not to publish this interesting conglomeration of dialogue between the Philosopher and Sophia and philosophical essays (with marginal automatic and mediumistic writings), he subsequently refined many of its ideas and presented them in his major work, *La Russie et l'Eglise Universelle* (1889 in French; 1911, trans. to Russian by G. A. Rachinskii; see *Rossiia i Vselenskaia Tserkov'* 11: 143–348). "Sophie" and "La Sophia; principes de la doctrine universelle" were finally published in 1978 in the French original. These seemingly unusual works were not really unusual for Soloviev, who continued throughout his life to combine philosophical speculation (derivative and original) with satire, parody, poetry, and literary prose (see Kornblatt, this volume).

In "Sophie" Soloviev described the creation of the world in a clearly gnostic manner, consistently equating Sophia with the rebellious Aeon and then with the World Soul (Sophia's primary role in the world of Darkness):

By itself, the Soul is feminine, and its bliss and power lie in its submission to the active male force of the Divine Nous. Liberating in herself blind desire, affirming herself in her autonomous selfness [*samost'*], the Soul leaves her state of passivity and potentiality and enters an active state, she herself becomes Spirit, but the Spirit of Evil—she is no longer Soul, but *spiritus*, the spirit of darkness and evil. "The Soul is Satan, here is wisdom." In her fall, the Soul gives birth to Satan, the blind cosmic spirit, and to the Demiourgos, an intelligent force, but negative and external, the source of purely external forms, order, and relation. And the cosmic process begins, *bellum omnium contra omnia*. (Sergei Solov'ev 138; see below for clarification of use of the word "Soul")

In Soloviev, as in the Valentinian gnosis, the ensuing struggle between the Demiourgos and Satan then creates time and space, while the fragmenting Soul becomes the world's material substratum. The remainder of Soloviev's manuscript goes on to describe the Valentinian paradigm of telluric creation in considerable detail. Soloviev later cleared out many of the more sensational aspects of this Valentinian paradigm, but left the discussion of the World Soul and the Sophia, the particular redemptive role of Divine Logos, and other aspects of his theory intact in both the *Lectures on Godmanhood* (*Chteniia o bogochelovechestve*) and *La Russie et l'Église Universelle*.

The unpublished "Sophie" is a very rough draft and thus, while jejune in many ways, is more than a little revealing of Soloviev's early direction. That he considered his early attempt an important text is clear from his original (and most unsuitable, given contemporary circumstances) intention to defend it as a doctoral dissertation (Sergei Solov'ev 149); it would never have been accepted.

Despite her "sin," the gnostic Sophia remains a perfect emanation of the All-Unity and a bearer of Divine Light. Because of this particularly interesting complication (she is both sinner and sinless), Valentinian cosmology "found it necessary, in view of the wide span of the conditions represented by the female aspect of God (Sophia), to differentiate this aspect into an upper and a lower Sophia" (Jonas 177). Thus Valentinian Gnosticism postulates an Agia Sophia, the Holy Wisdom of God that remains in the glory and perfection of the Pleroma, and her antitype, the Sophia Prouneikos, Wisdom the Whore, the "formless" entity who, in being pushed out of the Light of the Pleroma and into the Darkness of the Void beyond, thrusts a spark of Divine Light into the Darkness.[7]

The fall into Darkness, Matter, and Evil of the lower Sophia, the Sophia Prouneikos, or Achamoth, was the very event that necessitated the creation of the world and of man for one very important purpose: to facilitate the eventual redemption of the fallen Light from the Darkness (the restoration of the complete Sophia to the Pleroma). Darkness and matter are defined as evil not absolutely, but relatively (for the physical world is the world of relativity): their distance from the perfection of the Pleroma means that they are less perfect, hence relatively more evil. Because of this state of events, the world and the universe exist, but within them also exist the means of returning the divine spark to the Godhead.

Once fallen into the realm of Matter and Darkness, the lower Sophia became nostalgic for her divine form and existence. In order to facilitate her return to the Light, she gave birth to the Demiourgos, who then created the earth and a human race to inhabit it.[8] Sophia splintered her divine Light and placed one spark of it into the soul of each human being, thereby herself becoming the Anima Mundi, the Soul of the World. In the world, then, the lower Sophia lost the original state of All-Unity and dwelt in a state of multiplicity and fragmentation (the basic feature of matter in mystical systems). She lost all but intuitive memory of her divine nature, although from time to time a reflection of her divine nature would penetrate the world to remind both the World Soul and the human souls of their great mission. The World Soul, the lower Sophia, or Sophia Prouneikos, became utterly sensual and was eventually assimilated to the various forms of the Great Goddess and the Tellus Mater of oriental and ancient religions (Jonas 176). This Sophia was "enclosed in human flesh and migrated for centuries as from vessel to vessel into different female bodies. And since all the Powers contended for her possession, strife and warfare raged among the nations wherever she appeared" (Jonas 107, quoting Irenaeus).

In this interesting mythology we see the source of the Russian symbolists' belief that Sophia could and would actually be incarnated in a particular woman, as Belyi, Blok, and Sergei Soloviev believed she might be incarnated in Liubov' Dmitrievna Blok or as the admittedly eccentric Anna Nikolaevna Schmidt believed she might be incarnated in herself (see Shmidt). Such a view also explains why it was not contradictory for Aleksandr Blok to search for her in cabarets and whorehouses and among sectarians as well as in drawing rooms and churches. Sophia is the Eternal Feminine, found in its divine aspect in Agia Sophia, and in its demonic, dark aspect in the World Soul, the seductive whore marked by the spark of divinity, Sophia Prouneikos. Soloviev's terminology reflects the gnostic paradigm, for he clearly made this same distinction between two Sophias, naming the two aspects Sophia (Wisdom of God) and World Soul: "As the world, which this soul attempts to create, is fragmented, divided, and held together only by purely external means; as this world is the antithesis and the opposite of divine universality; so the soul of the world itself is the antithesis or the antitype of the essential Wisdom of God. This soul of the world is a creature [*tvar'*] and the first of all creatures, the *materia prima* and the true *substratum* of our created world," he wrote as late as 1889 (Solov'ev, *Rossiia i Vselenskaia Tserkov'* 11:295). This is pure gnosticism.

According to the gnostics, it was the goal of world history to redeem Sophia. She had opened a gateway between the Pleroma, the World of Light, Spirit, and Goodness, and the World of Darkness, Matter, and Evil. She had crossed the boundary and left the periphery of the perfect Pleroma open to infiltration by the Powers of Darkness. The lower Sophia, the World Soul, and through her, the Spiritual Light imprisoned in Darkness and Matter, would be redeemed by the descent into Matter of the Christos (a form related to the Aeon Logos; Soloviev's Divine Logos). There the Christos would unite with the soul of the man Jesus; in "human garments" (material form) he would undergo a passion and be crucified (symbolizing the rejection of Matter for Spirit). In the gnostic paradigm, the Aeon Logos-Christos united with the mortal Jesus at the latter's baptism; in this way Jesus became the Christ. Soloviev pointed out in a notebook entry from 1875 that "The restoration of Christ, as an individual man = the union of the Divine Logos with the individual soul of Jesus" (Sergei Solov'ev 120). The voluntary descent of the Christos and his seeming self-sacrifice bring the liberating gnosis to mankind, making redemption possible. This gnosis is Wisdom; men who "know" (*gnostiki*) search after it.

Through his voluntary descent, the Christos effects the redemption of the Sophia; he becomes her consort (*syzygos*) on the marriage bed of the Cross (Limit, Boundary). Ultimately, the Christos reascends into the Fullness of the Pleroma, leading the lower Sophia with him as his Bride. This event is to occur at the end of History, and signals the completion of the redemption of Divine Light from Demonic Darkness, the final redemption of Spirit from Matter. This act would unite the divine and the human and would lead to a new heaven and new earth inhabited by a divine humanity (Soloviev's *bogochelovechestvo*, toward which it is the purpose of mankind to strive). Since man was created originally as a repository for the spiritual fragments of the World Soul, the marriage of the lower Sophia with the Christos signifies the reestablishment of the original, precosmic status quo and symbolizes the syzygy of human spirit and divinity (as the divine spark, placed in man by the fallen World

Soul, is reunited with its original source in the Godhead). Thus is the Sophia the "bridge" by which man comes (returns) to God.

The Gnostic Logos-Christos suffers not for the original sin of mankind (for there is none),[9] but for the precosmic guilt of the Sophia, whose original fall required the making of the world and of man so that the Christos would have a platform to which he could descend and a stage on which he could act out the drama of mankind's/Sophia's redemption. His coming brings a gnosis by means of which man (if sufficiently "awakened") can identify the spark of Divine Light that resides in him, purify himself of earthly, material dross, and restore the Light within to the All-Unity by completely identifying with the spiritual act of the Christos (i.e., descent into matter, passion, crucifixion, syzygy with the Sophia, and return to the Godhead). The coming of the Christos was thus the central event of human history; the restoration of the divine spark in man to its original source in the All-Unity became the very basis of the *imitatio Christi* and the only purpose of human existence.

The successful completion of this process of redemption is by no means predetermined or automatic (although some gnostic speculations assume it must and will happen). The descent of the Christos into the realm of matter, understood as an individual, inner spiritual event taking place in each human heart, means that the Christos is now subject to the illusions and temptations of material existence.[10] The Christ Feeling may not be strong enough to enable the individual to overcome the bondage of matter and awaken to his true spiritual nature; he may perish, trapped in the web of the World Illusion.[11] This is the risk that every mystic faces: the courage to descend into the abyss does not guarantee the strength to escape from it; the possibility of annihilation or eternal entrapment in matter is ever-present. Soloviev, toward the end of his life, felt this danger and at times despaired of man's ever having the strength to achieve a state of Divine Humanity (*bogochelovechestvo*).

In this way Soloviev's personal cosmogony derived to a great extent from this traditional gnostic paradigm. He continued to view the cosmic process, the creation of the world, and the redemption of the world in terms of the precosmic fall of Sophia (in her gnostic variant as the dark and demonic *anima mundi*, Achamoth), her separation from her heavenly bridegroom (Nous), her role as the Soul of the World in the creation of the material world, her nostalgia for her heavenly state, her creation of the Church on earth, her eventual redemption by the Bridegroom (Logos-Christos). In Soloviev's later works, the more sensational and clearly "mythological" gnostic elements disappear, some replaced by more traditional Christian vocabulary (although not always by traditional Christian meanings), some by patristic theological vocabulary, as Richard

Gustafson's chapter in this volume makes clear. But certain essential aspects of the gnostic cosmogony remain.

An examination of gnostic cosmogony elucidates why Soloviev was able to call his Sophia by many names: Agia Sophia; the World Soul (Anima Mundi); the Bride of the Lamb, Christos; the New Jerusalem; the Universal Church; the Wisdom of God, an Eternity (as aeonic emanation); and the Creative Principle, the *prima materia* of creation (for the world is *created* from the body of Sophia for one reason only: to facilitate the redemption of divine light trapped in matter through her fall), etc. Soloviev's Sophia is *not* (as some critics, like Vasily Zenkovsky [47–48], have claimed) fragmentary, inconsistent, and ambiguous. She is entirely consistent within the framework of a particular and very ancient gnostic pattern with which Soloviev was clearly familiar.

The profoundly moving and poetic Sophia Prayer, cited at the start of this essay, more than any dry didactic discourse, reveals the depth of Soloviev's debt to gnostic ideas. The poem begins with an invocation of the "Unutterable," Ineffable One. It refers to "the priceless pearl of Ophir" (the Pearl of Great Price, a well-known gnostic metaphor for the soul [Jonas 125–29]). It names the Rose, symbol of the perfection of the Pleroma; the "Rose of Sharon" is Ecclesia, the Church, while the Lily of the Valley represents the Advent of Christ (Cooper 98, 141–42). The Divine Sophia is "the bright body of Eternity" (Eternity being another name for Aeon; see above); she is the "Soul of worlds and the one Queen of all souls" as the *anima mundi* and the *prima materia*. She requests that her beloved, Jesus Christ (Christos-Logos), descend into the "prison of the soul" (the gnostics called the human body the "tomb" or the "prison house of the soul") and "fill our darkness with thy radiance" (descend into material reality with divine light), and "melt away the fetters that bind our spirit" (bring the gnosis that liberates the spirit from matter), "incarnate thyself in us and in the world, restoring the fullness of the Ages" (the perfection of the Aeons, the Pleroma), "so that the deep [the Void, the Cosmos] may be confined and that God may be all in all." When the reader learns the vocabulary, the gnostic power of the Sophia Prayer becomes clear.

Gnosticism, although heretical in the view of traditional Christianity, has exercised a tremendously seductive power over many thinkers within the Orthodox tradition; moreover, the gnostic heresy seems to be a "natural" heresy for Orthodox Christianity. The mystical theology of the Eastern Church was flexible enough to accommodate what would become the sophiology of Sergei Bulgakov and other post-Solovievian thinkers. But from the point of view of the traditional Orthodox church, Father Georges Florovsky was correct to point at

Soloviev as a "pernicious influence" in his *Ways of Russian Theology* (*Puti russkogo bogosloviia* 469).

Certain aspects of gnosticism certainly affected Soloviev and his literary heirs. Gnosticism is also present in the various occult doctrines, notably Theosophy and Anthroposophy, which attracted converts from among the Russian intelligentsia during the early twentieth century (most of whom were, not surprisingly, fervent Solovievians; see Carlson). The vocabulary and symbology of gnosticism continued to be profoundly appealing to poets of all times and places, including the Russian symbolists. While most readers are acquainted with the Sophia paradigm as expressed by the "Beautiful Lady" (Prekrasnaia Dama) and "The Stranger" (Neznakomka) poems of Aleksandr Blok (1880–1921), the young, impressionable, and mystically inclined Andrei Belyl (Boris Bugaev, 1880–1934) took more from Soloviev's total system. This is especially clear in his First Symphony, whose heroine is a Sophia figure who gives the gnostic "Call of Eternity"; his short story "Adam" actually narrates the story of the precosmic fall into matter as an anecdote; and in the novel *Silver Dove*, the Logos-hero, Petr Darialsky, finds himself literally trapped in matter as in a spiderweb (the veil of Maya), then hears "The Call," and returns to his true home in eternity by dying to material existence.

Although the younger symbolists emphasized Soloviev's concept of Sophia as primary, others recognized in Soloviev's system of metaphysics the primacy of the Christ idea and the secondary role of the Sophia as the Herald of His Coming or the Bridge between man and God. For Soloviev, as for the Christian Gnostics, Christ was not a founder, not a teacher; Christ was the very *content* of Christianity. The life of the true Christian, if he desires to participate in that content, must be lived *in imitatio Christi*. Soloviev's Sophia, a figure whom many modern commentators erroneously endow with a primacy it does not possess in his system, is only a link, a mediating principle between the human and divine; Sophia is but the *means* of uniting man with Christ.

More recently, gnosticism has attracted the attention of analytical psychologists. Elaine Pagels has pointed out in her book *The Gnostic Gospels* that "the gnostic movement shared certain affinities with contemporary methods of exploring the self through psychotherapeutic techniques. Both gnosticism and psychotherapy value, above all, knowledge—the self-knowledge which is insight" (124). Other scholars of gnosticism, notably Hans Jonas, have also noticed the "parallel vocabularies" of gnosticism and depth psychology, as both seek words to describe the indescribable and to express complex psychic contents. C. G. Jung wrote extensively about gnosticism and "deciphered" its symbology, translating it into the vocabulary of depth psychology, in numerous essays (see, for example, the anthology *The Gnostic Jung*; also Jung's *Psychology and Alchemy* and *Aion*). Gnostic thought repeatedly returns to enthrall human consciousness, as it does today in the manifold syncretic systems of New Age mysticism.

This essay has left many subjects (about which gnosticism had something to say) unexplored. These include Soloviev's understanding of the nature of divine and human love, syzygy, and abstract eroticism; morality and ethics; the nature of evil; the role of asceticism. The essay has focused instead on the contributing role played by gnostic cosmogony and the gnostic Sophia concept in the evolution of Soloviev's understanding of man's divine and human essences, of the nature of sin and redemption, and of the Sophia's particular role as bridge between the Godhead and humanity.[12] Soloviev's fundamental notion of divine humanity (*bogochelovechestvo*) may, ultimately, be understood only when its gnostic as well as its traditional Christian context is fully explored.

Soloviev was an essentially eclectic (even syncretic) thinker, and he found in the gnostic Sophia and her poetic genesis a rich vocabulary and imagery for spiritual events and experiences. This gnostic vocabulary and imagery he combined creatively with those of other religious, mystical and philosophical systems that attracted him and his contemporaries of the *fin-de-siècle* (including Kabbalah, the thought of Boehme and Swedenborg, mystical Orthodox theology, and even, occasionally, occultism, among others); the result was a system unique to Vladimir Soloviev. Thus Soloviev's syncretic sophiology may fruitfully be viewed in the context of a search for a *modern gnosis*, a search for new forms of meaningful spiritual knowledge, which, arguably, the Russian religious renaissance was.

Notes

1.   Translation mine; the Russian original is given in Sergei Solov'ev 118–19. Sergei Soloviev included this material in the sixth and seventh editions of his uncle's *Stikhotvoreniia*; it can be found in Vladimir Solov'ev 12:148–49.

2.   Concepts and vocabulary are particularly troubling. In *Adversus haereses*, Irenaeus writes, "Certainly they [the Valentinians] confess with their tongues the one Jesus Christ, but in their minds (*sententia*) they divide him" (cited in Rudolph 154–55). Kurt Rudolph points out that, indeed, for the gnostics Christ is Jesus Christ, the earthly manifestation of the Christos; Christ is a higher being, an Aeon, who dwells in the Fullness of the Pleroma; and finally, Christ is the "Perfect Fruit" of the Pleroma, who becomes the consort of the fallen Sophia. This scarcely conforms to the traditional Christian concept of the Christ.

3. Rudolf Steiner even wrote the introduction to the first German edition of Soloviev, emphasizing Soloviev's role as mediator between Eastern and Western spirituality. See Solov'ev, *Ausgewählte Werke*.

4. That the one fallen Aeon, or Eternity, is feminine is interesting. Perhaps it reflects Aristotelian belief in a hierarchy of physical perfection in which the male human being was the acme. The female, as a step away from male perfection, was a step toward imperfection and deformity. Such a view seems to be present in the gnostic paradigm of the emanating Aeons, with the last, "sinning" Aeon being the feminine Sophia. The names of the Aeons, or Eternities (Christos, Holy Spirit, Divine Logos, Nous, Sophia, Achamoth, etc.), differ slightly in the various renderings, but their functions remain essentially the same.

5. The Valentinian speculation preserves the antique Greek view of the double soul, sometimes called the *psyche* and the *pneuma*. The former is a body soul, which endows life and consciousness, then perishes with the body; the latter is the imperishable spiritual soul.

6. The concepts of parody, grotesque, and the satiric are central to Soloviev's own work, as well as to the writings of the second-generation symbolists. Gnostic laughter (the laughter of the gnostic Christos at the moment of crucifixion, laughter as creative substance) is certainly an important element in the works not only of Soloviev, but also of Andrei Belyi, Sergei Soloviev, and Aleksandr Blok.

7. In some gnostic variants, Agia Sophia and Sophia Prouneikos are replaced by Sophia and her female offspring, Achamoth. Sophia then remains in the perfection of the Pleroma, but Achamoth must live with her mother's sin in the Darkness.

8. The gnostics thus viewed the God of the Old Testament as the evil Demiourgos, the Creator who would keep the World Soul and mankind enslaved eternally in matter. They viewed the "fall" of Adam and Eve as a happy event, brought about by the wise serpent. Only by tasting of the fruit of the Tree of Good and Evil could Adam and Eve understand their divine origin and begin the work that was to restore the Divine Light.

9. In a gnostic cosmogony, there is no human "fall," only the fall of the Sophia from the Pleroma into the Cosmic Void. The serpent in the Garden of Eden is the hero of the gnostic paradigm, not the villain. In the gnostic Genesis, "God" is the material Demiourgos who places the divine spark of the World Soul into Adam and Eve, and then attempts to hide from them their divine origin in the Pleroma and to trap them forever in matter. The serpent (symbol of Wisdom), by encouraging them to taste of the Tree of the Knowledge of Good and Evil (Spirit and Matter), ensures that the human race will eventually become aware of the trap of matter, recognize its spiritual home, accept the gnosis, and hearing The Call, return to the Godhead (see Pagels *Adam* 65ff.; Jonas 93–94).

10. The Valentinian speculation did not intend for its initiates to take the Sophia story literally. The story functions as an allegorical paradigm for the redemption of the human spirit, pining in ignorance until redeemed by

the knowledge (gnosis) of the Christ. This macrocosmic drama has its counterpart in the microcosmic tribulations of the human heart.

11.   This is one of the many points at which gnosticism, Theosophy, Buddhism (all important at the fin-de-siècle), and other occult doctrines intersect. Theosophy and Buddhism both posit Maya, the cosmic Spider who spins the web of World Illusion which must be overcome. The image appears in a number of symbolist works, notably Andrei Belyi's *Serebrianyi golub'*, where the entrapping web literally sends its viscous strands into the hero's breast. The web of World Illusion holds its victim trapped in matter and occludes the higher, "real" reality that stands behind illusion.

12.   The understanding of theosis conspicuously highlights the difference between traditional Orthodoxy and gnosticism. Stated in extreme terms, the gnostic *is* God, albeit a fragmented and imprisoned God; his earthly task is to discover this fact, to reject and overcome the material world that keeps him prisoner in his physical body and in nature (which are evil, having been created by an evil demiourgos), and to return to the unknowable Godhead. Most gnostic doctrines have no concept of grace or resurrection, let alone resurrection in the despised flesh. The gnostic path is a return, not a trial or a quest. In Orthodoxy, on the other hand, man is made in the image of God, but he *is not* God. Man dwells in nature, which is good, for it was created by God; man acquires the Holy Spirit only through divine grace and "dwells in" God, as God dwells in him. Man partakes of divine nature, joins with the divine energy of God, but is not himself divine.

Works Cited

Allen, Paul M. *Vladimir Soloviev: Russian Mystic*. Blauvelt, N.Y.: Steinerbooks, 1978.

Belyi, Andrei [Boris Bugaev]. *Simvolizm: kniga statei*. Moscow: Musaget, 1910.

Carlson, Maria. *"No Religion Higher Than Truth": A History of the Theosophical Movement in Russia 1875–1922*. Princeton: Princeton University Press, 1993.

Cioran, Samuel D. *Vladimir Solov'ev and the Knighthood of the Divine Sophia*. Waterloo, Ontario: Wilfrid Laurier University Press, 1977.

Cooper, J. C. *An Illustrated Encyclopedia of Traditional Symbols*. London: Thames & Hudson, 1978.

Florovsky, Georges. *Puti russkogo bogosloviia*. Paris: [YMCA Press], 1937.

Jonas, Hans. *The Gnostic Religion: The Message of the Alien God and the Beginnings of Christianity*. 2d rev. ed. Boston: Beacon Press, 1963.

Jung, Carl Gustav. *Aion: Researches into the Phenomenology of the Self*. Trans. R. F. C. Hull. 2d ed. Vol. IX,2 of the *Collected Works*. Bollingen Series 20. Princeton: Princeton University Press, 1959.

Jung, Carl Gustav. *The Gnostic Jung*. Ed. Robert A Segal. Princeton: Princeton University Press, 1992.

Jung, Carl Gustav. *Psychology and Alchemy*. Trans. R. F. C. Hull. Vol. XII of the *Collected Works*. Bollingen Series 20. Princeton: Princeton University Press, 1968.

Mead, G. R. S. *Fragments of a Faith Forgotten.* New York: University Books, 1960. Rpt. of orig. 1921 ed.

Merezhkovskii, Dmitrii. "Nemoi prorok." *Polnoe sobranie sochinenii,* ed. I. I. Sytin. 24 vols. Moscow: I. D. Sytin, 1914. 16:122–35.

Pagels, Elaine. *Adam, Eve, and the Serpent.* New York: Vintage, 1988.

Pagels, Elaine. *The Gnostic Gospels.* New York: Random House, 1979.

Rudolph, Kurt. *Gnosis: The Nature and History of Gnosticism.* Trans. R. McL. Wilson, P W. Coxon, and K. H. Kuhn. San Francisco: Harper and Row, [1985].

Shmidt, Anna Nikolaevna. *Iz rukopisei Anny Nikolaevny Shmidt. Budushchnosti. Tretii Zavet. Iz dnevnika. Pis'ma i pr. S pis'mami k nei V1. Solov'eva.* Ed. S. Bulgakov. [Moscow]: Put', 1916.

Solov'ev, Sergei. *Zhizn' i tvorcheskaia evoliutsiia Vladimira Solov'eva.* Brussels: Zhizn' s Bogom, 1977

Solov'ev, Vladimir [Solowjew, Wladimir]. *Ausgewählte Werke.* 4 vols. Trans. Harry Köhler (Harriet von Vacano). Stuttgart: Der kommende Tag, 1922.

Solov'ev, Vladimir. *Pis'ma.* Ed. E. L. Radlov. 4 vols. St. Petersburg: "Obshchestvennaia pol'za," 1908. Reprinted with appendix, Brussels: Zhizn' s Bogom, 1970.

Solov'ev, Vladimir. *Sobranie sochinenii.* Ed. S. M. Solov'ev and E. L. Radlov. 2d ed. 10 vols. St. Petersburg: Prosveshchenie, 1911–14. Reprinted with 2 additional volumes, Brussels: Zhizn' s Bogom, 1966–1970.

Solov'ev, Vladimir. *"La Sophia" et les autres écrits français.,* Ed. François Rouleau. Lausanne: La Cité, 1978.

3

Soloviev on Salvation
The Story of the "Short Story of the Antichrist"

Judith Deutsch Kornblatt

"God made Himself man so that man might become God." The Eastern Orthodox Church understands this statement, spoken by many of the early Fathers, including Irenaeus, Athanasius, Gregory of Nazianzus, and Gregory of Nyssa, to refer to human salvation as *theosis*, or deification (see Ware 236–42; Lossky 97; and Gustafson's article in the present volume). We are made in the image and likeness of God, and our godlike countenance can and will again shine through our earthly life.[1] The doctrine of salvation as deification plays a key role for Vladimir Soloviev, and through him in the religious philosophy of the early twentieth century, for, as Semën Frank asserts, Soloviev "can be considered the sole intellectual thread connecting the religious thought of the twentieth century with the thinkers of the nineteenth" (Frank 12).

In Soloviev's well-documented view, the deification of creation cannot occur through divine grace alone. We must participate in our own salvation, both individually and socially. Godmanhood (*bogochelovechestvo*) wrote Soloviev early in his philosophical career, "is the real mutual activity of God and man" (*real'noe vzaimodeistvie Boga i cheloveka* 3:36).[2] The true relationship between humanity and divinity, as Soloviev repeatedly asserted, was one of mutual interpenetration (*vzaimoproniknovenie*), not absorption of humanity into the divine, and not of human passivity in the face of supernatural grace. Like his theological mentor Maximus the Confessor, Soloviev aggressively opposed any monothelite tendency that would remove human nature or human will from Christ (see 12:598–99, 10:421–26). Equally, he rejected any notion of theodicy that ignores human participation, and of history that does not include the responsibility of individuals and nations for their own salvation.

History, for Soloviev, is a process culminating in the realization of the potential for divinity within humanity. This emphasis on human activity and cooperation with the Divine—delivered in an essentially optimistic tone—continued throughout his life. It is why, for one, he repeatedly praised the Jews; Abraham entered into a covenant with God as a partner: "as two beings, although not of equal strength, nonetheless morally akin" (4:144). It forms the core of his vision in the 1880s of a future theocracy; it continues in his articles on "Christian politics" during the following decade.

Recognizing the centrality of human-divine interaction for Soloviev, this article examines the theme of salvation in perhaps Soloviev's most famous work, published just one year before his death: *Three Conversations* (*Tri razgovora*, 1899), a series of dialogues roughly based on the platonic genre, the third of which includes the reading of a story titled "Short Story of the Antichrist" ("Kratkaia povest' ob antikhriste"). Most critics, following Soloviev's symbolist heirs, understand this work with its imagery of the final apocalypse as a deathbed reversal of the optimistic tone and content of his earlier writing. Presumably, Soloviev suddenly abandoned his idealistic emphasis on the process of human history and, focusing instead on the existence of unrelenting evil in this world, sadly turned his attention to the end of time.

"In his new understanding, we no longer find that earthly completion of progress that earlier seemed so necessary to the philosopher," writes Evgeny Trubetskoi (2:302). Soloviev finally recognized that, although the Divine may have become man within human history (Christ as Godman or *Bogochelovek*), the universal realization of Godmanhood (*bogochelovechestvo*) is possible only by God's judgment at the end of time. His vision turned dark. All admit, of course, that the central polemic with Tolstoy on passive resistance to evil was not new to this work. But, according to Konstantin Mochulsky, "In denouncing Tolstoy, Soloviev castigated himself as well. . . . That is why the tone of *Three Conversations* rises to tragic passion; Soloviev could not have died without writing it. It is his repentance" (Mochul'skii 256).

Critics extol Soloviev's alleged repudiation of earlier beliefs for various reasons: Mochulsky on the assumption that Soloviev finally recognized the sole power of resurrection; Lev Shestov for Soloviev's

supposed confirmation of the supremacy of revelation over philosophy
(Shestov 22, 32); Trubetskoi for Soloviev's new understanding of the
importance of Golgotha (Trubetskoi 2:381). Stremooukhoff attributes
Soloviev's change of mood (to which the philosopher himself refers
in his author's preface, 10:83) to demonic visions in the spring of 1898
and to disillusionment on his final trip to Egypt (Stremooukhoff 318,
and Losev 178–79); Soloviev recognized at last that "theocracy will not
be realized in history" (Stremooukhoff 331).

It is my contention, however, that *Three Conversations* and its imbed-
ded story reinforce rather than repudiate Soloviev's lifetime of beliefs.
We need only allow ourselves to read it as a clever example of self-
parody, instead of self-negation. Since deathbed reversals make great
drama but are in fact quite rare, and none of Soloviev's other writings
in the last two years of his life expresses the supposed tragic tone of the
"Short Story of the Antichrist" (see Gaut 93), I will argue that Soloviev
did not suddenly abandon his former faith in human cooperation in our
own salvation. True, the Antichrist appears for the first time in Soloviev's
work, and the story is based in part, as Soloviev himself admits, on
imagery from Revelation 10:89, leading readers to assume that *Three
Conversations* relays the dramatic message that only divine intervention
can save humanity from its own inclination toward evil. It is also true
that Soloviev's earlier vision of theocracy and of a Universal Church
appears in the story only as a *false* theocracy permeated with evil instead
of God. Nonetheless, salvation comes, even in this most apocalyptic of
works, only because of, and by means of, human participation.

Why have critics so consistently understood *Three Conversations* as
a repudiation of Soloviev's former faith? We must remember that it
was the symbolists, especially Aleksandr Blok, Andrei Belyi, and Sergei
Soloviev, the philosopher's nephew, who took up Soloviev's banner
following his death in 1900. Reading Soloviev through their own otherwordly eyes, they showed little interest in the full breadth of Soloviev's
work, and concentrated narrowly on his mystical writings about the
Divine Sophia, on his poetry, his "gnosticism," and on this last dramatic
story of apocalypse.[3] What is more curious is that we, to this day, tend
to read Soloviev through the symbolists' eyes, showing interest in his
ethics and social philosophy only with difficulty.[4] It is perhaps not
without significance that Soloviev's major biographers emerged from
the symbolist movement and, immersed in a decadent worldview, chose
to impose a tragic curve upon the life of their subject.[5]

Furthermore, later critics have not questioned this early picture because they have failed to see the obvious: Soloviev experimented in
his dialogues and in the short story not with new ideas, but with

new genres.[6] Both the setting for the story and the story of the end
of history itself are fiction—neither a "scholarly-philosophical paper"
nor "religious homily," as the author himself admitted ("Predislovie"
10:83)—and we should read them as such. In fact, Soloviev invites
us to ask literary questions about *Three Conversations*, as we will see,
and we are therefore justified in employing literary-critical tools on
his last famous work.[7] Such a critical reading can reveal more to us
about Soloviev's larger view of reality than have those that insist on
ignoring generic, narrative, and general literary considerations. We will
find evidence, as already stated, of self-parody, not self-negation, of
extreme self-consciousness regarding the literariness of this work, and
an intricate interplay between author, narrators, and characters who
themselves narrate. Most important, we will note the significance of
the supposed unfinished state of the short story's manuscript, and of
the tension between its written and oral stories. Together, these literary
issues show that Soloviev remained dedicated in *Three Conversations* to
belief in salvation as the deification of humanity, and to the crucial role
of human and social action in the attainment of that goal.

The Dialogue

In light of his concurrent work on Plato's dialogues, we must assume
that Soloviev's choice of the dialogue form was not accidental. Sparked
by his desire to master Plato's thought, and encouraged by his friend
Afanasy Fet to "give Plato to Russian literature" ("Predislovie," *Tvoreniia
Platona* 12:360), Soloviev began an ambitious translation project in 1897.
In conjunction, he published a major essay entitled "The Life Drama of
Plato" ("Zhiznennaia drama Platona" 9:194–241) in 1898.

Plato, for Soloviev, was a consummate stylist on the level of Pushkin,
a "born artist of the word" ("O pervom otdele platonovykh tvorenii"
12:467–68). According to Soloviev, the philosopher began his career as
an erotic poet, but consciously turned from the orgiastic poetry of his
youth, as well as from the dry prose of his contemporaries:

And thus he created a new form—the philosophical dialogue—that most closely
suited Socrates' lively, upwardly striving thought. A philosophical conversation
controlled by Socrates, in which he leads his various collocutors to the truth, was
the best and, we might say, the only direct, "adequate" means for the expression
of Plato's own internal experience. (12:467)

Regarding his own choice of the dialogue, Soloviev wrote in his
preface to *Three Conversations*, published only after the separate printing
of the three dialogues: "For a long while I could not find the proper

form for the accomplishment of my plan. . . . This verbal form then appeared spontaneously, as the simplest expression of what I wanted to say" (10:83).

For Soloviev, the genre of the dialogue fit perfectly his expressed polemic goal: to discredit Tolstoy's attitude toward evil in the world. Like Plato through the character of Socrates, Soloviev as author could manipulate the conversation of his characters so that the Prince (who rather transparently represents Tolstoy) eventually would expose the internal contradictions of his own arguments.[8] In fact, the Prince is forced to absent himself from the conversation at several crucial moments, and has totally disappeared by the end of the last dialogue. Like the speakers in Plato's *Symposium*, at the end of which all but the strongest literary representatives (Agathon for tragedy, Aristophanes for comedy, and Socrates for philosophy) have fallen asleep, the representative of the "weakest" position in *Three Conversations* simply fades away.

Besides his polemic with Tolstoy, Soloviev also had what he called a "positive" goal for his work: "to present the question of the struggle against evil and the meaning of history from three different points of view" (10:87). What is significant for us here is that the dialogue provided Soloviev with an interactive form to represent graphically, as it were, this struggle. As he claims:

Although I myself stand firmly behind the latter point of view [that expressed by Mr. Z], I recognize the relative truth of the first two, and thus could with equal impartiality relay the opposing arguments and declarations of the Politician and the General. The highest unconditional truth does not exclude nor does it negate the preparatory conditions of its appearance, but rather justifies, interprets, and sanctifies them. (10:87)

Critics usually emphasize Soloviev's first statement here—that he stands behind the views of Mr. Z. (In fact, they often assert that he *is* Mr. Z.) Occasionally they acknowledge Soloviev's recognition of the relative truth of the positions of the Politician and the General. Almost never do they analyze Soloviev's historiographical statement, however, and therefore miss the very Solovievian emphasis on process as struggle—he also uses the terms "rivalry" and "battle" (*tiazhba, bor'ba*, 10:87)—created by the interaction of opposing principles. As Soloviev goes on to say, we must understand the various players in this process as instruments or weapons (*orudiia*) to be judged on their efficacy, not their inherent truth value (10:88). We can arrive at the "highest unconditional truth" only through the interaction, that is, the struggle, of the discussants, just as Good can be victorious only through the struggle with Evil. The Platonic dialogue, therefore, provided Soloviev with the form necessary to express a dearly held belief about progress. Although some have called Soloviev's historiographical ideas deterministic, in fact optimism about the eventual interpenetration of human and divine principles should not be confused with lack of belief in human will. Only *with* human struggle will the goal of *bogochelovechestvo* be reached. These beliefs have not changed, but have found new expression in the genre of *Three Conversations*.

The Short Story

The preface to *Three Conversations* next discusses the second genre with which Soloviev experiments: the "short story" (*kratkaia povest'*) in "Short Story of the Antichrist." The conversations, he states, had to end on an indication (*ukazanie*) about evil in history, and on a presentation of evil's brief triumph and decisive fall (*predstavlenie ego kratkago torzhestva i reshitel'nago padeniia*, 10:88). This "indication" and "presentation" take fictional form. Why did a polemic about the existence of evil in the world require a short story (*kratkaia povest'*) to represent the short triumph (*kratkoe torzhestvo*) of that evil? In other words, what is the relationship between the literary genre and the content?

In his preface, Soloviev asserts that the reason is drama. He claims that he first wrote the third conversation without a story, but became convinced that the dialogue form was not sufficiently serious, and its frivolity would inappropriately interrupt the dramatic buildup:

At first I placed this subject into the same conversational form as the previous ones, with the same admixture of humor. Friendly criticism convinced me, however, that such an exposition was doubly inept here: in the first place because the interruptions and inserted comments required of the dialogue would hinder the dramatic interest of the story [literally, aroused interest, *vozbuzhdennyi interes*], and, in the second place, because the wordly and especially the humorous tone of the conversation did not correspond to the religious significance of the subject. (10:88)

Must we, however, take Soloviev's word here for the way in which we should read the short story? For one thing, does Soloviev not give ample evidence that a humorous tone is precisely the one with which to approach "serious" subjects? At about the time Soloviev worked on his *Three Conversations*, he also wrote *Three Encounters*, the famous poem that beautifully recreates at the same time as it parodically mocks his alleged visions of Divine Sophia. At the end of the composition, he included the following note:

An autumn evening and the dense forest inspired me to reproduce in humorous stanzas the most significant moments of my life up until today. Memory and consonance rose up irrepressibly in my consciousness for two days, and the third day delivered this small autobiography that has appealed to some poets and ladies. (12:86)

It seems unlikely in light of Soloviev's repeated use of humor in any number of his more literary pieces that he would reject it here (see Gusev 6). In fact, we need not look far to find humor even in this "serious" short story. Might then the requirement of a work of literary prose here have less to do with drama and/or seriousness of content, and more with a desire to reinforce through genre an essential truth, just as the Platonic dialogue allowed Soloviev to depict the interactive struggle that he called progress? Might not also the short story be a genre that allows for a certain *type* of humor—parody—not present in the tame repartee of the "casual social conversation" that is the dialogue (10:83), so that its inclusion would permit Soloviev to sharpen his message by turning his humor against himself? We would then more profitably turn our attention to an interpretation of form and context, instead of apocalyptic content, and see how the short story uses parody in conjunction with other narrative tricks to manipulate its readers toward a true understanding of human involvement in salvation.

The Context of the Short Story

We can turn now to the placement of the short story embedded in the third dialogue. Throughout the conversations, Soloviev gives ample evidence that we are to attend to the formal aspects of his work. The Lady in particular frequently brings up questions of style, metaphor, tone, and irony. She is the facilitator in the dialogues, representing no single view; she is present, we might say, solely for form, not at all for content. In addition to the Lady's foregrounding of literary issues, Soloviev embeds within the dialogues frequent references to and quotations from other literary genres. We have a story from the chronicles, with much comment about style (is it or is it not vulgar? 10:107–8); a chilling war story (10:109); an anecdote from contemporary life about the death of a writer that includes the story of another character, the wanderer, half-*iurodivyi* Varsonofius (10:121–25). The latter himself is turned into narrator, as Mr. Z relates a story about yet another character, a European-educated old Russian woman, who had been told a "story from the life of ancient hermits" by Varsonofius that Mr. Z now summarizes (10: 125–28). The second conversation includes lines of poetry, plays on words, a discussion of grammar, and a reference to the theater.

The third conversation contains additional discussion of metaphor and includes the recital of an unpublished poem of A. K. Tolstoy.[9] Not insignificantly, Mr. Z argues that the farcical form of the poem does not negate its "serious and, what is most important, truthful and realistic content" (10:168). In fact, "the actual relationship between goodness and evil in human life is depicted with these humorous lines better than I could depict it in my serious prose" (10:168). We are thus alerted to Soloviev's own use of a humorous tone. "I have not the least doubt," Mr. Z continues, "that when the heroes of other world-renowned novels that skillfully and seriously plow the black soil of psychology are no more than literary reminiscences for bibliophiles, then this farce, which has touched the subterranean depth of the moral question with its humorous and wildly caricaturelike features, will preserve all of its artistic and philosophical truth" (10:168).

The Lady is frustrated by Mr. Z's "paradoxes" (10:168), but the contradictions that he expresses here about the relationship of form, tone, and content are in fact preparation for our interpretation of the coming story of the Antichrist: form interacts with content, fiction with reality, the sublime with the profane, ultimately reinforcing Soloviev's belief in the actual, not metaphoric coactivity of human and divine in the creation of the story of our future salvation. If laughter is uniquely human, as Soloviev writes elsewhere, and we are all by essence "laughing animals,"[10] then humor's penetration into doctrinal seriousness shapes the created work toward true *bogochelovechestvo*.

In the third conversation, the General recites a soldier's song, and a biblical parable is first retold, then read directly from the Bible (10:174, 10:177–78).[11] At last, we are introduced to the "Short Story of the Antichrist." Mr. Z claims that portraits of the Antichrist (like those of Christ) are unpaintable, and that Church literature gives us no more than a "passport with his general and particular features" (10:191). He will satisfy us instead with a manuscript (again, the depiction *requires* a story instead of some other genre or artistic medium) written by a former classmate-turned-monk who, on his deathbed, willed the work to Mr. Z. "Although in fantastic form, in the shape of an imagined historical forecast,[12] this composition presents everything, in my opinion, that Scripture, Church tradition, and common sense could say with any kind of surety about the subject" (10:192).

Thus Soloviev removes the narration of the story from himself, attributing the writing of the fantastic forecast of history to the fictional monk Pansofius, and relinquishing the reading of it to the fictional Mr. Z. Let us remember that, despite Soloviev's assertion in the preface that he stands most closely by the views of Mr. Z, the author is *not* his fictional character, just as he is not his more primary narrator, who remains a silent eavesdropper on the (fictional) discussions recorded in *Three*

Conversations (10:92). We cannot miss the artificiality of a literary device long ago made trite; an "editor" or lay reader simply reproduces, and therefore is not responsible for, the content of the material before us. Pushkin had already parodied the device seventy years earlier with his *Tales of Belkin*. In *Three Conversations*, the narrator's ridiculous claim to truth only reinforces our recognition of his fictionality: he arrived too late to hear the opening of the first conversation and now refuses to "make it up": "I decided not to fabricate [the opening] out of my own head after the model of Plato and his imitators, and thus began my recording with the words of the General that I heard as I approached the group" (10:92). Soloviev is thus able to play humorous one-upmanship with his acknowledged mentor.

At the same time, however, as the author distances the story from himself—Pansofius to Mr. Z to narrator to us—Soloviev inserts himself back into the narrating loop, now with parody. He draws attention to the fictional author with the following exchange:

POLITICIAN: And is this the work of our acquaintance Varsonofius?
MR. Z: No, this one's name is even more refined: Pansofius.
POLITICIAN: Pan Sofius? A Pole?
MR. Z: Not at all. From the Russian clergy. (10:192)

We must assume that Soloviev considers his readers smarter than his Politician, who unknowingly separates Pansofius' name into its two semantic parts: Pan for "all" (although the Politician assumes "Pan" to be the Polish form of "Mr.") and Sofius for "wisdom." Is the monk then not a parodic combination of Soloviev's most dearly held mystical beliefs: all-unity (*vseedinstvo*) and Divine Wisdom (Sophia)?

The Written Text

Mr. Z begins his reading with the title and an epigraph:

SHORT STORY OF THE ANTICHRIST
Panmongolism! Although the name is wild,
It caresses my ear,
As though filled with a portent
Of God's great destiny.

The Lady interrupts: "Where did he get that epigraph?" "I think," answers Mr. Z, "that the author of the story composed it himself" (10:193). We would be hopelessly immersed in the fictional drama of the situation were we to ignore Soloviev's second humorous intrusion back into the story by means of these four lines from his 1894 poem "Pan-mongolism."[13] Can we not then see the "Short Story of the Antichrist" as Soloviev's own "deathbed" testament entrusted, *parodically*, to his readers? Poking fun at himself, he is "all-wise" and will instruct us now on the final appearance of evil in the world. As a "laughing animal," Soloviev proves his own creative potential for partnership with God. His "wisdom" in this fiction is the true stuff of *bogochelovechestvo*; parody leads to truth.[14]

Mr. Z reads the manuscript, an annotated resume of which I lay out here. The story begins with a dry retelling of future history; four pages without paragraph break describe a devastating war between Asia and Europe, exacerbated by the fact that the countries of the West could not get along. The decidedly unexciting tone of the story's beginning gives the lie to Soloviev's ex post facto statement in his preface that the purpose of the story form was to provide tension and not to hinder the "aroused interest" of the content. The new genre, as we have already assumed, has some other purpose. Like the battle of opinions in the dialogue, the fictional genre allows for an interplay of narratives that make up the story of history.

The manuscript then turns to the description of a thirty-three-year-old "Superman" who believed in good, God, and the Messiah, "but who *loved* only *himself*" (10:198; emphasis in original). Because of the tremendous popular response that fanned his egoism, the Superman begins to see himself as the ultimate salvation of mankind. When he receives no sign from God to this effect, he becomes a prime candidate for approach by the Evil Power, whose literary portrait here is familiar to the point of triteness:

A figure appeared before him, shining with a phosphorescent, hazy light. Its eyes penetrated his soul with an unbearably sharp brilliance.

He saw these two piercing eyes and heard a strange voice, not exactly from within him, and not exactly from without. The voice was thick, at once muffled and distinct, metallic and completely lifeless, as though from a phonograph. (10:200)

Through the new authority granted him in an apparent pact with Satan, the Superman becomes yet wiser, more beneficent, and more powerful. Importantly, his power comes not as much from himself as from the abdication of responsibility by all the inhabitants of the earth. Like Dostoevsky's Grand Inquisitor (and the parodied parallel is so close as to be indubitably intentional),[15] the Superman solves the "socio-economic question" for all times by providing for "the most basic of all equalities—the equality of universal satiation" (10:205).

To assist him with both the true and the sometimes illusory provision of his flock, the newly elected Emperor-Superman takes on the services of Apollonius, a half Asiatic and half European miracle worker. Apollonius is shown to control a vast arsenal of magic tricks, including the ability to conjure up death-dealing lightning bolts from the heavens. As Soloviev reminds us in the preface, we cannot know the marvel of mechanical skill two or three centuries hence, and therefore must not dismiss his description of Apollonius as fantasy (10:89). In fact, Soloviev's use of fantastic "details" to flesh out the "bare schema" of his story is more sophisticated than this prefatory remark indicates, as he makes clear elsewhere in an analysis of the fantastic in poetry.[16] Not only are the fictional observers of Apollonius' wizardry helpless to evaluate the source of the wizard's power (even the narrator can do no more than describe how Apollonius fumbles with something inside his robes and finally confesses that "the new Pope-Wizard accomplished feats so wonderous and unbelievable that it would be useless even to relay them," 10:217), but the readers of the story of the wizard are equally at a loss. In his analysis of the fantastic, Soloviev reminds us that the uncertain evaluation of phenomena—in life as in art—is in fact *more real* than simplistic "realism":

> But the presentation of life as something simple, rational, and transparent first and foremost contradicts actuality [*deistvitel'nost'*]; it is not *real* [*real'no*]. It would be very poor realism to assert, for example, that nothing but emptiness is hidden beneath the visible surface of the earth on which we walk and ride. Realism of this sort would be destroyed by every earthquake and every volcanic eruption, witnessing the fact that active [*deistvuiushchiia*], and thus actual [*deistvitel'nyia*], forces hide beneath the earth's visible surface. ("Predislovie k 'Upyriu' Grafa A. K. Tolstogo" 9:376)

Considering the fact that the article above and the "Short Story of the Antichrist" were published in the same year, it is probably no coincidence that the Emperor and Apollonius ultimately succumb precisely to an earthquake and a volcano. By using the fantastic in his story, Soloviev places his readers and his characters in a similar predicament. We must distinguish between the falsely or simplistically real and the actually real, the hidden earthquake, that is, the fantastic but simple truth.

To continue: the satanically empowered Emperor sets about uniting the three major Christian denominations in a crude mockery of Soloviev's own Universal Church. He offers spiritual authority to the Catholics, sacred tradition to the Orthodox, and to the Protestants—a world institute of free scriptural investigation. We should note here what is not seen by those who concentrate only on the "philosophical" content, which might be taken here as the story's "surface value": the ridiculously unsophisticated nature of the Superman's plans within this "story," which, as an imitation of Dostoevsky's "poem" (as the author calls the Grand Inquisitor section of his *Brothers Karamazov*), is purposefully poor.[17] The evil vision in "Short Story of the Antichrist" again suggests self-parody on Soloviev's part, not negation. And if we miss the humorous spectacle in the scene in which the helpless Pope Peter, Starets John, and Professor Pauli huddle together, virtually alone in their rejection of the one they now label the Antichrist, we nonetheless cannot dismiss the overblown rhetoric of the revelation of the Emperor's true nature:

[His face] expressed some evil [*chto-to nedobroe*]. Within him a hellish storm arose, identical to the one he experienced that fateful night [when he first encountered the Evil Powers]. He completely lost internal equilibrium, and all his thoughts focused on maintaining outward self-control so as not to give himself away too soon. Only an inhuman effort prevented him from howling wildly, throwing himself on the speaker and tearing him apart with his teeth. Suddenly he heard a familiar, unearthly voice: "Be silent and fear not." He was silent. Only his deadened and darkened face remained distorted, as sparks flew from his eyes. (10:213)

Pansophius' story is pure melodrama, hardly the "serious" genre Soloviev playfully claimed he sought, and critics assumed he found.

At this point, the wizard, soon to be named Pope Apollonius, produces an artificial storm within the hall, and both John and Peter collapse as though struck by lightning. Pauli retreats to the desert with a small entourage and returns after four days to retrieve the bodies of his brothers, which he finds miraculously untouched by corruption and which soon rise from the dead (cf. Revelation 11:7–11). Unlike the biblical analogue, however, the bodies do not ascend directly to heaven (Revelation 11, 12), but shake hands.

"And thus," reads Mr. Z,

the unification of the Churches was accomplished in the dark of night, on a high and deserted spot. But the night darkness was suddenly lit by a brilliant brightness, and a great sign appeared in the heavens: a woman, clothed in the sun, under her feet the moon, and on her head a crown of twelve stars [cf. Revelation 12:1]. The apparition stood still for several moments, and then quietly moved toward the south. Pope Peter raised his staff and exclaimed: "Here is our banner! Let us follow her." And he set off after the vision, accompanied by both elders and the whole crowd of Christians—to the divine mountain, to Sinai. . . . (10:218)

So ends Pansophius' manuscript, since the monk died before he could complete his task. The written work that exists within the fictional world of the conversations is indeed a "short story" about the "short triumph" of evil in the world, and it ends on an apocalyptic vision of supernatural resurrection and divine intervention. No wonder critics sense a change of tone toward capitulation and tragedy, and praise Soloviev's return to orthodox belief in divine grace. The manuscript ends here, however, but the story itself does not; the written story is incomplete, just as is the future history it retells.

The Oral Story

Mr. Z merely summarizes the remainder of the story, which he remembers "only in its main outlines" (10:218). True believers stream into the desert from all corners of the earth. In the meantime, the Pope-Wizard uses his powers on all the remaining inhabitants of the earth, convincing them that he has opened the door to the dead (a parody of Nikolai Fedorov's literal interpretation of resurrection, with which Soloviev expressed sympathy?), and allowing all manner of debauchery. But: "Just as the Emperor began to consider himself firmly rooted on religious turf and had declared himself the single, true incarnation of the supreme divinity of the universe based on the persistent encouragement of the secret voice of the "Father," a new trouble fell upon him from a direction no one would have guessed: an uprising of the Jews" (10:219). Breaking away from his narration, Mr. Z now suggests that perhaps Pansophius imagined this section with too much simplicity and realism (*s izlishneiu prostotoiu i realizmom*, 10:219). No such internal stylistic comment had been made before about the story, and we are thus cued to ask what Soloviev might mean by "too much" simplicity and realism. Had not Soloviev in fact praised simplicity in his preface ("This verbal form then appeared spontaneously, as the simplest expression of what I wanted to say," 10:83)? Might we not reverse Mr. Z's judgment, and assume this simplicity and realism are *good*, in fact, the opposite of the "rational" and "transparent" realism, of the false simplicity of those with no belief in a subterranean world? It would seem that Mr. Z's critical insertion does not evaluate content as much as alert us to a significant change of tone: from the melodrama of the written manuscript to more complex humor in the oral one, i.e., to that which is more "real."

What is it that is real here? The author behind the narrator of the story by Pansophius humorously inserts a parody of another of his dearest beliefs—the role of the Jews in the establishment of *bogochelovechestvo*—into the very climax of his otherwise dramatic story. The Jewish people, we learn, had previously supported the Superman's rise, but "the fact is that the Jews, who considered the Emperor a true Israelite, accidently discovered that he was *not even circumcised*" (10:219;

emphasis in original). In other words, it is an accident that reveals a technicality that spurs the traditionally defenseless nation to take up arms and ultimately cause the fall of the Antichrist himself. Instead of a sign from above, Soloviev gives us one from below![18] What could be more simple and realistic? A serious short story relates the short triumph of the Antichrist, as Soloviev warns us in the preface, but his "decisive fall" is related in nothing other than a joke.

Mr. Z continues that a huge army of Jews (an oxymoron in post-biblical, pre-1948 terms—so unthinkable as to be funny) conquered Jerusalem and imprisoned the Antichrist. The Pope-Wizard assists in the Emperor's escape, only to witness his defeat at the Dead Sea (as opposed to the Jews' biblical triumph at the Red Sea?): "The crater of a huge volcano opened up and its fiery flood flowed into a single flaming lake, swallowing up the Emperor, his countless forces, and his ever-present companion, Pope Apollonius, all of whose magic could help him not in the least" (10:220). The Jews run to Jerusalem, praying to the God of Israel for salvation. As they approach, lightning splits the sky from east to west, revealing Christ dressed in emperor's robes, with stigmata exposed on his outstretched hands. From Sinai to Zion the Christian crowds stream in, led by Peter, John, and Pauli, and met by all who had been unfairly condemned by the Antichrist. "They came to life and ruled with Christ for a thousand years" (10:220).

Let us look back now at the moment at which the story moves from written to oral. We might assume provisionally that the written text represents human history, i.e., that which is written down about humankind. The manuscript ends on the glory of the Antichrist, implying that his reign has already begun on earth, within our historical conception. This is generally understood as Soloviev's conclusion regarding Tolstoy; the false, transparently simplistic Christianity that Tolstoy preached is the work of the Antichrist, who perverts the words of the Gospels. In the future history that is the written story, the Antichrist is in the past and the present. The oral text, then, is the future, that which is not yet written. Ahead lies divine intervention in the form of volcano and earthquake, followed by the Second Coming of Christ. In this interpretation, the end of the story narrated by Mr. Z represents sacred, as opposed to human, history.

We might begin with a different assumption, however. The manuscript was written by a monk, and is a work of creation, as is all fiction, thus imitative of God's own creative act in Soloviev's essentially classical aesthetics. It is based, as well, on sacred text, as Soloviev reminds us in the preface: "All of this is found in the word of God and in ancient tradition" (10:89). Perhaps, then, we need to understand the oral text, narrated by Mr. Z only "in its broad outlines," as the opposite: as human, in contrast to sacred, history. Where does the Woman Clothed in Sun from Revelation lead the Christian leaders just at the point where the written manuscript breaks off? She takes them to Mt. Sinai, to the sacred spot where the people of Israel received the Torah, and thus began their written history.

What can we learn, then, about the end of this history to be created by humanity, the one that is narrated by Mr. Z? Final divine intervention is precipitated in the oral story only by human action: a military uprising. Furthermore, the Jews at the end of the narration run westward from the Dead Sea to Jerusalem, and could see the vision of Christ in the sky rent from east to west by lightning only by looking behind themselves. Christ's Second Coming is indeed related in the oral story, but He comes following human action, and walking behind human beings. He then leads the rest of the world to Zion for the millenarian reign of the Messiah, brought about by the intervention of humanity in its own story of salvation.

To draw attention to the significance of humanity's role, Soloviev resorts to humor in the detail relayed with "too much simplicity and realism" about circumcision, and chooses for his liberators—the all-too-mundane Jews. The leaders of the three Christian denominations had retreated to the desert, unable to oppose the force of the Antichrist and his magician. The Churches eventually unite—Soloviev's dream—but only in the dark of night on a "high and deserted spot," and follow *behind* a divine revelation illuminated not on earth, but in the sky. According to E. Trubetskoi, *Three Conversations* reverses Soloviev's earlier "false" beliefs in the establishment of heaven on earth: "On the contrary, in *Three Conversations* the idea of progress is revealed not in some kind of external organization, and not in the life of the broad masses, *but in the heroic deeds of individuals* [*a v podvige lichnostei*], led by the grace of three men chosen by God, around whom gather a small flock of Christians who have remained true to Christ to the end" (Trubetskoi 2:403; emphasis in original). But the text, as we have seen, may also be read in the opposite way. The "three men chosen by God" follow instead of lead. It is the Jews, the traditional chosen people, condemned in Soloviev's present to humiliating inaction, who openly oppose evil.

Soloviev's choice of the Jews as the turning point of his story of salvation is not arbitrary. The Jews figure prominently in a number of Soloviev's works. His reasons for praising the Jews are complex, and sometimes contradictory, but for the purpose of the present study we must note that he believed that the Jews of history, into whose midst Jesus was born, were the true model of the interpenetration of material and divine principles:

Firmly believing in the essence of God, Israel attracted to itself the divine manifestation and His revelation. Believing also in itself, Israel could enter into a *personal* relationship with Jehovah. It could stand before Him face to face, confirm a convenant with Him, and serve Him as an active partner instead of a passive instrument. Finally, by the strength of that active faith striving toward the final realization of its spiritual principle through the purification of material nature, Israel prepared in its midst a pure and holy abode for the incarnation of God the Word. ("Evreistvo i khristianskii vopros" 4:150; emphasis in original)

About the role of the Jews in history Soloviev wrote:

The life and religious history of mankind is concentrated in this single nation because only they sought a living God within the Unconditional, a God *of history*: the ultimate future of mankind was prepared for and revealed within this nation because it alone saw in God not only *that which is* but also *that which will be*, Jehovah, the God of the future. Salvation came from the Jews, and could come only from them, because they alone understood true salvation—not in nirvanic *absorption* through moral and physical suicide, and not in the *abstraction* of the spirit and the pure idea through theoretical contemplation, but in the sanctification and rebirth of the whole human being and of all of his existence through living moral and religious activity, in faith and deeds, in prayer, labor, and charity. (*Rossiia i Vselenskaia Tserkov'* 11:321–22; emphasis in original)

In Soloviev's eyes, the Jews paved the way for the coming of Christ the *Bogochelovek* in history, and it is their actions that bring about His Second Coming in the oral story that completes the "Short Story of the Antichrist."

To summarize, the written manuscript of Pansophius tells the story of human *inaction* and *passivity* in the face of a false messiah. The oral story does the opposite: it glorifies human *responsibility* and *interaction* in the divine plan of salvation, no matter how "simple," no matter how "realistic." Humor—and the surprise of generic dissonance—leads us to our conclusions: the serious confession of a dying monk is a parody of failure; the joke that completes urges us toward active responsibility. The believers in the manuscript huddle in the desert and wait for a divine sign to follow. Those who believe in God in the oral story take up arms and lead the divine sign. That sign is Christ fully divine *and* fully human, robed in the splendor of the kingdom of God, but physically wounded from his death on the cross ("coming toward them in royal dress and with nail wounds on his extended hands," 10:220).[19]

The *Bogochelovek* in the "Short Story of the Antichrist" is neither simply a human figure from past history—as the Prince (a.k.a. Tolstoy) would like to read Jesus—nor a divine character about whom Soloviev can write only in future history, and whose glory contrasts sharply to the author's supposed deathbed disillusionment. The latter interpretation is, of course, that of Soloviev's heirs cited at the beginning of this article who have largely determined our reading of the philosopher's last great work. Rather, Soloviev's choice of philosophical dialogue and short story allowed him to illustrate through these literary forms—"simple," "realistic," and, above all, humorous—that in the story that is our past and future history, our salvation is no less than *bogochelovechestvo*, that is, "the real mutual activity of God and man" (3:36). At best we should recognize, with Soloviev himself, that the philosopher had become disenchanted with the external forms into which he had tried to place his beliefs (he had moved from preaching a "Universal Church" in the eighties to faith in liberal institutions in the early nineties),[20] but not with the beliefs themselves. So he wrote about his study of Plato in the late 1890s: "With the accumulation of life experience, but with no change in the essence of my convictions, I came more and more to doubt the usefulness and the possibility of accomplishing those external notions to which I had given over my so-called 'best years.' To become disillusioned with them meant to return to the philosophical activities that had felt less pressing in the interim" (12:360). Soloviev returned to Plato to find a new expression for divine and human reconciliation, and thus for salvation in terms of *bogochelovechestvo*. At the same time, he experimented with conversation, argument, and laughter: a humorous anecdote to parody a serious genre, a joke for the true story, fantastic reality for that which is simply, but not simplistically, real.

Notes

This research was assisted by grants from the National Endowment for the Humanities and from the Joint Committee on Soviet Studies of the Social Science Research Council and the American Council of Learned Societies with funds provided by the U.S. Department of State under the Russian and Soviet Studies Research and Training Act of 1983 (Title VIII).

1.   The greater emphasis placed on the doctrine of transfiguration by the Eastern Church supports its view on salvation; mortal flesh can shine with divine light. For more on Soloviev and transfiguration, see Kornblatt, "Transfiguration of Plato" 45–48.

2.   All quotations from Soloviev will be from the Brussels reprint unless otherwise noted, and cited in the text with title of work where appropriate, volume, and page number.

3.   As Carlson's essay in this volume shows, Soloviev's interests were wide-ranging, from gnosticism to Pushkin, from patristics to epistemology. But interest does not equal identity, and we cannot fully understand Soloviev through gnosticism and mysticism any more than we can through Western liberalism or Catholicism.

4.   For confirmation of this statement, see Cioran, whose book on Soloviev is largely devoted to analysis of the symbolists. For a significant exception, see

Walicki's work on Western liberalism in Russia. I am currently at work on a book about Soloviev and his heirs, that examines how Soloviev's followers focused on only one or another strand of their mentor's philosophy.

5. Ironically, Soloviev argues against the tendency of the "new" Nietzscheans and the "latest" (i.e., decadent) critics to impose a story of tragic fate upon Pushkin's life. See "Sud'ba Pushkina" 9:48–49. He would no doubt have felt the same about the majority of his supposedly friendly critics.

6. To be entirely accurate, neither the humorous dialogue nor the short story was totally new, although Soloviev never developed them to this sophisticated literary level. Compare his earlier plays and the story "Na zare tumannoi iunosti . . ." (12:289–302). The use of a jocular tone for serious subjects was also not new, as will be discussed below.

7. Miłosz calls *Three Conversations* Soloviev's "most literary work except for his poems" (Miłosz, "Introduction" 11).

8. See Bori for an extended discussion of the conflict between the "hermeneutics" of Soloviev and Tolstoy.

9. What better irony than to publish a poem by one Tolstoy while admonishing another?

10. "Among the many characteristic peculiarities of human nature, only one belongs uniquely to man and constitutes his unequivocal distinction from other living beings. This characteristic is not sociability, as Aristotle defined it when he said that man is a social animal. . . . The characteristic peculiarity of man is found in the fact that only he has the ability to laugh. This ability is extremely important and lies at the very essence of human nature. I therefore define man as a *laughing animal*" ("Lektsiia ot 14 ianvaria 1875 g" 12:526).

11. The differences between the Prince's interpretation of the parable based on his oral retelling and Mr. Z's interpretation after reading directly from the written text have great bearing on our interpretation of the oral and written sections of the "Short Story of the Antichrist," but cannot be elaborated here.

12. Regarding the "future past tense" of the story, see Miłosz, "Science Fiction and the Coming of the Antichrist" 16.

13. "Panmongolism" was not published until five years after the author's death, in *Voprosy zhizni* 8 (1905):27. He was well-known, however, for including stanzas from his own poems in his letters and essays, and he made sure that his contemporaries knew the context by discussing the epigraph in his written response in *Vestnik Evropy* to criticism of *Three Conversations* ("Po povodu poslednikh sobytii: Pis'mo v redaktsiiu, 1900" 10:222–26).

14. The editors of the German edition of Soloviev's collected works also identify Soloviev and Pansofius (*Werke* 8:539–41, 542). Based on the comment that Mr. Z's friend is now buried in the Daniil Monastery (*Tri razgovora* 10:218), they also speculate that Nikolai Gogol, initially buried in the monastery, served as a model for the monk-author (8:582). The editors point to the apocalypticism of the earlier author, but his humor, and especially his tendency to unite humor with serious moral and metaphysical questions, is also worth citing. In general, the notes to the German edition are invaluable.

15.   The reference to Nietzsche's Superman must also be intentional. In a critique of Nietzsche written in 1899, Soloviev wrote: "A single word can contain within itself both the falsity and the truth of this astonishing doctrine. Everything depends on how we understand, on how we pronounce the word 'superman' " ("Ideia sverkhcheloveka" 9:268). We should keep in mind the ambiguous nature of verbal forms when we discuss Soloviev's own Antichrist. As Mr. Z tells us at the end of the story: "All that glitters is not gold" (10:220).

16.   See Soloviev's comments on the fluctuation between mundane and supernatural explanations of the fantastic in an introduction to Aleksei Tolstoy's story "Upyr' " (9:376–78). Soloviev's definition of the fantastic was embraced by Tzvetan Todorov and cited as a significant precursor to the latter's still canonical study of the genre (Todorov 25–26).

17.   Some critics claim that Dostoevsky used Soloviev as the model for Alesha Karamazov, and others that the philosopher forms the basis of Ivan's character. Soloviev, for his part, greatly admired his older contemporary, but was not averse to criticizing him. See especially his complex and sometimes contradictory assessment in "Three Speeches in Memory of Dostoevsky" (3:184–223).

18.   My thanks to Gary Rosenshield for uncovering this hidden joke.

19.   I recognize, of course, that Soloviev runs the risk inherent in a bad comic strip. Good and evil on an apocalyptic scale are "funny" only to a certain extent. Still, given his (well-deserved) serious reputation, and, even more, the seriousness with which he was read by his symbolist heirs, Soloviev might not have gone *far enough* in using humor to jog us out of our own passivity.

20.   My thanks to Gregory Gaut for pointing out this caveat to my interpretation of Soloviev's consistency.

Works Cited

Bori, P. Ch. "Novoe prochtenie 'Trekh razgovorov' i povesti ob antikhriste Vl. Solov'eva, konflikt dvukh universalizmov." *Voprosy filosofii* 9 (1990): 27–36.

Cioran, Samuel D. *Vladimir Solov'ev and the Knighthood of the Divine Sophia.* Waterloo, Ontario: Wilfred Laurier University Press, 1977.

Frank, S. L. *Iz istorii russkoi filosofskoi mysli kontsa XIX i nachala XX veka.* Washington, D.C., and New York: Inter-Language Literary Associates, 1965.

Gaut, Gregory Arthur. "A Christian Westernizer: Vladimir Solovyov and Russian Conservative Nationalism." Ph.D. diss. University of Minnesota 1992.

Gusev, V. A., and A. A. Boiko. "Ironiia v khudozhestvennom tvorchestve Vl. Solov'eva." *Voprosy russkoi literatury* 1, no. 57 (1991): 3–10.

Kornblatt, Judith Deutsch. "The Transfiguration of Plato in the Erotic Philosophy of Vladimir Solov'ev." *Religion and Literature* 24, no. 2 (1992): 35–50.

Losev, A. F. *Vl. Solov'ev.* Moscow: Mysl', 1983.

Lossky, Vladimir. *In the Image and Likeness of God.* Crestwood, N.Y.: St. Vladimir's Seminary Press, 1974.

Miłosz, Czesław. Introduction, in Vladimir Solovyov, *War, Progress, and the End of History: Three Conversations Including a Short Story of the Anti-Christ.* Trans.

A. Bakshy. Revised by Thomas R. Beyer, Jr. Hudson, N.Y.: Lindisfarne Press, 1990.

Miłosz, Czesław. "Science Fiction and the Coming of the Antichrist." In *Emperor of the Earth: Modes of Eccentric Vision*. Berkeley: University of California Press, 1977.

Mochul'skii, Konstantin. *Vladimir Solov'ev: Zhizn' i uchenie*. 2d ed. Paris: YMCA Press, 1951.

Shestov, Lev. "Speculation and Apocalypse: The Religious Philosophy of Vladimir Solovyov." In *Speculation and Revelation*. Trans. Bernard Martin. Athens, Chicago, London: Ohio University Press, 1982.

Solov'ev, Vladimir [Solowjew, Wladimir]. *Deutsche Gesamtausgabe der Werke von Wladimir Solowiew*. 8 vols. Ed. Wladimir Szyłkarski, Wilhelm Lettenbauer, and Ludolf Müller. Munich: Erich Wewel Verlag, 1953–79.

Solov'ev, Vladimir. *Sobranie sochinenii*. Ed. S. M. Solov'ev and E. L. Radlov. 2d ed. 10 vols. St. Petersburg: Prosveshchenie, 1911–14. Reprinted with 2 additional volumes, Brussels: Zhizn' s Bogom, 1966–70.

Stremooukhoff, D. *Vladimir Soloviev and His Messianic Work*. Ed. Philip Guilbeau and Heather Elise MacGregor. Trans. Elizabeth Meyendorff. Belmont, Mass.: Nordland, 1980.

Todorov, Tzvetan. *The Fantastic: A Structural Approach to a Literary Genre*. Ithaca, N.Y.: Cornell University Press, 1975.

Trubetskoi, Kn. E. *Mirosozertsanie Vl. S. Solov'eva*. 2 vols. Moscow, 1913.

Walicki, Andrzej. *Legal Philosophies of Russian Liberalism*. Notre Dame: University of Notre Dame Press, 1992.

Ware, Timothy. *The Orthodox Church*. New York: Penguin Books, 1963, 1964; rpt. 1978.

FLORENSKY

Background

Pavel Aleksandrovich Florensky (1882–1937) occupies a somewhat unusual place in the Russian religious renaissance. Unlike that of many of his contemporaries who came to religious philosophy through law and the social sciences, and often as a reaction to Marxism, Florensky's early experience—and continuing interest—was in the hard sciences and mathematics, beginning as a gymnasium student in Tbilisi. He graduated from the physics and mathematical faculty of Moscow University in 1904 and continued throughout his life to be involved in scientific work. Florensky's mathematical contributions, and his association with N. V. Bugaev—professor of mathematics and father of the symbolist Andrei Belyi—and N. N. Luzin, the "father" of the Moscow School of mathematics, are only now being explored.

Despite a nonreligious upbringing, Florensky graduated from the Moscow Theological Academy four years after completing Moscow University, and was appointed to the chair of philosophy there. Florensky had wanted to become a monk, but was counseled to marry by his confessor. This he did, and he was ordained a member of the "white" (or married) clergy in 1911. In 1914 he published his major philosophical work, *Stolp i utverzhdenie istiny* (*The Pillar and Foundation of Truth*).

Although the leap from mathematics to religious philosophy might seem an unlikely one, we must consider that Florensky saw all knowledge and truth as interrelated, and favored an eclectic and interdisciplinary approach to philosophical and scientific endeavor. Indeed, Florensky's work was controversial partly because of its attempt to embrace many aspects of knowledge. In addition to being an excellent mathematician, Florensky mastered a variety of both ancient and modern languages (including Iranian and Indian languages), became a professor of art history, and even taught perspectival art at the Moscow Arts Academy. He often supported his theological points with heavily documented linguistic and art-historical arguments, which rendered his work dilettantish to some, and incoherent to others. Indeed, the rather eccentric points in his thinking (for instance, his astronomy argued for geocentrism) sometimes caused scholars to underestimate Florensky's work. In addition to noting his scientific work, we must also recognize how his interest in language and linguistics played into the poetry that he published in symbolist journals, and most of his pre-Revolutionary work should be read against this symbolist background.

After the Revolution, Florensky lost his academic positions but was allowed to remain in the Soviet Union and to continue lecturing (albeit almost exclusively in scientific and technical venues) into the early twenties. He supported himself with scientific work; in 1927 he invented a noncoagulating machine oil that he named Dekanite in honor of the tenth anniversary of the Revolution, and he served as the editor of the Soviet *Tekhnicheskaia entsiklopediia* (*Technical Encyclopedia*) from 1927 until 1933. In 1935, after a lengthy series of legal difficulties, Florensky was arrested and sentenced to ten years in a Siberian labor camp, where he continued his scientific work, including important research on permafrost and on the production of agar and iodine, for which he received, at the time, no credit. He dated his last letter to his family June 4, 1937; his execution occurred half a year later. This date, significantly earlier than that usually assumed, is based on documents from KGB archives published only in 1990.

Despite the relative dearth of scholarly attention to Florensky's works, there is no doubt that he was a major influence in Russian intellectual history. Florensky was well-known to the symbolist poets, and many of their views on art were directly rooted in his works. In addition, a large portion of the pre- and immediately post-Revolutionary intelligentsia knew Florensky personally.

Finally, Florensky's conception of all truth as essentially antinomial, as discussed in the following essays, and of the Trinity as the embodiment of the one antinomial Truth (since it is both one and not one) with which all other truths participate, marked, in Zernov's words, "the beginning of a new era in Russian theology" (101). For seventy years that era was played out in exile. The religious and thus dissident Russian intelligentsia of the late sixties and seventies rediscovered Florensky only gradually. In post-Soviet Russia, the publication of the Florensky archives is closely controlled by members of his family, some of whom have engaged in xenophobic rhetoric, a theme discernible in some of Florensky's own writings as well. Although the extent to which these new materials will influence our understanding of Florensky's personality and biography remains to be seen, it is clear that his contributions to Russian theological, mathematical, scientific, semiotic, and philosophical discourse are of tremendous importance.

—Peyton Engel

Bibliography

Major Works

V vechnoi lazuri, 1904. (Poetry)
Stolp i utverzhdenie istiny, 1914.
Smysl idealizma, 1914.
Ikonostas, 1922.
Mnimosti v geometrii, 1922.

English Translations

"On the Holy Spirit." *Ultimate Questions: An Anthology of Modern Russian Religious Thought*. Ed. Alexander Schmemann. Crestwood, N.Y.: St. Vladimir's Seminary Press, 1977.
"On the Icon." *Eastern Churches Review* 8 (1976): 11–37.
The Pillar and Foundation of the Truth. Trans. Boris Jakim. Princeton: Princeton University Press, forthcoming.

Secondary Sources in English, Selected

Andronik, Hierodeacon. "The Personality, Life and Work of Father Pavel Florensky." *Journal of the Moscow Patriarchate* 5 (1982): 18–29.
Bychkov, Victor. *The Aesthetic Face of Being: Art in the Theology of Pavel Florenskii*. Trans. Richard Pesear and Larissa Volkhonsky. Crestwood, N.Y.: St. Vladimir's Seminary Press, 1993.
Cassedy, Steven. *Flight from Eden: The Origins of Modern Literary Criticism and Aesthetics*. Berkeley and Los Angeles: University of California Press, 1990. 114–20.
Cassedy, Steven. "Pavel Florenskij's Philosophy of Language: Its Contextuality and Its Context." *Slavic and East European Journal* 35, no. 14 (1991): 537–52.

Ford, Charles, E. "Pavel Florensky: Priest, Mathematician, Theologian." *Isis*, forthcoming.

Lossky, N. O. "Father Pavel Florenskii. " *History of Russian Philosophy*. New York: International Universities Press, 1951. 176–91.

Sabaneeff, Leonid. "Pavel Florensky: Priest, Scientist, and Mystic." *Russian Review* 20, no. 4 (1961): 312–25.

Slesinski, Robert. *Pavel Florensky: A Metaphysics of Love*. Crestwood, N.Y.: St. Vladimir's Seminary Press, 1984. (Includes extensive bibliography.)

Zenkovsky, V. V. [Zen'kovskii]. *A History of Russian Philosophy*. Trans. George L. Kline. 2 vols. London: Routledge & Kegan Paul, 1953. 2:873–90.

Zernov, Nicolas. *The Russian Religious Renaissance of the Twentieth Century*. London: Darton, Longman & Todd, 1963. 101–3.

4

P. A. Florensky and the Celebration of Matter

Steven Cassedy

Russian religious thought as it evolved in the nineteenth century was fond of directing our eye at the material world only to remind us that matter could at best be a sign for a truth that lay elsewhere. When the term *kenosis* was taken from nineteenth-century German Protestant theology and introduced into Russian theology in the 1890s, it immediately filled a terminological need that had been there for many years.[1] For *kenosis*, the "emptying" suggested by Saint Paul in Philippians 2:7, where Christ is said to have "emptied himself" (of divinity) in order to assume the form of a servant, is a term that perfectly describes the "emptiness" of flesh, of all matter, the reason that proximity to earth and flesh means distance from divinity. The kenotic tradition in Germany in the nineteenth century is the one that produced so many scholarly works on the "life of Jesus," in which Jesus was seen historically, as a man.[2] In Russian theology the term serves as a sort of negative corollary to incarnation, which emphasizes the divine presence in matter.

Few writers had as vivid an intuition of the kenotic principle and its ramifications as did Dostoevsky, who recorded that intuition as he kept vigil over the body of his first wife in April of 1864. For Dostoevsky the sign of our fleshliness and our humanity was the fact of individuality, the ineluctable separation between the self of one individual and that of every other individual. It meant, in short, the impossibility, on earth, of perfect Christian love. Here is what he wrote in his notebook:

To love a person *as oneself*, according to Christ's commandment, is impossible. The law that there must be such a thing as an individual person [*zakon lichnosti*] is binding on earth. The self is the obstacle. Only Christ could, but Christ was an eternal ideal toward which man strives and, by a law of nature, must strive. After the appearance of Christ as the *ideal of man in the flesh*, however, it became as clear as day that the highest, the ultimate development of the individual person [*lichnost'*] must progress precisely to the point . . . where man can find out, recognize, and, with all the force of his nature, be convinced that the highest use he can make of his individual person, of the fullness of the development of his self, is, as it were, to annihilate this self. . . . (Dostoevskii 20:172; emphasis in original)

"An eternal ideal toward which man strives and, by a law of nature, must strive." This is the essence of the kenotic problem. Of all those who have walked on earth, Christ alone was able to love according to his own commandment, but this is because the godly component of his dual nature allows him to love selflessly. Our fleshly nature reminds us that we cannot do what is purely ideal, but it also reminds us that we must strive always to approximate that ideal while remembering piously (not to remember would be impious) that we cannot attain it. For to attain the ideal in question, namely, selfless, Christian love, would mean to annihilate one's self, and thus the meaning of "I have attained selfless love" would be lost as one's *I*, one's individual person [*lichnost'*], dissolved.

The status of icons in the Eastern Church is another example of the traditional status of matter in Orthodox theology. Icons are material objects bearing visual representations of various holy beings. The proper attitude toward them, we are always reminded, is one that stems from looking beyond the physical icon to something infinite and invisible that lies beyond it. The wood and paint are matter; our awareness of what the icon stands for, its infinite and invisible prototype, is the essential component of our experience of it. The material icon simply points to something that is entirely immaterial.

Florensky's view, however, is different. He stands at the summit of the modern Russian Orthodox tradition as that tradition examines the kenosis and the nature of matter. He has provided us with some of the most profound statements on the relation between matter and the divine. But by contrast with many others in the Russian tradition he never loses sight of the source from which the kenosis proceeds. Florensky resists the temptation to view matter as wholly despicable, because for him it is part of God's creation, and so, instead of regarding matter as "merely" the physical sign that points beyond itself, that in effect invites us to reject it altogether, Florensky sees matter as cause for celebration.

One of the most valuable texts by Florensky to appear in recent years is something the author called an *avtoreferat*.[3] The title is apparently meant to be taken literally, as a "report" (*referat*) on oneself, and not in its usual sense as "abstract" (of a dissertation). Florensky wrote it some time in 1925 or 1926 as an entry on himself for an encyclopedia.[4] This is how he characterizes his philosophical outlook: "Florensky regards the continuation of the path toward a future integral worldview as his life's task. In this sense he may be called a philosopher. But in contrast to the devices and objectives of philosophical thought that have become entrenched in the modern period, he rejects abstract constructs and a schematically exhaustive universe of problems. In this sense he should be regarded rather as a researcher or investigator" (Florenskii, "P. A. Florenskii's Review of His Work" 41).[5]

Here, without any specialized philosophical or theological terminology, is a description of the basic dualism underlying all of Florensky's thought. For Florensky was an idealist and a materialist at the same time. The phrase "integral worldview" (*tsel'noe mirovozzrenie*) in early-twentieth-century Russian philosophy immediately suggests an idealist perspective, like the one we find in Andrei Belyi, who also spoke of worldviews. "Philosopher" in this passage might be read as "idealist." Opposed to this is Florensky's role as *issledovatel'*, a role in which he spurns the sort of abstractions that one finds in idealist thought. A "researcher" or "investigator" is someone who gathers information about the material world, as Florensky, an accomplished scientist, did.

His remarks toward the end of the text emphasize the dualism once again:

Florensky sees in mathematics the necessary and prime premise of a worldview, but he also sees in the self-sufficiency of mathematics the reason for its cultural barrenness: mathematics must receive its guiding impulses on the one hand from a general conception of the world, and on the other from an empirical study of the universe and from technology. Florensky's own pursuits were in both these directions, with the subject matter in technology being electrical engineering, mainly electrical fields and their material environment. The theory of fields in an expanded sense is related to the problems of geometry, natural philosophy, and aesthetics, while materials technology is related to the histology of materials, a domain that applies set theory and the theory of functions. (45)

Something else in the "Avtoreferat" is worth mentioning. Florensky feels that no self-portrait is complete without an account of his interest in language. He says this about his language studies:

Finally, a few words should be said about language studies: rejecting the idea that language follows the principles of abstract logic, Florensky sees the value of thought to lie in its concrete manifestation as the revelation of personality. Hence his interest in the stylistic study of the products of thought. In addition, rejecting the idea of thought without language, Florensky regards the study of language as a prime tool for penetrating into the thought of others and for formulating one's own thought. Hence his interest in etymology and semasiology. (45)[6]

The "Avtoreferat" refers to two essential elements of Florensky's outlook: first, his dual gaze at the ideal and the material, and, second, his concern with language. It is appropriate that Florensky should juxtapose these two elements, since his theory of language is one place in his work where the ideal-material duality shows up most prominently. His theory starts out as an essentialist, Platonist theory in the established tradition of nineteenth- and early-twentieth-century Russian language philosophy, but it takes a surprising turn at one point and ends up focusing on what Florensky regards as the antinomic quality of language. I will return to this later.

A first-time reader of Florensky's overtly theological writing would readily come to the conclusion that this writing is purely idealist, if only because of the strength of the Platonic tradition in Russian Orthodox theology. Florensky's major work, *The Pillar and Foundation of Truth* (*Stolp i utverzhdenie istiny*), with its subordination of everything to the supreme, divine principle of Love (which is at the root of the concept of Truth), is easy to read in this way. But there is a subtradition in Orthodox theology that is often overlooked and that had considerable influence on a great many Russian religious thinkers (as well as on a number of sects within Orthodoxy). It is a tradition that stresses that the material world as an epiphany of God is to be venerated.

The best pre-Russian elaboration of this line of thought can be found in the writings of Saint John of Damascus, the eighth-century defender of icons. Saint John elaborated in clearer form than perhaps any of the other Church Fathers a theology of icons whose logic has remained standard throughout the history of the Eastern Church. The fundamental fact of Saint John's theology is the incarnation. The result of the incarnation is a being who is fleshly but who carries in him the divinity of the Father. He is accessible to human perception in his physical form, but human perception cannot apprehend the essence that is incarnate in him, since that essence is invisible. Saint John's system thus takes as its point of departure the simple opposition between God's nature, which is invisible, immaterial, and infinite, and God's creation, which is visible, material, and finite.

The incarnation then serves as an analogy for other concepts. Icons are analogous to Christ, because, even though they are material objects, they are thought of as embodying within themselves a "prototype, " which is ultimately God. In his treatise on iconoclasm, *On the Divine Images*, Saint John says that we do not *worship* icons. In John's terminology, *worship* (*latreia* in Greek) is a form of honor that is due God alone; to icons we show *veneration* (*proskynēsis* is literally a "bowing down before," a form of honor we show people and things).[7] But when we venerate an icon, the honor we show it "passes over to the prototype" (that is, to God) (John of Damascus, *Pro sacris imaginibus* 1269/40).[8]

For "why should the icon [*eikōn*] not be honored and venerated, not as God, but as the image [*eikōn*] of God made flesh?" (1269/40). The same is true for matter in general, since God became matter and therefore dwells in it. "I venerate the Maker of matter, who became matter for me, who established his dwelling in matter, and who accomplished my salvation through matter" (1299/61). "I therefore grant matter to be the work of God and thus a good thing" (1297/60–61). "I honor [matter], not as God, but as something filled with divine energy and grace" (1300/62).

Perspective is everything here. One can take the separation between God's immaterial nature and God's material creation either as evidence that the material creation is profane, because it is humbler than God, or as evidence that it is to be venerated, because its source is God. Saint John adopts the second point of view. For him, the incarnation and the implicitly divine origin of such material beings as Christ, icons, and the whole material world are evidence that material things are "filled with divine energy and grace." Thus, when viewed from this perspective, the cosmic dualism is a sign that we must celebrate and honor matter, not despise it.

This is one of the arguments Saint John uses against the iconoclasts. Those who prohibit the veneration of images, he says in *On the Divine Images*, assume that matter is despicable. But matter is not despicable, because it was created by God, and so were all human beings and all their institutions. "You see that the law and everything accomplished by it, all our worship, the things we have made with our own hands, are sacred and lead us through matter [*hylē*] to the immaterial [*aülos*— literally "nonmatter"] God" (1309/67).

The same basic dualism that is at the heart of the doctrine of incarnation serves time and again as the point of departure for Florensky's theories. "Two Worlds" ("Dva mira") is the title of the first "letter" of *The Pillar and Foundation of Truth* (the work is divided into twelve "letters"), and in it Florensky refers to the separation between God's truth and our understanding.

Florensky's long essay on icons, called "Iconostasis" ("Ikonostas") (1922), is devoted precisely to the problem of the division between the two worlds, which he calls here the visible world (*mir vidimyi*) and the invisible world (*mir nevidimyi*). He begins the essay with a reference to God's creation of heaven and earth in Genesis 1:1 and then goes on to observe that "this division of all that is created into two has always been acknowledged as fundamental" (193). He then explores a series of objects, concepts, and experiences that mediate between the two worlds or somehow straddle the border between them. Dreams, for example, are an experience that takes place on the border between the visible world and an otherwise invisible one, and they thus serve as a model for the mediation that can occur between the visible world and the world of God's truth. As with the other objects and experiences that Florensky will shortly discuss, the position of dreams on the border between visible and invisible means, depending on our perspective, either they mark the separation between the two realms or they mark the point of contact between them. "Thus dreams are also the sort of images that divide the visible world from the invisible world, divide and at the same time unite these worlds" (202). The dream is a symbol, Florensky says. Of what? "From the heavenly a symbol of the earthly, from the earthly a symbol of the heavenly" (*iz gornego—simvol dol'nego, i iz dol'nego—simvol gornego*, 203).

Florensky then lists and categorizes other objects whose state of being is transitional between two realms. He gives an ontological analysis of the distinction between *litso* (face), *lik* (a theological term translated variously as "countenance," "face," or "image"), and *lichina* (mask). The details of this discussion are not important here. What is important is that the three concepts show varying balances of ideality and materiality, but that all three display the transitional character I have described (209–12). The same may be said of a temple (*khram*), which, Florensky says, is like Jacob's ladder: "from the visible it elevates [us] to the invisible" (*ot vidimogo ona vozvodit k nevidimomu*, 217).[9]

The most interesting transitional objects for Florensky are icons, and Florensky spends the bulk of his essay discussing their nature. In an Eastern Orthodox church most of the icons are displayed on an iconostasis, the partition that separates the section of the church where the sanctuary is located from the rest of the church. The iconostasis supplies the title image for Florensky's essay, because in it he has found the perfect example of a mediating object, an example that allows him to pursue the issue of the two worlds and the issue of the veneration of matter. The iconostasis does more than just separate the most consecrated portion of the church from the part where the worshipers congregate. As Florensky says, it is "the sanctuarial barrier, separating the two worlds." It is "the border between the visible world and the invisible world, and this sanctuarial barrier is made real, becomes accessible to consciousness, through a throng of saints that have come together, through a cloud of witnesses who have gathered around the throne of God, that sphere of heavenly glory, and who proclaim a mystery. The iconostasis is a *vision*" (219; emphasis in original).[10]

The ultimate reason for the iconostasis's mode of being, however, is the mode of being of the objects it is designed to display, namely, icons, and Florensky offers one of the most penetrating philosophical discussions of these objects ever written. We might appropriate the word *ontic* (as an adjective for "being," as opposed to *ontological*, which refers to the study of being) from the phenomenological movement and say that the objects and experiences Florensky describes in this essay are *ontically transitional*, since their mode of being marks a transitional moment between the infinite, invisible, divine world and the finite, visible, material world.[11] A sign that they are ontically transitional is that they are also *ontically ambiguous*, since their mode of being is not simple, like that of, say, a rock, which clearly inhabits this world, or some sort of idea that clearly inhabits the other world (although Florensky's belief that matter is to be venerated complicates this simple division). The ontically transitional object par excellence would be the icon, which, in the eyes of Florensky and other theologians, represents both the essence of Russian Orthodoxy and the line of demarcation between Russian Orthodoxy and other forms of Christian belief.

This demarcation can be seen in the different ways in which the two traditions have visually represented the reality of the spiritual world. Religious painting in the West, Florensky says, has been an "artistic untruth." Artists in the West, having no contact (*kasatel'stvo*) with the reality they presume to represent, have not paid attention even to the few indications the Catholic Church has given them of what the spiritual world is like. Icon painting, by contrast, is "the making-flesh [*oplotne-nie*], on a board, of the living cloud of witnesses that billows around the throne [of God]. Icons materially signal to us these countenances [*liki*] permeated with significance, these supersensible ideas, and make visions accessible, almost universally accessible. The witnesses of these witnesses—icon painters—give us images, *eidē, eikones* of their visions. Icons, by means of their artistic form, immediately [*neposredstvenno*] and visually testify to the reality of this form: they speak, but with lines and paints" (225).[12]

As Florensky defines the essence of icons he returns again and again to the ontic ambiguity of these objects. He reminds us over and over of the fundamental distinction between icon painting and traditional art. Icons don't represent, as paintings can do. Instead, "there is a board with paints, and there is the Mother of the Lord Herself." Nowhere is the paradox of iconicity clearer than in this passage: "A window is a window, and the board of an icon is a board, paints, and drying oil. But *behind* the window the Mother of God Herself is contemplated" (226; emphasis in original). And just as icons don't represent, icon artists don't create or express themselves, as other artists do. Instead, the icon painter seeks "the embodied [*voploshchennoi*] *truth of things*" (236; emphasis in original). Iconicity thus always gives a kind of unmediated access to the immaterial, and yet it can do so only because an immaterial prototype has been made flesh. The miracle of the incarnation works both ways: the ontically ambiguous objects it produces are humble and fleshly, like us, but they may be venerated both because of their divine origin and because of the access they give us to that divine origin.

Thus the essence of iconicity for Florensky is what it was for Saint John. Icons and similar objects dwell at the transitional point between two worlds, where they mark the separation between the spiritual and the material, but where they also show the point of contact that testifies to the divine origin of matter. Here, as in Saint John, perspective is everything.

This is hardly surprising in a thinker for whom ambiguity, doubt, and contradiction are at the heart of truth itself. In *The Pillar and Foundation of Truth* Florensky had elaborated a theory of truth that took doubt and contradiction as its point of departure. Florensky's theory of truth is ultimately based on the structure of the trinity, but the foundation of his trinitarian structure is always an initial duality. The sixth "letter" of *The Pillar and Foundation of Truth* is called "Contradiction" ("Protivorechie"). In it Florensky distinguishes between Truth (*Istina*, capitalized), by which he apparently means God's Truth, and truth (*istina*, with a lowercase initial letter), by which he apparently means earthly truth. "There is no doubt," he says, "that together with Truth there necessarily exists *truth* as well, if together with God there exists *the world of creatures* [*tvar'*]. The existence of *truth* is simply another expression of the very fact of the existence of creation as such . . ." (143; emphasis in original). Florensky then proceeds to demonstrate that truth must always anticipate, and respond to, all objections to itself and that it is a "self-contradicting proposition." "Thesis and antithesis *together* form the expression of truth," Florensky says, and so truth is in reality an antinomy (147; emphasis in original). Florensky will make it his purpose in *The Pillar and Foundation of Truth* to show that Truth (capitalized) depends on the intercession of a third element to break the antinomic duality he describes here, but three things are clear at this early stage in the construction of Florensky's system in *The Pillar and Foundation of Truth*. The first is that ordinary truth is related to matter (*tvar'*, the world of creatures) as God is related to His Truth, which means that truth itself is an ontically transitional or ambiguous quality. The second is that the very structure of truth is ambiguous, since it rests on the principle of contradiction. The third is that, if truth is to Truth as matter is to God, then truth offers the same sort of "window" to Truth as matter offers to God. The mode of being and the structure of truth are thus characterized by the same ambiguity as icons and are thus subject to the same play of perspective as icons. Ordinary truth is grounded in matter just as icons are, and its structure is deeply antinomic just as that of icons is.

Even Florensky's use of the term *kenosis* is, at first glance, strangely equivocal. In an early passage in *The Pillar and Foundation of Truth* he discusses love as an illustration of the principle of Truth. The true nature of love, he says, rests in a process whereby one self (one "I") departs from itself to enter into another self (or "I"), but somehow avoids becoming simply identical to that other self. Identities for Florensky are empty. "Rising *above* the logical, contentless-empty law of identity and identifying with the beloved brother, the Self [*Ia*] by this very act freely turns itself into a non-Self or, to use the language of the holy Scriptures, 'empties' itself," he says, citing the verse in Philippians from which the word *kenosis* is derived (*Pillar and Foundation of Truth* 91–92; emphasis in original). Florensky then describes how through love the now impersonal "nonself," the result of the emptying, as the earthly Christ was the result of an emptying, becomes a person by becoming another self, this other self being "Thou." It is here that Florensky uses the word *kenosis*: "But in this 'impoverishment' or 'draining' of the Self [*Ia*], in this 'emptying' [*opustoshenie*] or 'kenosis' of itself, an opposite restoration of the self takes place in its own norm of being, by which this norm is now no longer just given, but justified, that is, it not only is present in a given place and moment, but has a universal and eternal significance" (92).

Kenosis here is used as an analogy for what seems to be merely a transitional stage between the solitary state of an unloving and unloved self and the "supralogical" joining of that self, through love, with another self. It clearly has an affirmative meaning, since one self empties itself only for the purpose of establishing a mystical union with another.

Later in the same work Florensky returns to the concept of kenosis, once again citing the kenotic passage from Philippians. This time, however, he refers to the actual kenosis, instead of merely using the concept as an analogy. The subject is *tvar'*, the created world or world of creatures. "Christ took the idea of God's humility to its ultimate limit: God, by going into the world, sets aside the form [*obraz*] of His glory and takes on the form of His creatures [*tvar'*] (Phil. 2:6–8)," he says, paraphrasing the kenotic passage, "submits to the laws of creaturely life, does not disturb the world's course, does not dazzle the world with lightning or deafen it with thunder . . . but merely glimmers before it with a modest light, gathering to Himself His sinful and weary creatures, showing them reason, but not chastising them" (289).[13]

This is the literal sense of kenosis for Florensky. He has in mind God's humility, but he does not use the fact of that humility as cause to indulge in the heresy of the nineteenth-century German biographers of the historical Jesus. And the reason he does not is that, unlike the kenotic theologians, Florensky emphasizes the corollary of the kenosis, namely, the incarnation and the miracle of creation. Later in *The Pillar and Foundation of Truth* he tells the story of a pilgrim who through continued prayer came to see the entire surrounding world in an entrancing new light. Florensky tells the meaning of the story. "In a word," he says, "all the world of creatures [*tvar'*] revealed itself to our pilgrim as an eternal, divine miracle, as a living being [*sushchestvo*] praying to its Creator and Father" (317).

Kenosis thus has a dual sense for Florensky. He sees it both as a transitional stage to a higher, transfigured state and as a true act of humiliation. But even when he views it as the "ultimate limit" of God's humility, as the act by which God took on the form of his creatures and submitted to their laws (including, of course, death), he speaks in celebratory tones, and this is because the world of creatures (*tvar'*), the world of matter, is something to be venerated and celebrated.

Among Florensky's most remarkable contributions to contemporary thought is his theory of language. As his own notation in the "Av-toreferat" showed, language was central to his worldview, and one reason for its centrality was its ability to mediate between the imma-terial (thought) and the material (the "concrete appearance" [*iavlenie*] of thought). It is not surprising that Florensky titled one of his most cogent analyses of language, an essay that he wrote some time be-fore 1922 and that was first published only in 1986, "The Antinomy of Language" ("Antinomiia iazyka"). The "antinomy" that Florensky refers to in the title stems from language's dual existence as what he calls *veshchnost'* and *deiatel'nost'*.[14] These terms are Florensky's attempt to translate into Russian Wilhelm von Humboldt's distinction between language as *ergon* and language as *energeia*. Language, as Humboldt put it in *Über die Verschiedenheit des menschlichen Sprachbaues* (1827–29) was traditionally viewed as "ein totes Erzeugtes," as a mere dead, created thing, or *ergon* (work). Instead, Humboldt believed, language must be regarded as a dynamic, living thing, as constantly evolving energy, or *energeia* (Humboldt 7:44–46). Florensky's *veshchnost'* effectively renders *ergon* as something like "thinghood," and *deiatel'nost'* renders *energeia* as "activity." His departure from Humboldt's theory consists partly in his use of terms with a slightly different sense from Humboldt's, but also in the relation he sees between the two terms. Humboldt preferred the *energeia* conception to the *ergon* conception. Florensky, however, stresses the *antinomy* (at least in this essay). For Florensky language is both *veshchnost'* and *deiatel'nost'*. It exists as a kind of object, a fixed means of communication with established and unchanging principles and meanings, but at the same time it exists as a fluid process, changing every time it is used in any type of communication.

As we might expect, the ontic ambiguity of language suggests that it, too, has something to do with iconicity and that the *veshchnost'-deiatel'nost'* opposition can be correlated with the standard iconic opposition between the two worlds. Even though *veshchnost'* has to do with the material dimension of language (its "thinghood"), it represents the changeless quality in language and will thus correspond to the divine, infinite pole of the two-world duality. And even though *deiatel'nost'* has to do with activity, which is immaterial, it represents the changing, contingent quality of language and will thus correspond to the material, finite pole. The opposition comes down to *fixed and eternal* like God's truth, on one side, and *fluid and temporal* like God's world of creatures, on the other.

Florensky presents a similar duality in another important text on language, "The Construction of the Word" ("Stroenie slova"), also written some time before 1922. In this essay Florensky describes the "antinomy of language" with a different pair of terms. Language, he says, has *monumental'nost'* and *vospriimchivost'*. The first of these terms, *monumental'nost'*, refers to the status of language as a "monument," that is, as a fixed, enduring object. The second, *vospriimchivost'*, with its emphasis on perception (*vospriiatie*) and on the "receptive" (*vospriimchivyi*) aspect of communication, refers to the status of language as something fleeting and unstable that has a unique meaning at the moment of perception/reception.

Florensky soon abandons the *monumental'nost'-vospriimchivost'* distinction for a more traditional one borrowed from Aleksandr Afanas'evich Potebnia (who in turn had borrowed it from Humboldt): the distinction between inner and outer form. But Florensky will reverse an important set of features in the inner form–outer form opposition. Humboldt had used the term "inner form" in a rather vague sense to indicate the essential feature of language that mediates between the individual subjectivity of the speaker and the objectivity of the outside world. In *Thought and Language* (*Mysl' i iazyk*, 1862), Potebnia had identified the inner form of the word with its timeless, essential core, something he called the *etymon*, or "closest etymological meaning." "Closest etymological meaning," in the case of Russian, means something like "proto-Slavic root." The outer form for Potebnia is simply the sound of the word, its most external and temporal quality. Florensky, however, identifies the *etymon* (which he defines as "the root meaning of the word, its original or true meaning") with the *outer* form of the word ("Stroenie slova" 351). Inner form, on the other hand, the true essence of the word, is something that is unique to an individual act of speaking. Florensky renames this essential core of the word its *sememe*, saying that the sememe "has no independent meaning that exists separately from *this* speech of mine, spoken right *here* and *now*, in the whole context of lived experience and also in the *present* place of this speech" (352; emphasis in original). Because of its rootedness in the present, the sememe does not survive a given utterance. Neither, for that matter, does a word. "Words are unrepeatable; in every instance they are spoken anew, that is, with a new sememe. . . . Only the *outer* form of a word can be objectively one and the same thing in conversation, but never the inner form" (353).[15]

For Florensky what really counted in language was the part that was immersed in history and materiality, rooted to the concrete here and now of verbal expression. "Matter is not despicable," his theory seems to say, or perhaps "history is not despicable." On the contrary, in "The Construction of the Word," matter and history are valued over the surviving and the "monumental" in language. Since Florensky views history as a dynamic process, that is, history conceived as the progressive revelation of Holy Spirit, it is hardly surprising that he took this view.[16]

Florensky does not consistently assign the individual, changing aspect of language a higher place. In "The Antinomy of Language," as I mentioned earlier, he stresses the duality, the "antinomy." But in either case he celebrates what he regarded as the underrated quality of language, that is, the quality that is individual and material (*deiatel'nost'*, *vospriimchivost'*). "In language everything lives, everything is flux, everything moves," Florensky says in "The Antinomy of Language," characterizing the thought of Humboldt (130). Here is how he puts it in another place in the same essay: "We value language in so far as we recognize it as something objective, something given to us, as if it were a condition of our life that had been imposed on us; but we truly speak only when we ourselves reduce language to its slightest nuances, cast it anew *in our own way*, while continuing, however, to believe completely in its objectivity. And we are right in doing so: for our individual thought rests not on solitary reason, which in and of itself does not exist, but on Communal Reason [*Razum Sobornyi*], on the universal *logos*, and the individual word is articulated through no other activity than the one that gives birth to and cultivates language. No individual language could exist that was not at the same time universal in its foundation; no universal language could exist that was not at the same time individual in its appearance" (135; emphasis in original).

Casting language as an antinomy, as Florensky does in his essay, makes our view of it an issue of perspective, as with other ontically ambiguous objects. Just as the iconostasis inhabits this world but appears to make contact with the other world, just as dreams are visible images but bring us into a world that is not visible, so language involves us in the world of historical accident while dwelling in a world that is fixed and unchanging.

Even the experience that language gives us in the world of historical accident, however, is dual and iconic, because such experience is at once individual and communal. When Florensky says that individual thought rests on Communal Reason (*Razum Sobornyi*) and the universal *logos*, he shows that even the private experience that serves as the basis for an act of speech has contact with a larger realm of enduring qualities. His choice of the expression *Razum Sobornyi* shows that here, too, his thinking is iconic and that here, too, the celebration of matter is present. *Sobornost'* is the communally shared, conciliar (*sobor* means "council," among other things), brotherly experience of Christ. It stems from the joyful recognition that the incarnation gives fleshly beings a point of contact with the divine. That point of contact is the Son of God (the Word of God made flesh), whose sojourn on earth provided the human community with a corporeal form of the invisible and allowed that human community to share—in the only way it could, namely, a fleshly way—the experience of this archetypally iconic being, the humbled, kenotic divinity. *Sobornost'* is thus communality with other worshipers and with the Son of God himself, because he was made flesh and he shared communally the experience of a fleshly being.

Once again, it is a question of perspective. From the fact of the humbled divinity, one may reach the conclusion that, as fleshly beings, we are base and ignoble, because we are completely separated from the invisible world of the divinity; or one may reach the conclusion that, as fleshly beings, while we can never *know* or *see* the world of the divinity, we enjoy contact with it through the experience of a shared communality in the kenotic Christ. *Sobornost'* takes the second route. Its beauty is that it recognizes the boundary between matter and the divine, while it celebrates matter as a gift from God. This is the sphere in which Florensky places language when he derives all individual acts of communication from a universal *Razum Sobornyi*. Language itself is thus a joyful celebration of matter, accident, presence, contingency. Its dual foundation in this world and in a world of fixed qualities makes it a model for the communal celebration of kenotic humility and fraternity.

The Pillar and Foundation of Truth and many of the writings I have mentioned here were designed to construct a trinitarian worldview. Florensky's method was always to start with duality (two worlds, the two members of an identity, I and Thou, the Father and the Son, and so on) and demonstrate the metaphysical inadequacy of that duality. The two members of a duality simply reflect each other and offer no chance for movement to a higher state. A third member is always needed to transcend this aporia, and the result is the completeness of trinity: I-Thou-Other, Father-Son-Spirit, and so on. What is remarkable, though, is how deeply entrenched in the pretrinitarian stage of his thinking Florensky's mind seems to be. It is as though he knew in good conscience that a Christian worldview required trinity for completeness, but put the third member of the trinity in its place almost by a kind of intellectual artifice.

Where he is truly comfortable is in states and things that in his view are characterized by duality: *Sobornost'* in the human community, antinomy in language, or the boundary between two worlds in a church. Florensky never explains why, if all matter is to be venerated and if the world of creatures (*tvar'*) stands in relation to God as ordinary truth stands to God's Truth, then certain material objects, like icons, appear to possess a different mode of being from that of ordinary objects. Presumably one could establish a hierarchy on the basis of his principles. But the mind that dwells in *Sobornost'* tends to overlook distinctions of this sort, and one can only conclude that the uncertainty of duality and the ambiguity of matter hold a greater value for Florensky than the rigor of theological systems.

Notes

1. For a history of the term *kenosis* in Russian theology, see Valliere 60–99. Valliere cites Tareev, *Iskusheniia Bogocheloveka*, and its use of the term *kenosis*. Florensky cites Tareev, in *Stolp i utverzhdenie istiny*, in a note to the passage where he first uses the term *kenosis* in that book. For the note, see *Stolp* 653–54 n. 117; for the passage, see *Stolp* 92.

2. For a list of nineteenth-century works on the historical Jesus in several languages, see Valliere 64–65 n. 3.

3.   "P. A. Florenskii. Avtoreferat." The "Avtoreferat" is preceded by a preface by A. I. Abramov, "Predislovie k publikatsii 'Avtoreferata P. A. Florenskogo.' " The "Avtoreferat" was published by M. S. Trubacheva, A. S. Trubachev, and P. V. Florensky. The preface and the "avtoreferat" were published in English translation as "Preface to the Publication of 'P. A. Florenskii's Review of His Work' " and "P. A. Florenskii's Review of His Work."

4.   For the date, see "Avtoreferat" 117 n. 1; "P. A. Florenskii's Review of His Work" 47–48 n. 1.

5.   The translator of "P. A. Florenskii's Review of His Work" omitted the last sentence in this passage. I have translated it from "P. A. Florenskii. Avtoreferat" (114).

6.   It is not clear in what sense Florensky understands "semasiology." When Florensky wrote the "Avtoreferat" the word had been around for a good half century in a sense that made it roughly synonymous with "semantics." More recently, Anton Marty had used the term as the basis for a theory of meaning derived from the psychological theories of Husserl's teacher, Franz Brentano. See *Untersuchungen zur Grundlegung der allgemeinen Grammatik und Sprachphilosophie* (51–95). And in Russia, Gustav Shpet, apparently borrowing from Marty, had used the term at least as early as 1917, in "Predmet i zadachi étnicheskoi psikhologii" (243).

7.   Both *latreia* and *proskynēsis* carry the general sense of service, obeisance, worship. Lampe lists "worship" under both words but also calls attention to the distinction that Saint John made in the iconoclastic controversy. See Lampe 793, where, in the context of this controversy, Lampe defines *latreia* as "being directed to God dist. from προσκύνησις of saints, sacred objects, etc."; and Lampe 1177, where he cites passages showing the special use of *proskynēsis* as distinguished from *latreia*. Here is how Saint John distinguishes between *proskynēsis* and *latreia*: "Veneration [*proskynēsis*] is a sign of submission and honor. We recognize various types of it. The first is by means of worship [*latreia*], which we direct only to God, Who is by nature to be bowed down before [*proskynētōi*]. The second is the one that, by means of God, Who is by nature to be bowed down before (*proskynēton*), is directed to His friends and servants" (*Pro sacris imaginibus* 1244/21). All translations from the Greek are mine.

8.   Further references are to the Migne edition and the Anderson translation.

9.   The reference to Jacob's ladder is from Genesis 28:12, where Jacob dreams of a ladder that stretches from earth to heaven.

10.   *Sanctuarial*, a nonexistent word, is my attempt to translate Florensky's *altarnyi*, an exceedingly rare word that serves as the adjective for the Russian *altar'* (sanctuary). Florensky took the phrases "cloud of witnesses" and "throne of God, " as well as many other images in this passage, from Heb. 12:1–2.

11.   *Ontic* (or *ontisch*) in this sense appears several places in Husserl, *Ideen I*, though Husserl does not stop to define it or to distinguish it from *ontological* (*ontologisch*). See *Ideen* 362, where Husserl speaks of formal ontology (*formale Ontologie*) and the connection of ontic forms (*ontische Formen*) with noetic forms. The distinction I am using has nothing to do with the Heideggerian ontic-ontological distinction.

12. The word *oplotnenie* does not occur in Dal'. It clearly comes from a verbal form (also not in Dal') that would mean "to make flesh." Normally the word *voplotit'*, "embody," "incarnate," is used for this purpose, but Florensky clearly wanted to convey more vividly the act of turning something into flesh. The word *obshchedostupnyi* in its everyday sense means "cheap" (because of the basic sense of "generally attainable"). The two Greek words are spelled incorrectly in the printed text. The first one means "shape" or "form," and the second one means "icon."

13. See Slesinski 172–74, for a discussion of creation as kenosis in Florensky.

14. See Bonetskaia. This publication consists of an introductory essay on Florensky by A. S. Trubachev (117–18), an essay on Florensky's philosophy of language by N. K. Bonetskaia (118–23), and the text of Florensky's essay (123–63). The terms *veshchnost'* and *deiatel'nost'* first appear on 125.

15. See also Cassedy, "Pavel Florenskij's Philosophy of Language," and *Flight from Eden* 114–20.

16. See especially *Stolp* 134–36, where Florensky quotes at length from Saint Gregory the Theologian and then presents his own modification of Gregory's views. I am grateful to Frank Poulin for calling my attention to this passage.

Works Cited

Abramov, A. I. "Predislovie k publikatsii 'Avtoreferata P. A. Florenskogo.'" *Voprosy filosofii* 12 (1988): 108–12.

Abramov. A. I. "Preface to the Publication of 'P. A. Florenskii's Review of His Work.'" *Soviet Studies in Philosophy* 28, no. 3 (Winter 1989–90): 31–39.

Bonetskaia, N. K. "'Antinomiia iazyka' P. A. Florenskogo." *Studia Slavica Academiae Scientiarum Hungaricae* 32 (1986): 117–63.

Cassedy, Steven. *Flight from Eden*. Berkeley and Los Angeles: University of California Press, 1990.

Cassedy, Steven. "Pavel Florenskij's Philosophy of Language: Its Contextuality and Its Context." *SEEJ* 35 (1991): 537–52.

Dostoevskii, F. M. *Polnoe sobranie sochinenii v tridtsati tomakh*. Leningrad: Nauka, 1972–1990.

Florenskii, P. A. "Ikonostas." *Sobranie sochinenii /sviashch. Pavel Florenskii*. Ed. N. A. Struve. Paris: YMCA Press, 1985. 193–316.

Florenskii, P. A. "P. A. Florenskii. Avtoreferat." *Voprosy filosofii* 12 (1988): 113–19.

Florenskii, P. A. "P. A. Florenskii's Review of His Work." *Soviet Studies in Philosophy* 28, no. 3 (Winter 1989–90): 40–51.

Florenskii, P. A. *Stolp i utverzhdenie istiny. Opyt pravoslavnoi feoditsei v dvenadtsati pis'makh*. 2 vols. Moscow: Put', 1914; rpt. Moscow: Pravda, 1990.

Florenskii, P. A. "Stroenie slova." *Kontekst 1972*. Moscow, 1973. 344–75.

Florenskii, P. V. "Zametki o simpoziume v Bergamo." *Voprosy filosofii* 10 (1988): 169–73.

Humboldt, Wilhelm von. *Gesammelte Schriften*. Ed. Albert Leitzmann. Berlin, 1907; rpt. Berlin: Walter de Gruyter, 1968.

Husserl, Edmund. *Ideen zu einer reinen Phänomenologie und phänomenologischen Philosophie. Husserliana*, vol. 3. The Hague: Martinus Nijhoff, 1950.

John of Damascus, Saint. *Pro sacris imaginibus. Patrologiae Cursus Completus: Series Graeca*. Ed. J.-P. Migne. Paris, 1857–66. 94:1227–1419. *On the Divine Images: Three Apologies against Those Who Attack the Divine Images*. Trans. David Anderson. Crestwood, N.Y.: St. Vladimir's Seminary Press, 1980.

Lampe, G. W. H. *A Patristic Greek Lexicon*. Oxford: Clarendon, 1961.

Marty, Anton. *Untersuchungen zur Grundlegung der allgemeinen Grammatik und Sprachphilosophie*. Halle: Max Niemeyer, 1908.

Shpet, Gustav. "Predmet i zadachi etnicheskoi psikhologii." *Psikhologicheskoe obozrenie*, 1917:27–59, 233–63, 405–20.

Slesinski, Robert. *Pavel Florensky: A Metaphysics of Love*. Crestwood, N.Y.: St. Vladimir's Seminary Press, 1984.

Tareev, Mikhail Mikhailovich. *Iskusheniia Bogocheloveka, kak edinyi iskupitel'nyi podvig vsei zemnoi zhizni Khrista, v sviazi s istorieiu dokhristianskikh religii i khristianskoi tserkvi*. Moscow: Izdanie Obshchestva liubitelei dukhovnogo prosvesheniia, 1892.

Tareev, Mikhail Mikhailovich. *Unichizhenie gospoda nashego Iisusa Khrista*. Moscow: Pechatnia A. I. Snegirevoi, 1901.

Valliere, Paul. "M. M. Tareev." Ph.D. diss. Columbia University 1974.

5

Florensky and Dante
Revelation, Orthodoxy, and Non-Euclidean Space

David M. Bethea

Voi non andate giù per un sentiero
filosofando: tanto vi trasporta
l'amor de l'apparenza e 'l sup pensiero!
—*Paradiso* 29:85–87

Below, you do not follow one sole path
as you philosophize—your love of show
and thought of it so carry you astray!
—Mandelbaum translation

Tam, na zemle, ne napravliaiut razum
Odnoi tropoi: nastol'ko nas vlekut
Strast' k vneshnosti i zhazhda zhit' pokazom.
—Lozinsky translation

He de gnosis agape ginetai
(And knowledge is love)
—Saint Gregory of Nyssa

Few figures outside Russian literary and cultural life held a greater fascination for the generation symbolists than the man with the fabled *orlinyi profil* (acquiline profile),[1] the poet Pushkin called *"surovyi Dant"* (stern Dante). Pamela Davidson has recently argued in her book on Viacheslav Ivanov that "For the religious Symbolists Dante—as the supreme representative of medieval culture—was the prototype of the ideal artist who succeeded in integrating religion and art on the deepest level" (Davidson 15). The semantic field of "Italy-Catholicism-Dante" supplied persistent motifs in the works of, among others, Annensky, Merezhkovsky, Gippius, Volynsky, Bal'mont, Baltrushaitis, Kuzmin, Voloshin, Briusov, Blok, Bely, Sergei Soloviev, Ellis, and Ivanov. And the *Commedia* was nothing less than a *nastol'naia kniga* (book in constant use) for the later Akhmatova and Mandel'shtam. What was the specific lure of Dante, this medieval Catholic in a post-Nietzschean world? These Russians, Davidson continues, were eager "to present Dante in Russian terms, to adapt him to meet the particular needs of the age." Most of all they were attracted to what, in Dante and the Latin tradition, was *not theirs*— "the intellectual aspect of [his] religion . . . [its] blend of philosophy and theology" (Davidson 16). One might even say they were attempting to appropriate a Western-style humanism by adopting, centuries after the fact, its ultimate father figure. Likewise, the ascetic, flesh-despising aspects of Catholicism were bound to appeal—by their very novelty—to an Orthodox tradition that viewed matter as spirit-bearing, on the one hand, and to a decadent/symbolist ethos that was fixated on the body-soul dichotomy and on the erotic, not to say sadomasochistic, aspects of mystical experience, on the other. No less important, the Catholic version of hell, purgatory, and, heaven, so elaborately exfoliated in Dante's great work, became a "fruitful source of inspiration for those who felt drawn to a more intellectual, structured and hierarchical view of the spiritual life" (Davidson 17) than that offered by the rather contourless "other world" of Russian Orthodoxy. We will return to these distinctions in due course.

It is into this symbolist ethos and pathos that, mutatis mutandis, the work of Father Pavel Florensky enters. To cite just two examples, Florensky was at one time close friends with Viacheslav Ivanov and in a letter of 1914 mentions the plans of Ivanov and the philosopher Vladimir Ern to do a translation of the *Convivio* for the "Monuments of World Literature" series at the Sabashnikov publishing house (Davidson 252). Even more intriguing for our purposes, at the turn of the century Florensky studied mathematics under Andrei Bely's father N. V. Bugaev at Moscow University, where the latter's presentation of the new field of "arithmology" (the combined analysis of the theory of numbers [teoriia chisel] and calculus [ischislenie beskonechnykh velichin]) served as a powerful stimulus for both Bely's and Florensky's subsequent attempts to bring far-flung metaphysical concepts under the vault ot post-Kantian mathematics and physics (Szilard 227).[2] It is precisely this connection between mathematics, Dante, the symbolist epoch, and Florensky's little book *Imaginaries in Geometry* (*Mnimosti v geometrii*, 1922) that I would like to explore in this chapter.

But first a brief note about Florensky the person. As far as we know, Florensky shared none of the symbolists' decadent or prurient tendencies, their hothouse blurring of the boundaries separating life and art against a background of fin-de-siècle apocalypticism. He was, after all, a priest, and seemed not at all interested in the secular "middle space" of social intercourse. At least one memoirist, however, has suggested there was something "clever and cruel," even "awesomely creepy" about him—"demoniac or diabolical, and yet holy" (Sabaneeff 312). This same Leonid Sabaneeff gives one of the few genuinely nonpartisan views of Florensky (Sabaneeff, a scholar of mysticism, was simultaneously fascinated and repulsed by Florensky), so perhaps it is well to cite him at some length:

From him [Florensky] emanated clearly perceptible vapors of a highly complex nature: one had an impression of genius, of unusual depth and power of thought, and at the same time there was something of black magic, dark, devoid of divine grace. . . .

I felt that Florensky possessed immense spiritual experience and was endowed with hypnotic power. His own asceticism was beyond doubt. It was manifest that he had undergone a complete and thorough training in "religious intellectual practice," possibly following the Russian Orthodox monastic tradition, but more probably also in other ways. He regarded himself as Orthodox, but to me his views always appeared much broader than the dogma of Orthodoxy.

His erudition was vast. He held degrees from two university departments (philological and mathematical) as well as from a theological academy. He was a philosopher, theologian, historian, mathematician, physicist, but he apparently took little interest in the biological sciences and none whatever in sociology. He lived in his closed, ascetic, intensely intellectual world and in the world of his secret "spiritual exercises." . . . In his tastes and psychological attitudes he seemed close to the early medieval gnostics (Origen, Basilides, and others), much closer probably than to pure and naive Orthodoxy.

His mind was complex, many-storied, and to some extent even hostile to simplicity. One might even call it a cabalistic mind. . . . His extravagant and excessively luxuriant thoughts often contradicted one another, but this did not embarrass him in the least. He often spoke of the "many facets" of any true thought and of the compatibility of contradictions on the deepest level. . . . Logic is valid for the "earthly life," for the lower levels; but the true world is one where contradictions are compatible—a realm of antinomies. He obviously regarded antinomy as the basic law of the universe, encompassing all others.

. . . Outside his chosen sphere, science and mysticism, he generally talked very little and would keep silent for long periods. I do not remember ever having talked with him about an everyday matter. (Sabaneeff 313–14)

Sabaneeff's memoir is based on notes and resumes of approximately thirty-five talks (totaling some hundred hours) with Florensky. The talks took place primarily during the early 1920s before the author's emigration in 1926. Though he published his piece on Florensky only in 1962, Sabaneeff claims—and we have no reason to doubt him— to have listened attentively to each talk and then to have committed immediately the contents to paper. His memory at the time was, in his words, "exceptionally exact." Some of the facts in Sabaneeff's account may be disputed (e.g., he gives 1948 as the year of Florensky's death, while the official date is now given as December 8, 1937),[3] but its overall "vector" seems to correspond rather convincingly with other sources. Thanks to their early date and to the relative lack—until recently—of subsequent information about Florensky, there is nothing cloying in Sabaneeff's "secular" admiration, no attempt to "iconize" the priest as two-dimensional martyr at the hands of the Soviets.[4] As we shall see, Sabaneeff was prescient about Florensky's ascetic streak, his dark erudition (coupled as it was with a total lack of interest in the more "human" sciences of biology and sociology), his affinities with medieval gnostics, his "desire to reconcile scientific and revealed truth" (Sabaneeff 317), and his near obsession with contradictions and antinomies—what he calls in *The Pillar and Foundation of Truth* (*Stolp i utverzhdenie istiny*) the *coincidentia oppositorum*. What is particularly interesting for our argument is the apparent absence of *love for the concrete other*, except as an intellectual construct, in Florensky's learned schemas and ever more attenuating formulas. "By nature he was . . . possessed rather by the spirit of cognition on a grand scale than by that of kindness and charity; Lucifer was closer to him than Christ. This increased rather than diminished his fascination for me" (Sabaneeff 316–17).[5]

As recent studies have made abundantly clear, every crucial question of ontology has for Florensky an antinomial structure to it.[6] Whether he is speaking about icons, language, dreams, the creative process, non-Euclidean geometry, the interior of a cathedral, or even Sophia, his way is to *visualize* two separate and as it were self-canceling categories and then to show, against logic (*rassudok*), how these categories can suddenly occupy the same space in a privileged "crossover zone," what Steven Cassedy calls, following Husserl, the "ontically transitional" (see essay in this volume). Thus we have the board, glue, gesso, and gold leaf of an icon on the one hand, and the unmediated "Mother of God" on the other; or the composition (*kompositsiia*) of a work of art on the one hand (that which the artist, with the concrete materials at hand, *conceives* from his vantage), and its construction (*konstruktsiia*) on the other (that which the viewer *perceives* from his vantage), etc. Florensky constantly asks the reader/viewer of his spatially arranged arguments to see two or more points of view *at the same time*, to, as it were, look back from the far side and forward from the near. The icon is a sacred object because the viewer sees the boards qua boards *and* the Mother of God qua Mother of God; this is achieved by *stepping through the window of faith/belief* where separation equals identification.

Pivotal to Florensky's antinomial thinking-cum-faith system is the notion of "sanctuarial barrier" (see Cassedy), the *limen* without which the philosopher cannot imagine his crossover zone. The iconostasis is an ideal expression of this precisely because of its *flat* surface and its function as threshold separating sacred from nonsacred space. And as Cassedy perceptively points out, while Florensky's method was consistently based on the metaphysical inadequacy of duality and hence the necessity of a transcending third member, his mind seemed to remain almost stubbornly "pretrinitarian"—it proposed the third member by a sort of "intellectual artifice."[7] In this regard, in the sense that a symbol can be figured as the crossover zone between the phenomenal and the noumenal, Florensky was a true child of his epoch: "A symbol is larger than itself. . . . A metaphysical symbol is that essence whose energy bears within itself the energy of another, higher essence, and is dissolved in it; its joining with it and through it manifestly reveals that higher essence. A symbol is a window to another, not immediately given essence" (cited in Genisaretskii 47).

This is where Dante and Florensky's discussion of the *Commedia* enter the picture. In 1921, on the six hundredth anniversary of the death of Dante, Florensky wrote a short but remarkably dense and provocative pamphlet in which he tried to prove that the latest theoretical discoveries in mathematics and physics actually confirm what Christian mystics had for centuries been calling revelation—namely, *that infinity could be knowable*. His term for this was *aktual'naia beskonechnost'* (actual infinity). The booklet, which has since become a bibliographical rarity, was called *Imaginaries in Geometry* and was published in 1922 by the Moscow publishing house Pomor'e. Several of the names that Florensky cites às points of departure for his ideas are well-known in modern accounts of the geometry of space and anticipate in interesting ways Einstein's general theory of relativity: Carl Friedrich Gauss, Bernhard Riemann, A. F. Moebius, etc. In essence, what Florensky argues, contra Euclidean geometry and contra its variations in Leibniz-Newton-Kant (cf. the "antinomy of space" in the *Critique of Pure Reason*), is that the universe can and should be imagined as "a finite homogeneous galactic system" (Callahan 93). That is to say, we can conceive of a universe that is both finite, in that it is bounded, and homogeneous, in that it has no fixed center. To put it another way, there is no other space beyond space, and yet space is not infinite. How can this be so? By seeing space as *curved*, as non-Euclidean, as having no properties *extrinsic* to itself by which to fix its dimensions, by imagining the intrinsic *relativity* of any position one is able to take in space. Those visual prompts, including Klein bottles, Moebius strips, and Escher drawings, that fascinate us because we cannot isolate their boundaries do so precisely by playing with or "bending" our perspective. From our three-dimensional space we look on their two-dimensional surfaces as optical illusions, for their bending does not pierce our space (i.e., it is not measurable outside of itself), just as the Einsteinian 3-sphere cannot be *empirically* charted.

These were some of the ideas Florensky was engaging in his booklet. Intriguingly, the print by Favorsky decorating the cover of *Imaginaries*

The cover of *Imaginaries*. Reprinted from Favorskii/Faworski, N. Rozanova (Leningrad: Aurora, 1970).

is itself a kind of non-Euclidean geometrist's Moebius strip: it presents *two* sides of a plane—the left side which is visible (*zrimaia*) and the right side which is imaginable/imaginary (*myslimaia*). Florensky asserts the integrity (*tselostnost'*) of the plane that can be seen from *both sides simultaneously*. Certain details from the visible side (the letter O) show up on the imaginary side, but fragmented, reversed in perspective, and, most important, bent or distorted. Here the author is trying to suggest, as on a chart, the essential curvature of space. Whereas the basic distinction in the Gauss-Riemann-Einstein model is a universe that is finite and homogeneous, that is, there is no fixed center (all galactic units being bounded equally by all other units) and thus no outer limit to be crossed over or pierced, the Orthodox and otherwordly Florensky still telescopes these antinomies in perhaps his most audacious crossover zone: "A shred of the real side, while located on the border of imaginary [space] . . . conveys the fluctuation of the geometrical figure at the point of its collapsing through the plane, when it has not yet been fixed in place [or "defined" or "determined"—*opredelilas'*], being at once both real and imaginary" (*Mnimosti* 63–64; cited in Szilard 233). If the modern scientist must conclude that "it is hopeless [in the absence of extrinsic criteria] to imagine curved space as being mysteriously bent through a fourth dimension" (Callahan 94), no such doubts assailed this believer, for that is precisely what he is asserting—that the intrinsic becomes extrinsic at this "crossover zone." In short, Florensky, with the aid of Favorsky, has constructed a mathematical icon: rather than the antinomies of boards versus Mother of God, we have the antinomies of three-dimensional versus four-dimensional space. When Florensky says of the cover sketch that it "does not merely decorate the book, but *enters* as a constitutive part into its *spiritual* make-up" (*Mnimosti* 58; emphasis mine cited in Szilard 232), he is asking his reader to step through that same *limen* of faith we have witnessed elsewhere.

Florensky concludes *Imaginaries in Geometry* with a fascinating discussion of how Dante's work, in its presentation of the other world, was not only "ahead of contemporary science" (*Mnimosti* 53) but in fact startlingly prescient about such notions as the bending or breaking of space at conditions—*imaginary yet no less real*—beyond the speed of light. In this regard, the Russian scientist-priest anticipates by almost sixty years the work of such recent physicists and mathematicians as J. J. Callahan and Mark A. Peterson, who have argued in their publications that Dante's vision, in the *Paradiso*, of the harmonious interrelation between the heavenly spheres (which increase in size and turn more rapidly the higher the pilgrim goes) and the Empyrean (whose nine concentric circles decrease in size but, paradoxically, *increase* in rotating speed the closer they come to the blinding point of light at their center) is in fact a rather accurate replica of Einstein's "finite and homogeneous" galactic system known as the 3-sphere (Callahan 99). The reader is left with "the almost inescapable impression that [Dante] conceives of these nine angelic spheres [of the Empyrean] as forming one hemisphere of the entire universe and the usual Aristotelian universe up to the Primum Mobile as the other hemisphere, while he is standing more or less on the equator between them. . . . Taken all together, then, his universe is a 3-sphere" (Peterson 1033). Or, as Florensky himself formulates the paradox of relativity in his own remarkably similar terms,

Dantesque space is precisely like elliptical space. This [realization] casts a sudden bundle of light on the medieval notion of the finite character [*konechnost'*] of the world. But these ideas concerning geometry in general have recently received an unexpected concrete interpretation through the principle of relativity [*printsip otnositel'nosti*], and from the point of view of modern physics universal space should be conceivable [*myslimo*] precisely as elliptical space, and is acknowledged to be finite, just as time is finite, enclosed in itself. . . . The realm of imaginaries [i.e., imaginary space] is real, comprehensible, and in the language of Dante is called the Empyrean. (*Mnimosti* 48, 53)

Thus far we having been making a case for the powerful typological links between Florensky's antinomial thinking and the themes of religious revelation and the "geometry of salvation" in Dante's *Commedia*. In the remainder of this chapter I would like to stress the opposite—the profound and irreconcilable *differences* between Dante's medieval Catholic worldview and Florensky's symbolist-tinged Orthodoxy. Ultimately, I would like to show that what is paradigmatically incompatible about these faith systems and their expressions in words is deeply implicated in their respective histories and particularly in their negotiations of a "middle space" on earth.

I will be using two works by Iury Lotman to support my argument.[8] First, his well-known study of binary models of culture (co-authored with Boris Uspensky), from which the following passage is taken:

In Western Catholicism, the world beyond the grave is divided into three spaces: heaven, purgatory, and hell. Earthly life is correspondingly conceived of as admitting three types of behavior: the unconditionally sinful, the unconditionally holy, and the neutral, which permits eternal salvation after some sort of purgative trial. In the real life of the medieval West a wide area of neutral behavior thus became possible, as did neutral societal institutions, which were neither "holy" nor "sinful," neither "pro-state" nor "anti-state," neither good nor bad. The neutral sphere became a structural reserve, out of which the succeeding system developed. . . .

The Russian medieval system was constructed on an accentuated duality. To continue our example, one of its attributes was the division of the other world into heaven and hell. Intermediate neutral spheres were not envisaged. Behavior in earthly life could be either sinful or holy. This situation spread into extra-ecclesiastical conceptions: thus secular power could be interpreted as divine or diabolical, but never as neutral. ("Binary Models" 31–32)

This absence of a neutral space, *not only purgatory itself but any middle ground over which one makes one's way to the destination of salvation/revelation*, has direct application, as we shall see, to Florensky's reading of Dante.

The second is an article in which Lotman advances the thesis, primarily from within the Orthodox worldview, that "a religious act has as its basis an unconditional act of self-giving" (" 'Agreement' and 'Self-Giving' " 125). This idea of religiously inspired behavior as being *one-sided* and *noncompulsory*, that is, bearing no signs of an implied quid pro quo, will, again, be implicated in the possibility or impossibility of imagining an axiological middle space:

In the West the sense of agreement, though having its remote origin in magic, had the authority of the Roman secular tradition and held a position equal to the authority of religion; in Russia, on the other hand, it was felt to be pagan in character. . . . It is significant that in the Western tradition an agreement as such was ethically neutral. It could be drawn up with the Devil . . . but one might also make agreements with the forces of holiness and goodness. . . . [In the Russian context, however,] an agreement may only be made with a Satanic power or its pagan counterpart. (126–27)

Now, to return to Florensky and Dante. It is perhaps not by chance that Florensky focuses on a turning point in the *Inferno* rather than in the *Paradiso* to make his case about non-Euclidean optical illusion and revelation. One recalls in this connection Sabaneeff's insight that Florensky was "possessed rather by the spirit of cognition on a grand scale than by that of kindness and charity; Lucifer was closer to him than Christ." The following passage, for example, is especially representative of Florensky's brilliant yet eccentric mapping of the Dantesque cosmos:

And so let us recall the path taken by Dante and Virgil. It begins in Italy. Both poets descend along the steep slopes of the funnel-shaped Inferno. The funnel culminates at the last, narrowest circle of the Lord of the nether regions [*Vladyka preispodnei*]. What is more, all the while during the descent down a vertical position is preserved by both poets—their heads are turned in the direction of the point of departure, i.e., toward Italy, and their feet toward the center of the Earth. But when the poets reach approximately Lucifer's waist [*poiasnitsa*], they both suddenly *turn over* [*perevorachivaiutsia*], proceeding now with their feet toward the surface of the Earth, whence they entered the subterranean kingdom, and with their heads in the opposite direction (*Inferno*, canto 34).[9] Having crossed this border . . . i.e., having completed the path [down] and crossed the center of the world, the poets find themselves beneath the hemisphere whose counterpart is the place "where Christ was crucified": they [now] rise up along the crater-shaped way [*po zherloobraznomu khodu*]. . . . Mounts Purgatory and Zion, diametrically opposed to one another, arose as the result of that [i.e., Lucifer's] fall, which means that the path to heaven is directed along the line of Lucifer's fall, but has an opposing meaning. In this way, Dante constantly moves along a straight line and [comes to] stand in heaven, turned with his feet in the direction of his descent. But having looked out from there, from the Empyrean, at God's glory, in the end he finds himself, without any particular movement of turning back [*bez osobogo vozvrashcheniia nazad*], in Florence. His journey has been a reality, but if anyone would deny the latter, then the least that can be said is that this journey must be acknowledged as a poetic reality, i.e., as something conceivable and possible to imagine, which means that it contains in itself the givens for an elucidation of its geometrical premises. And so, moving constantly ahead in a straight line and turning over once en route, the poet comes to his prior place in the same position in which he left it. (*Mnimosti* 45–47)

Notice, to begin with, that, whereas the physicists who speak of Dante's anticipation of the Einsteinian 3-sphere invariably single out the *Commedia*'s last book and the pilgrim's transit from the earthly to the heavenly spheres, Florensky fixes on an entirely different crossover zone—the end of the *Inferno* and Lucifer's waist (*poiasnitsa*) or, more precisely, the seam where the thigh/loin meets the bulge of the hip/haunch.[10] Moreover, as is his wont, Florensky *collapses* all the drama of the *Inferno* into this one point in space and time where opposites can be identities— where the pilgrim and the guide can turn upside down and still walk upright, where their heads and feet can turn in a diametrically different direction and yet they can still make forward progress in their journey, where Lucifer as the very symbol for the way down can suddenly provide an exit to the way up, and so on. Florensky takes pure intellectual pleasure in the posing of these paradoxical movements—Dante makes his way ever forward, turns upside down at one juncture en route, and arrives back at the original point of departure in the same position (*v tom zhe polozhenii*) in which he left. Salvation becomes a Moebius strip, and the point where the outer surface joins the inner surface is at Lucifer's waist.

In all this, Florensky differs from Dante in one significant way. Like Bakhtin, who imbibed the same currents of symbolist and postsymbolist spirituality, Florensky places great, even exclusive emphasis on Dante's so-called verticality, on the one moment of his transcendence rather than on the multitude of moments between any ultimate stepping across or over (see, e.g., Bakhtin 156–57). No mention is made by Florensky of the tremendous learning process Dante has passed through in order to get to this point, or the role of Beatrice (love, beatitude) in sending Virgil to guide him. Nor does it appear to register on this Russian reader that the underworld grows denser and, as it were, "fatter" (i.e., all the various pouches in the eighth circle and the rings in the ninth circle) the closer the two travelers get to the center of the earth (just as things will move more slowly the closer we get to the Earthly Paradise and the Empyrean later on). In other words, what is crucial to Dante's Catholic worldview but goes unattended by Florensky the Orthodox believer is that the steps of the pilgrim qua *homo claudus* have been agonizingly *incremental* and spread out over a massive *middle space*.

According to medieval tradition, one's soul has two feet, the *affectus* (will, carnal appetite) on the left, which clings to the things of the earth, and the *apprehensivus* (intellect) on the right, which tries to perceive the good in a postlapsarian world. These steps have been *measured out* to the ethical centimeter by the Catholic notion of sin and retribution, that very specific adherence to the rightness of the *contrapasso*[11]—the fitting of the punishment in hell to the unrepented sin on earth.[12] Thus, to cite the first few examples, those who refused to take sides in the battle between good and evil are, like the neutral angels, punished just beyond the Gates of Hell by chasing after banners that lead nowhere (they had no *telos* in life) and by being bitten by horseflies and wasps (they were themselves parasites of sorts) (canto 3); or the lustful, including the symbolists' beloved Paolo and Francesca, are blown about like birds (just as their passions tossed them about in life) because they have forfeited their right to choose (canto 5, second circle); or Ciacco and the other gluttons who were so well fed and indulged in Florentine life must now lie in the filthy and evil-smelling pigsty of the third circle and be flayed by the big-bellied Cerberus (canto 6), etc. The number of circles in Minos the judge's tail tell each sinful soul his or her precise destination below.

But all these measurements and portionings-out are, for the reasons outlined by Lotman, anathema to the spirit of Orthodoxy. To be punished in a way that fits one's misdeeds, just as to be rewarded in a way that fits one's spiritual *podvigi* (deeds), is to engage in the quid pro quo that the Slavic world associates with magic (the domain of the devil), Roman law, and the Catholic Church. Here Florensky very much follows Dostoevsky and the Slavophiles. As he writes in "Gehenna," his eighth letter in *The Pillar*:

I want to point out the decisive difference between the view expressed here . . . and the Catholic teaching about purgatory, where the person is saved *not* in spite of, but *thanks to, as a result of* the torments of purification. It is for this reason that, for the Apostle Paul, what is saved is not the person in his entire makeup, but only "he himself" [*sam*], his God-given "about oneself" [*o sebe*], while according to Catholic teaching it is the whole person that is saved, but only having bethought himself and changed for the better under [the influence of] the disciplined retribution of purgatory. The profoundly mysterious and suprarational metaphysical act of the separation of two moments of being ("about oneself" and "for oneself" [*dlia sebia*]) is transformed, in the vulgar conception of Catholic purgatory, into something psychological, thoroughly understandable—into justification through suffering and into education through punishment. (*Stolp* 233)

It should not be surprising, having read such statements, to find Florensky not mentioning the steps leading up to the way out of the Inferno—these latter would have evoked too readily the "false discipline," the "justification through torment," and the "edification through punishment" of Catholicism. It is not simply that these various mediating measures are too easily associated with the corruptions of the historical Church, including simony and the securing of one's place in the other world through negotiations in this one. Equally offensive to Florensky's mentality is the very notion that *there is or can be something in between*, that the "crossover zone" can be stretched out, arranged with signposts, made long or steep in its own right. Here Florensky joins hands with the Dostoevsky of *The Idiot* whose hero tells the tale of the peasant who murders his friend for a silver watch *at the same time* that he genuinely asks God's forgiveness *radi Khrista* (for the sake of Christ).

For Florensky, then, the concept of divinity and the sacred is always associated with the iconic and a clean, flat, and as it were "geometric" surface; for Dante, as we learn in the very last canto of the *Commedia* (30:85–87), *God is a book*, whose multitude of pages are scattered throughout the universe—the book is thick and its contents add up to a plot. At the end of the letter on Sophia, Florensky explains the phenomenon of her wisdom by first describing taxonomically the three primary categories of Sophia icons (typified by the Novgorod, Iaroslavl', and Kiev "Sophias," respectively) and then explaining what the symbolism in these icons means. Again, there is no plot, no story line. Instead there are one-to-one correspondences on the order of "Sophia's wings = closeness to a higher world," or "the caduceus = theurgic power," or "the crown in the form of a city wall = Earth-mother/civitas" (*Stolp* 374–75). One can only assume that a plot such as we have in the *Commedia*, where the salvation of one pilgrim soul is achieved through grace to be sure, but also through the intricately calibrated blend of poetic footsteps in terza rima and physical footsteps through three massive realms of the afterlife, is already, by definition, too human-centered, too "secular," for Florensky's tradition. Beatrice, as the *Vita nuova* tells us, is the ninth most beautiful woman in Florence—certainly the kind of hairsplitting in the aesthetic/potentially erotic realm in which Florensky would have absolutely no interest. Likewise, whereas Dante is very careful about the various female intercessors, their precise positions vis-à-vis the Godhead, and even their individual qualities—recall that it is Mary who sends Lucia who sends Beatrice—Florensky is apt to "telescope" (the *optical* element being crucial) the different incarnations of Sophia. To the poet who could not speak of feminine beauty, whether physical or spiritual, without remembering the lessons of *dolce stil nuovo* and the love poetry of Guinizelli and Cavalcanti, the following Sophia-inspired catalogue would seem very strange indeed:

If Sophia is all Creatures [/Creation], then the soul and conscience of Creation, Mankind, is chiefly Sophia. If Sophia is all Mankind, then the soul and conscience of Mankind, the Church, is chiefly Sophia. If Sophia is the Church, then the soul and conscience of the Church, the Church of Saints, is chiefly Sophia. If Sophia is the Church of Saints, then the soul and conscience of the Church of Saints, the Intercessor and Defender for all creatures before the Word of God . . . [that is,] the Mother of God . . . is once again chiefly Sophia. But the true sign of the Blessed Mary is Her Virginity, the Beauty of Her soul. It is this that is Sophia. (*Stolp* 350–51)

This is a remarkable passage when placed against the notion of Christian beatitude in feminine form in the *Commedia*. As Zenkovsky first pointed out, how can Florensky's version of Sophia be, at one and the same time, "the preexistent nature of creation," "the Church in its earthly aspect," and "creation that has been deified by the Holy Spirit" (see *Stolp* 350)? How can Sophia be both the ideal personality of the world (*ideal'naia lichnost' mira*), that is, unfallen, and that world's Guardian Angel (*Angel-Khranitel'*), a concept that presupposes there is some evil to guard against (Zenkovsky 2:889)? She cannot be, if any Christian plot or extended notion of theodicy is involved. The main point to keep in mind as we conclude this discussion of Catholic middle distance and Orthodox two-dimensionality is that the former stresses *the analogous that is different* (Mary is like Lucia who is like Beatrice, but still *they are different*) and the latter stresses the *different that is identical* (Sophia = humankind = Church = Church of the Saints = Mother of God = Virginity). The former cannot help but create space, especially over time as the later Church Fathers continue to weigh and measure the subtle differences on the path from secular to divine knowledge. The latter cannot help but consume and eliminate the potential for middle space.

Which brings us, finally, to the role of love in revelation. As numerous scholars have shown, including most recently Giuseppe Mazzotta in his fine study *Dante's Vision and the Circle of Knowledge*, Dante's works were continually implicated in the ongoing debates between the Augustinian tradition, on the one hand, a tradition that spurned rhetoric, logic, and the art of eloquence for their own sakes (see, e.g., *Confessions* 1:18), and the positions of Saint Bonaventure and Saint Thomas Aquinas, on the other, which were intent on establishing "links between logic and theological speculation and between theology and grammar," and which were vigorously contested by such Oxford Franciscans and neo-Augustinians as John Peacham (Mazzotta 10). These debates, which swarmed in the Scholastic air of thirteenth-century Paris, are important because they provided a palpable historical context for Dante's understanding of the interrelationship between intellect, love, and knowledge. They were, in Mazzotta's wonderfully apt phrase, "ideological crystallizations of his [Dante's] time" (Mazzotta 11).

This is not the place to revisit the massive Scholastic tradition that fed the *Commedia*. But if one may crudely express what was rigorously analyzed by the best late-medieval minds, for Dante (and the contemplative tradition influencing him) the substance of revealed truth could be told only by positing "a *coincidence* between intellect and love" (Mazzotta 13; emphasis mine). And this coincidence was not an optical illusion *tout court*, a turning upside down at Lucifer's hip or a stepping across from the earthly to the heavenly spheres. Rather it was, as I would like to argue, the entire great "middle space" of the *Commedia*. Dante has traditionally been viewed as Thomist in the sense that beatitude "depends / upon the act of vision, not upon / the act of love—which is its consequence" (*Paradiso* 27:109–11; cf. *Summa contra gentiles* 3, chap. 59, and Dante, *Divine Comedy* 414). "Thus there must be an act of intellection first, an 'act of vision' of an object, for it to be the possible object of an act of love" (my emphasis; Dante, *Divine Comedy* 414). This is the Thomist position *in nuce*, and because Dante's reiteration of it comes near the end of the *Paradiso*, most commentators have seen the poet and the theologian speaking here in one voice.

However, it is Mazzotta's intention to show that Dante is subtly polemicizing with Saint Thomas, even as the latter is one of the most privileged interlocutors in the *Commedia*. The kind of revelation that is Dante's quarry in the work cannot be achieved by the disciplines of philosophy or theology alone. Nor can one get there by love, if that love has not first been trained to contemplate the proper object. A *risk* is necessarily involved, one that in Dante's case *is* the "way down" into the world of the *imaginativa* (technically one of the five interior senses that Aristotelian psychology located in the sensitive part of the soul [Mazzotta 126]), the world of dark images, dense and threatening forests, in short, the *poetic* word and impulse that can lead astray. Only through the imagination, which is dangerous because its ties to the nether realm of the passions and dream visions can overwhelm the apprehension of the good, can the poet-pilgrim hope to join intellect to love. "Dante's contention is that psychologists and theologians, who claim that moral freedom can be reached by reason's overcoming of the sensuous realm of passions, in fact restrict the sphere of the imagination's powers and circumvent the possibility of imagination's dialogue both with experiences that lie above the grasp of reason and with those that he assigns to the darkness of unreason" (Mazzotta 127).

In a word, then, to take the path of the *imaginativa*, without guides like Virgil and Beatrice, is to run the risk of suffering the fates of Paolo and Francesca, who were reading about how love overcame Lancelot just before it overcame them as well. Dante's willingness to engage the potentially "vagrant faculty" of the imagination in order to make his long and perilous journey from darkness to light of course challenges those theologians, including Saint Bonaventure, Albert the Great, and Hugh and Richard of St. Victor, who believed their own discipline was the best means of "safeguard[ing] the operations of reason from the erratic intrusions of the imagination . . . under the authority and rigor of moral sense" (Mazzotta 127). And it was presumably this moving but also threatening blend of intellectual rigor and *poetic* visionariness, where love and mind are always simultaneously implicated in the steps of the *terza rima* and in the images floating before the pilgrim's inner eye, that forced the Dominican chapter at Santa Maria Novella to prohibit the reading of the *Commedia* as a heretical text in 1335.

My purpose in all this is not to suggest that Dante's Catholic vision of revelation and beatitude is superior to Florensky's Orthodox one because Dante is a poet and Florensky is a philosopher-theologian, or because Dante's vision is predicated on a middle space whereas Florensky's is not. After all, from the Orthodox point of view, the "crossover zone" we have been speaking about may be drained of spatial footsteps but it is filled instead with its own transformative energy. No, my purpose is rather to constitute what I take to be the somewhat startling fact that Dante is already, even in the early fourteenth century, deeply humanist, while Florensky, writing after the Revolution and fully aware of how secular powers wield apocalyptic models, is rather anti- (or perhaps better, "otherly"?) humanist. Even as Florensky is clearly intrigued, as a mathematician, by Dante's non-Euclidean vision, he would have little patience with the sensuous, concrete, quirky, almost palpable quality of Dante's imagery; as he writes in *The Pillar*:

If the Protestant destroys Christ, then the Catholic wishes to dress himself in the likeness [*lichina*] of Christ. Whence the sensuous [*chuvstvennyi*] quality of the church service, its dramatism, its open altar (the altar a stage, the priest an actor), the plasticity, the sensuous music, the mysticism that is not of the mind [*ne umnaia*] but of the imagination (/fantasy: *voobrazhatel'naia*], leading to a fixation on the stigmata (it is noteworthy that in the East there has been no such fixation . . .), the eroticism, the sense of hysterics, etc. Whence too the Catholic mysteries, the processions, all that which operates on the imagination—the action, the shameful display, but not contemplation, not *thoughtful* [*umnaia*] prayer. (*Stolp* 723 n. 400)

Despite Florensky's connections to the tradition of Saint John of Damascus and the eighth-century theologian's assertions that the material world is sacred and spirit-bearing (see Cassedy), there is apparently little room in Florensky's thinking for "matter," if that matter be a traditional love object in this world. What he selects out as damning in the Catholic service are precisely those elements that gave Dante's poem its middle space and its love plot *cum* Christian history: its sensuous (*chuvstvennyi*) images, its potential eroticism, its dramatism and incipient orientation toward a three-dimensional realism, its openness (note the lack of the iconostasis and the "ontically transitional"), its mysticism tinged with elements of a dark imagination (*voobrazhenie*) .

At least in its scriptive incarnation, Dante's love for Beatrice begins in the *Vita nuova* with references to flaming hearts, the god of love (*Amore*), convenient screen ladies, Guido Cavalcanti, and those "Donne che avete intelleto d'amore" (ladies who have understanding of love), and ends only in the *Paradiso* with the speech-stopping exclamation that

The loveliness I saw [as the pilgrim looks on Beatrice at the verge of the Empyrean] surpassed not only / our human measure—and I think that, surely, / only its maker can fully it enjoy. / I yield: I am defeated at this passage / more than a comic or tragic poet / has ever been by a barrier in his theme; / for like the sun that strikes the frailest eyes, / so does the memory of her sweet smile / deprive me of the use of my own mind [La bellezza ch'io vidi si trasmoda / non pur di là da noi, ma certo io credo / che solo il suo fattor tutta la goda. / Da questo passo vinto mi concedo / più che già mai da punto di suo tema / soprato fosse comico o tragedo: / ché, come sole in viso che più trema, / cosi lo rimembrar del dolce riso / la mente mia da me medesmo scema]. (*Paradiso* 30:19–27).

Lest we forget something very basic, Dante's great love was, first and foremost, a real person, and what began as adolescent swooning and ended in blinding revelation had a concrete signified to go with its multitude of signifiers.

This was not the case with Florensky. To be sure, he too had a private life, including a wife and family. Indeed, his confessor at the Moscow Theological Academy, Vladyka Antony, had set marriage as a condition to Florensky's ordination because apparently he sensed that this spiritual son, with all his gifts, could not minister to others until he experienced, in a concrete way, the humanizing sacrament of matrimony (Andronik 22). One of the fascinating paradoxes about Florensky the man is that over against the written traces of his profound and otherworldly thought is the record of his warm family life and the straightforward, touching letters written home from exile.[13] Why then, to return to our opening comments, did someone like Sabaneeff feel there to be a "Luciferian" aspect to Florensky's attraction to cognition per se and a kind of "cloying sweetness" to his language when it touched upon questions of the heart (Sabaneef 316)? Speaking speculatively, we could say that Florensky's language about love probably sounded unreal or disembodied to this man because it had never apparently known the *intermediate* steps where intellect and love come together and push and pull against each other in the pilgrim's progress so painstakingly described by Dante. As far as we know, Florensky's pious love never attached to, never *desired*, any one actual person, at least in the sense that that person provided a locus where sacred and secular have the potential to create plot (he was, to repeat, *instructed* to marry, and still the decision took him six years). Instead, it attached to the Person of the Mother of God, whose motivations and raison d'être always began *in the other world*. This is what Sabaneeff means when he says, "In him [Florensky] the motif of loving-kindness, of grace and forgiveness, sounded muted, and he disliked making it sound at all" (325). Dante experienced passion that could express itself in both love and wrath. Florensky's love, if it can be put this way, was finally as "iconic" as his tremendously erudite but also cool mathematical mind. That mind may have been two dimensional or it may have been even four-dimensional; what it was not was three-dimensional.[14]

Notes

The epigraph from Saint Gregory of Nyssa is found on the title page of the 1914 edition of Pavel Florensky's *Stolp i utverzhdenie istiny*. My thanks to Professor Stephen Baehr for drawing this detail to my attention. See Baehr, "On Love, Truth, and the Resolution of Antinomies."

1. See, e.g., Blok's "Ravenna."

2. The mathematician Charles E. Ford summarizes Bugaev's position in the following way: "Bugayev was familiar with the works of Kant, Hegel, Locke and

Leibniz. Taking as a starting point Leibniz's monadology, he created a system which he called 'evolutionary monadology.' He hoped to make it a universal system able to explain all phenomena. Mathematics entered his system mainly as the theory of functions, which, for Bugayev, has two branches: the theory of continuous functions and of discontinous functions, the latter theory he called arithmology" (Ford 2).

3. The precise date of Florensky's death was for decades a source of debate and conjecture. In 1989 the family of the deceased received word from the KGB (i.e., copies of the execution order and death certificate) that Florensky was executed on December 8, 1937. See Florenskii, "V. I. Vernadskii" 260.

4. More partisan accounts may suggest that what Sabaneeff saw as a lack of interest in others or as cold, "intergalactic" intellect was in actuality Florensky's otherworldliness, his inability to "fit in" to any social role or "middle space" (see Sheehan). Also, the more we know about Florensky's childhood and background, including his parents' avoidance of formal religion and his family's "hidden" history of the *proton pseudos* (the "great lie" of turning from the priesthood of his great-grandfather to the science of his grandfather), the more the synthesizing efforts of the priest-scientist become understandable and motivated (see Sheehan 5–6).

5. Even a supporter of Florensky, such as Lossky, senses a connection between this (in Sabaneeff's phrase) "spirit of cognition on a grand scale" and the potential sin of pride (Lossky 177). For a factual (though also somewhat "heroicizing") account of Florensky's life, see Slesinski, "Fr. Paul Florensky" 3–27, esp. 12–13. Slesinski mentions, for example, that such gifted thinkers as S. Bulgakov, Lossky, and Rozanov returned to the Church under Florensky's guidance; at the same time, Slesinski stresses the "complexity and outright enigma of his [Florensky's] character."

6. As Robert Slesinski has noted, an antinomy is, for Florensky, "an opposition whose terms remain incompatible in the logical order, but which find their resolution and, indeed, essential complementarity in the metalogical order" (*Pavel Florensky* 145).

7. To be fair to Florensky, he might respond, contra Cassedy, that the third member of the trinity appears not through "intellectual artifice" but through the mediating presence of the icon as it produces the "transcending vision" that draws the viewer across the threshold into its sacred space. Still, this aspect of the optical illusion and space-bending *perekhodnaia zona* is crucial to many of Florensky's arguments and does seem to have a strong cognitive/mathematical quality to it. For relevant passages on Florensky's understanding of iconic space, see his "Ikonostas" 91–91, 96–99, 101–3.

8. Curiously, Lotman briefly discusses Dante's notions of medieval space and Florensky's "retrofitting" of Dante to modern mathematics in *Universe of the Mind* (177–85). He also uses the same passage in *Inferno* (canto 34) (Dante and Virgil at Lucifer's haunch) that Florensky cites to make his case at the end of *Imaginaries* (see below). However, with his "positivist" streak, Lotman seems slightly critical of Florensky and says that the philosopher "in his eagerness to

show how much closer to the twentieth century is the medieval mind than the mechanistic ideology of the Renaissance gets somewhat carried away" (179).

9. There is an apparent error of Florensky's text at this point; this scene takes place in canto 34, not 23, as indicated in *Mnimosti* (46). I have made the change in the cited passage.

10. In the Italian: "Quando noi fummo là dove la coscia / si volge, a punto in sul grosso de l'anche . . ." (34:76–77); and in Lozinsky's translation: "Kogda my probiralis' tam, gde bok, / Zagnuv k bedru, daet uklon pologii." Florensky himself uses another translation (that of D. I. Min?), which foregrounds even more the notion of turning and crossing: "Kogda zhe my dostigli tochki toi, / Gde tolshcha chresl vrashchaet bedr gromadu. . . ."

11. Among other things, a kind of New Testament version of *lex talionis*.

12. "All sins, which Dante arranges in a strict hierarchy, have spatial attachment so that the weight of the sin corresponds to the depth of the sinner's position" (Lotman, *Universe of the Mind* 180).

13. "For Father Pavel his family was one of the main yardsticks with which he rightly assessed his attitude to people and events. . . . The family helped to mould him spiritually" (Andronik 22). For examples of Florensky's letters to his wife, see Florenskii, "V. I. Vernadskii" 236; "Pis'ma iz Solovkov" 118, 119; *Detiam moim* 413, 416, 420.

14. I would like to thank especially Professor Stephen Baehr of Virginia Polytechnic Institute, who read my paper carefully and made a number of valuable suggestions for improving it.

Works Cited

Andronik, Hierodeacon. "The Personality, Life and Work of Father Pavel Florensky." *Journal of the Moscow Patriarchate* 5 (1982): 18–29.

Baehr, Stephen. "On Love, Truth, and the Resolution of Antinomies in Florenskii: Discussion of David Bethea's 'Florenskii and Dante.'" Conference proceedings.

Bakhtin, M. M. "Forms of Time and of the Chronotope in the Novel." In *The Dialogic Imagination*, ed. Michael Holquist, trans. Caryl Emerson and Michael Holquist. Austin: University of Texas Press, 1981. 84–258.

Callahan, J. J. "The Curvature of Space in a Finite Universe." *Scientific American* 235 (August 1976): 90–100.

Dante Alig'eri [Alighieri]. *Bozhestvennaia komediia*. Trans. M. Lozinskii. Moscow: Khudozhesvennaia literatura, 1961.

Dante Alig'eri [Alighieri]. *The Divine Comedy*. A Verse Translation by Allen Mandelbaum. New York: Bantam, 1982.

Davidson, Pamela. *The Poetic Imagination of Vyacheslav Ivanov: A Russian Symbolist's Perception of Dante*. Cambridge: Cambridge University Press, 1989.

Florenskii, P. A. *Detiam moim. Vospominaniia proshlykh dnei*. Moscow: Moskovskii rabochii, 1992.

Florenskii, P. A. "Ikonostas." *Bogoslovskie trudy* 9 (1972): 80–148.

Florenskii, P. A. *Mnimosti v geometrii: Rasshirenie oblasti dvukhmernykh obrazov geometrii.* Moscow: Pomor'e, 1922.

Florenskii, P. A. "Pis'ma iz Solovkov. " *Nasha nasledie* 4 (1988): 115–29.

Florenskii, P. A. *Stolp i utverzhdenie istiny: Opyt pravoslavnoi feoditsei v dvenadtsati pis'makh.* Berlin: Rossica, 1929.

Florenskii, P. A. "V. I. Vernadskii i sem'ia Florenskikh." *Novyi zhurnal* 186 (1992): 226–61.

Ford, Charles E. "Pavel Florensky: Priest, Mathematician, Theologian." Article MS.

Genisaretskii, O. I. "Konstruktsiia i kompozitsiia v ikonologii P. A. Florenskogo." *Trudy VNIITE* (Seriia "Tekhnicheskaia estetika") 59 (1989): 44–142.

Lossky, N. O. *History of Russian Philosophy.* New York: International Universities Press, 1951.

Lotman, Iu. " 'Agreement' and 'Self-Giving' as Archetypal Models of Culture." In *The Semiotics of Russian Culture,* ed. Ann Shukman. Ann Arbor: Michigan Slavic Contributions, 1984. 124–40.

Lotman, Iu. "Binary Models in the Dynamics of Russian Culture" (with Boris Uspenskii). In *The Semiotics of Russian Cultural History,* ed. Alexander D. Nakhimovsky and Alice Stone Nakhimovsky. Ithaca: Cornell University Press, 1985. 30–66.

Lotman, Iu. *Universe of the Mind: A Semiotic Theory of Culture.* Introd. Umberto Eco. Trans. Ann Shukman. London: I. B. Tauris, 1990.

Mazzotta, Giuseppe. *Dante's Vision and the Circle of Knowledge.* Princeton: Princeton University Press, 1993.

Peterson, Mark A. "Dante and the 3-Sphere." *American Journal of Physics* 47 (1979): 1031–35.

Sabaneeff, Leonid. "Pavel Florensky: Priest, Scientist, and Mystic." *Russian Review* 20, no. 4 (October 1961): 312–25.

Sheehan, Donald. "An Introduction to Fr. Pavel Florensky's *Iconostasis*: A Complete Translation by Olga Andrejev and Donald Sheehan." Article MS.

Slesinski, Robert. "Fr. Paul Florensky: A Profile." *St. Vladimir's Theological Quarterly* 26 (1982): 3–27.

Slesinski, Robert. *Pavel Florensky: A Metaphysics of Love.* Crestview, N.Y.: St. Vladimir's Seminary Press, 1984.

Szilard, Lena. "Andrei Belyi i P. Florenskii." *Studia Slavica Hung.* 33 (1987): 227–38.

Zenkovsky, V. V. *A History of Russian Philosophy.* Trans. George L. Kline. 2 vols. London: Routledge & Kegan Paul, 1953.

BULGAKOV

Background

Father Sergei Nikolaevich Bulgakov (1871–1944) was born in Livny, in the province of Orel. His father was a priest, as the Bulgakov men had been for the previous six generations (indeed, they traced their name back to that of the Tatar Bulgak, who defected to the Russians during the Mongol wars and took holy orders), and Bulgakov's upbringing was strongly religious. Bulgakov had an unstable childhood—his father and two older brothers died from alcoholism, his mother was emotionally shaken by the deaths of several of her children in infancy, and still others of his siblings suffered from various ailments—but family troubles did not prevent him from entering the local seminary in 1884.

A year before Bulgakov was to graduate, however, he quit the seminary. It was to be many years before he returned to religion. In 1890, having completed his studies at gymnasium, he entered Moscow University to study law; by this time, he—like so many of his contemporaries—had embraced Marxism. Bulgakov graduated from Moscow University in 1894 and went on to receive his master's degree in 1897. In 1898, Bulgakov married Elena Ivanovna Tokmakova (with whom he eventually had two sons and a daughter) and went abroad.

In 1900, Bulgakov published his first major work, *Capitalism and Agriculture* (*Kapitalizm i zemledelie*), and in 1901 he received a position at the Polytechnic Institute of Kiev as a professor of political economics.

During his time in Kiev (1901–1905), Bulgakov became fully disenchanted with Marxism and published a collection of his own articles entitled *From Marxism to Idealism* (*Ot marksizma k idealizmu*) and, together with Nikolai Berdiaev, bought the journal *The New Way* (*Novyi put'*), which the two would later leave in order to found *Questions of Life* (*Voprosy zhizni*). In 1906, Bulgakov became a lecturer at Moscow University, but resigned his position in 1911 in protest over the university's restrictions on the expression of ideas.

From 1911 to 1916, Bulgakov devoted himself to his greatest philosophical work, *Unfading Light* (*Svet nevechernii*). Two years after its publication, Bulgakov was ordained a priest. In 1922, Bulgakov was banished from the Soviet Union and went to Prague, where he lived until 1925, when he moved to Paris to help found the Paris Orthodox Theological Institute. For the rest of his life, Bulgakov remained active in religious intellectual life, continuing on in Paris as chair of dogmatic theology and associate dean of the institute, and attending ecumenical conferences in Lausanne in 1927 and meetings in Edinburgh and Oxford in 1937 with Church of England hierarchs. He reacted to World War II and the Nazi threat with several articles condemning anti-Semitism. Even after an operation for throat cancer in 1939 left Bulgakov unable to raise his voice above a whisper, he continued to celebrate mass every morning at seven and even delivered Berdiaev's funeral address just a few months before his own death in 1944.

Although Bulgakov's fame as a religious philosopher rests largely on his contributions to sophiology (and it is this with which two of the articles in the present volume deal), some mention must be made of his critique of Marxism and his discussion of the intelligentsia. Bulgakov believed that there are two main religious paths possible. The first is theism, culminating in Christianity. The second is pan-theism, culminating in the worship of humanity and anti-Christianity. For Bulgakov, Marxism, with its focus on the unindividuated material side of human existence and the doctrine (borrowed from Feuerbach) that *homo homini deus est*, represented a modern-style chiliasm. In his article in *Signposts* (*Vekhi*), Bulgakov portrayed the intelligentsia as vital and heroic in its intellectual achievements and its stand against Russia's condition, but simultaneously tragic, seduced by Marxism's maximalism of ends and means into idealizing the revolutionary student instead of the religious ascetic. His specifically spiritual understanding of history in a dominantly materialist age places Bulgakov, as surely as his theology itself, at the heart of the Russian religious renaissance.

—Peyton Engel

Bibliography

Major Works

Filosofiia khoziaistva, 1912
Svet nevechernii, 1917.
Petr i Ioann dva pervykh apostola, 1926.
Neopalimaia kupina, 1927.
Die Tragoedie der Philosophie, 1927.
Drug novobrachnogo, 1928.
Lestnitsa Iakovleva, 1929.
Ikona i ee kul't, 1931.
Pravoslavie, 1933.
Agnets bozhii. O bogochelovechestve, vol. 1, 1933.
Uteshitel'. O bogochelovechestve, vol. 2, 1936.
Nevesta agntsa. O bogochelovechestve, vol. 3, 1945.
Avtobiograficheskie zametki, 1947.
Filosofiia iazyka, 1948.
Filosofiia imeni, 1953.

English Translations

"At the Feast of the Gods." *From the Depths*, trans. and introd. by William Woehrlin, preface by Bernice Glatzer Rosenthal. Irvine, Ca.: Charles Schlacks, Jr., 1986. 65–118.
A Bulgakov Anthology. Ed. James Pain and Nicholas Zernov. Philadelphia: Westminster Press, 1970.
Karl Marx as a Religious Type. Introd. Donald Treadgold. Belmont, Mass.: Nordland, 1979.
"Meditations on the Joy of the Resurrection." *Ultimate Questions: An Anthology of Modern Russian Religious Thought*, ed. Alexander Schmemann. Crestwood, N.Y.: St. Vladimir's Seminary Press, 1977.
The Orthodox Church. Trans. Lydia Kesich. Introd. Thomas Hopko. Crestwood, N.Y.: St. Vladimir's Seminary Press, 1988.
Social Teaching in Modern Russian Orthodox Theology. Evanston: Seabury-Western Theological Seminary, 1934. [Hale Memorial Sermons no. 20]
Sophia, The Wisdom of God: An Outline of Sophiology. Hudson, N.Y.: Lindisfarne Press, 1993.

Secondary Sources in English, Selected

Crum, Winston F. "Sergius N. Bulgakov: From Marxism to Sophiology." *St. Vladimir's Theological Quarterly* 22 (1982): 3–25.
Evtuhov, Catherine. *The Cross and the Sickle: Sergei Bulgakov and the Fate of Russian Religious Philosophy, 1890–1920*. Ithaca: Cornell University Press, 1996.

Kindersley, Richard. *The First Russian Revisionists: A Study of "Legal Marxism."* Oxford: Clarendon Press, 1962.

Lossky, N. O. "Father Sergius Bulgakov." *History of Russian Philosophy.* New York: International Universities Press, 1951. 192–233.

Newman, Barbara. "Sergius Bulgakov and the Theology of the Divine Wisdom." *St. Vladimir's Theological Quarterly* 22 (1978): 39–73.

Rosenthal, Bernice Glatzer. "The Search for a Russian Orthodox Work Ethic." *Between Tsar and People: Educated Society and the Quest for Public Identity in Late Imperial Russia,* ed. Edith W. Clowes, Samuel E. Kassow, and James L. West. Princeton: Princeton University Press, 1991.

Sutton, Jonathan. "Fr. Sergei Bulgakov on Christianity and Judaism." *Religion, State and Society* 20, no. 1 (1992): 61–67.

Zenkovsky, V. V. [Zen'kovskii]. *A History of Russian Philosophy.* Trans. George L. Kline. 2 vols. London: Routledge & Kegan Paul, 1953. 890–916.

Zernov, Nicolas. *The Russian Religious Renaissance of the Twentieth Century.* London: Darton, Longman & Todd, 1963. 137–50.

6

Sergei Bulgakov's Philosophy of Personality

Michael A. Meerson

The Russian concept of personality that emerged in post-Solovievian religious thought is grounded in two different traditions that are rarely considered together: the tradition of modern Western thought running from Descartes to Marx, on the one hand, and the tradition of Eastern Orthodoxy with its emphasis on the doctrine of the Trinity and *sobornost'*, on the other.[1] These two traditions merged into one religious-philosophical discourse in the writings of Sergei Bulgakov, a personalistic thinker and theologian who continually exposed the dangers of impersonalism in philosophies ranging from Marx's economic theory to the trinitarian doctrine of the Greek patristics and developed his own conception of personality.

The title of Bulgakov's first philosophical book, *From Marxism to Idealism*, is revealing. Having been disappointed in Marx, Bulgakov reconstrued the tradition of German classical idealism which the Marxists claimed as Marx's legacy. Bulgakov thus sought the foundation for personalism in idealistic dialectics. The discovery, made by Bulgakov the economist, that Marx's philosophical antipersonalism is the weakest point of his economic theory, is a departing point for Bulgakov's philosophical research. He then argues that economic activity is impossible without creative initiative. The creative act requires two conditions: design, or the freedom of will, and power, or the freedom of performance.

Both conditions in turn require the presence of personality, which, as Bulgakov points out, is notoriously absent in Marx's economic theory (*Filosofiia khoziaistva* 239). Following Werner Sombart and Max Weber, Bulgakov treats economics as a phenomenon of spiritual life, emphasizing the personalist dimension (*Filosofiia khoziaistva* 238; "Narodnoe khoziaistvo" 198–99). Bulgakov argues that Adam Smith's "economic man"—a notion on which Marx based his theory of political economy—is only one aspect of human personality, only one manifestation of the industrious "self." Human personality is in itself an independent factor of economics. Economics is the interaction between freedom, a person's creative initiative, and mechanism, the determinism of nature. In a word, every household is managed by a master, i.e., some person or *self* ("Narodnoe khoziaistvo" 183).[2]

The weakness of Marx's political economy led Bulgakov to criticize Marx's *philosophical* impersonalism. Bulgakov points to Marx's "theoretical disregard for the person, the elimination of the individual under the pretense of a sociological interpretation of history" (*Karl Marx* 51). Bulgakov sees Marx's antipersonalism as philosophically grounded in Marx's interpretation of Feuerbach. Bulgakov considers Feuerbach the real clue to Marxism and also "Marx's untold secret" (*Karl Marx* 76). For Bulgakov, Marxism is Feuerbach's philosophy "translated into the language of political economy and, in particular, that of Marx's economic system" (*Karl Marx* 103).

Feuerbach's philosophy claims to be personalistic. In fact, it has an important aspect of relationality, i.e., of the I-Thou relation that Martin Buber singles out as the very foundation of personalism. In modern thought, according to Buber, Feuerbach was the most important contributor to philosophical anthropology, next to Kant, because he posited Man as the exclusive object of philosophy, and discovered the THOU. Buber calls this discovery "the Copernican revolution" of modern thought, as "rich in consequences as the idealistic discovery of the *I*" in Fichte ("What Is Man?" 148). Buber also pointed to Feuerbach's limitations. Among all the problems of philosophical anthropology, Feuerbach focused only on the problem of relationality, "the connection of I and Thou," but failed to elaborate on it or to consider Man as an individual. And he did not ask Kant's fundamental question *What is Man?* and reduced the whole problem of being to the issue of "unproblematic man" ("What Is Man?" 147).

For Bulgakov, Feuerbach failed to substantiate his personalistic claim. Bulgakov exposes this failure, pointing to Feuerbach's reduction of theology into anthropology. If Buber stressed Feuerbach's continuity with Kant, for Bulgakov Feuerbach remained a theoretical offspring of

Hegel.[3] Translating theology into anthropology, Feuerbach substitutes man for God. However, as Bulgakov points out, Feuerbach substitutes for God not an individual man, a person, but humanity as a whole ("Religiia chelovekobozhiia" 17–20). Since for Feuerbach, as for Hegel, the ultimate representation and organization of human society takes place through the state, Feuerbach ends by positing the head of the state as the real head of humanity ("Religiia chelovekobozhiia" 20–21).

Bulgakov's overall attitude to Feuerbach was nonetheless far from negative. He maintained that Feuerbach was important for early Russian philosophical thought for two reasons: for his ardent zeal in confronting religion and for the positive content of his teaching, which Bulgakov called Feuerbach's "atheistic dogmatics" ("Religiia chelovekobozhiia" 5). For Bulgakov, Feuerbach is an "atheistic theologian" ("Religiia chelovekobozhiia" 3–4). He values Feuerbach's theological anthropology precisely because Feuerbach "humanizes" God; in our century this humanization would give rise to what Martin Buber called "believing humanism" ("Believing Humanism" 117–22). For Feuerbach, religion is empty without man. "To be sure," he writes in view of his prospective critics, "my work is negative and destructive; but, be it observed, only in relation to the *UNhuman*, not to the *human* elements of religion" (Feuerbach 3; emphasis mine).[4] For Feuerbach, this anthropological dimension of religion calls for trinitarian theology. While for Kant or Schleiermacher the doctrine of the Trinity is either unnecessary or without practical significance, Feuerbach considers the Trinity indispensable for man. "Only a divine Being who comprises in himself the whole man can satisfy the whole man," he argues. "Man's consciousness of himself in his totality is man's consciousness of the Trinity" (Feuerbach 31).

Feuerbach explains the trinitarian structure of God not only from the perspective of human needs, but also in terms of trinitarian theology itself. His point of departure is the idea of love. Following Hegel, he posits "the spirit of love" who connects the Father and the Son as the third person of the Trinity. This community of persons in God is then linked to the community of men, their life in fellowship: "God the Father is *I*, God the Son *Thou*. The *I* is the understanding intellect, the *Thou* is love. But a love rooted in understanding or an understanding rooted in love is what we mean by spirituality, and spirituality constitutes the totality of man as man. Only a life in fellowship is truly life, satisfying in itself, and divine . . . God is a life in fellowship, God is the living realization of love" (Feuerbach 32). This link between the divine and human community also suggests to Feuerbach a conformity between the human and divine natures. "If the object of God's love is man, is not then man, in God, an object to himself? If God is Love, and if the essential object of this love is man, is not then the inner essence of the Divine Being human nature" (Feuerbach 28)? This Feuerbachian train of thought, so significant for Bulgakov, was well characterized by Nikolai Berdiaev who connected Feuerbach's teaching with the modern Russian trinitarian theology of Pavel Florensky, Lev Karsavin, and Sergei Bulgakov. "The thought of Feuerbach that man projects his own nature upon God," Berdiaev wrote, "is not an argument in favor of the rejection of God; quite the opposite. It means only that God is commensurate with man, but not with man as a natural and social being, but rather with man as a free spirit. The existential dialectic of the Divine Triunity, as well as the dialectic of the divine and the human, takes place in the very depth of being" (*Ekzistentsial'naia dialektika* 47, 61).

Bulgakov also bases his understanding of religion on the famous idea that religion is humanity's projection of itself. Describing the religious phenomenon, Bulgakov points to its essential dualism discovered by Feuerbach. "Religion (as Feuerbach justly observed) is always a bisection of man with himself, man's relation to himself as to another, a second one who is connected and related to him" (*Svet nevechernii* 6). Bulgakov, however, defines this otherness of man and in man, in religious terms, as God. He rejects the Feuerbachian conception of human projection onto the transcendent and defines religion as the experience of the transcendent within, the experience of "the transcendently immanent." At this point, Bulgakov obviously disagrees with Feuerbach, who viewed religion as merely anthropomorphic and immanent. Bulgakov, however, develops his own philosophy of religion in view of and in opposition to Feuerbach's thought (*Svet nevechernii* 25, 34, 399), as well as to the thought of other German philosophers of religion: Kant, Schelling, Fichte, Schleiermacher, and Hegel. He credits Feuerbach for the idea that man created gods out of his own image (*Svet nevechernii* 326), but interprets this differently from Feuerbach. This different interpretation becomes the cornerstone of his own anthropology and theology: for Bulgakov, man is correlated with God (Zander 316). Human nature is commensurate with divine nature. God could create man after his own image and likeness, because humanity is not alien to God (Bulgakov, *Ikona* 63).

Bulgakov's development of the theory of personality in line with Feuerbachian "I-Thou" relationality is in fact "a voice from the choir," to use Andrei Siniavsky's phrase. Similar theories of personality that reject the notion of a mere isolated ego, and posit rather an open reality, or what Mikhail Bakhtin would later call an "unfinalized" (*nezavershennaia*) entity, a being who defies and negates the identity of "A=A" in which logic and objectified reality attempt to lock him (see, for example, Bakhtin 69), were emerging in this very period in Russia. Bakhtin himself refers to Viacheslav Ivanov's and Sergei Askoldov's personalistic interpretation of Dostoevsky (Bakhtin 11–15).

Ivanov develops his theory of relational personalism from an aesthetic perspective on the basis of Vladimir Soloviev's teaching on love as the act of transcending one's ego. For Ivanov, the antinomy of personality is revealed in religious ecstasy that splits "our self into realms of 'I' and 'Thou' " (V. Ivanov 264).[5] Askoldov emphasized the inner freedom of personality that differs from character, type, and temperament, as Bakhtin noted in the area of special interest to him, namely that of Dostoevsky's poetics (Bakhtin 13). Following his father, Alexei Kozlov, who under influence of Feuerbach, Schopenhauer, and Leibniz prepared the way for "a personalist metaphysics" in Russia (Zenkovsky 2:631, 639–40), Askoldov insisted on "the primary reality of the self" (Zenkovsky 642). Bulgakov, as we shall see, synthesized the ideas of both Ivanov[6] and Askoldov[7] in his treatment of 'self' as the unraveling of threefold 'I-Thou-He' relationality, revealed in religious experience. However, it was Pavel Florensky, himself a close friend of Bulgakov, Ivanov, and Askoldov, who came out with the productive synthesis in his famous *Stolp i utverzhdenie istiny.*[8]

Florensky develops his conception of personality in both epistemological and trinitarian contexts. He contrasts personality with thinghood. Thinghood can be defined, whereas personality is indefinable. Thinghood is conceivable because it can be grasped by a concept, whereas personality spills out beyond the limits of any concept (*Stolp* 83) and transcends the closed self-identity of A=A (*Stolp* 80). Florensky points out that thinghood is characterized by the external unity given in the sum of its features, whereas personality is characterized by an inner unity, given in its self-positing activity (*Stolp* 78). Ultimately for Florensky, only the divine triune personality is truly identical, or truly the same (*homoousios* in patristic terms), both in the sense of numeric identity, and in the sense of the dynamic identity[9] required in logic, where three elements A, B, C are needed because two elements would end up being undistinguishable from one other (Slesinski 113).[10] The numeric identity of the divine personality can be described only in the act of ontological love (*Stolp* 83). By going out of itself (in love) for the sake of another, the self expresses its own 'I' to the 'I' of another, which is 'not-I' for the self. The impersonal nonself becomes a person, another *self*, it becomes 'Thou' (*Stolp* 93–94). At this point Florensky follows the reasoning of Greek patristics (especially Saint Maximus and Saint Basil), but personalizes it. A personal God cannot dwell on the dyad, which is an eternal opposition of two terms that cannot signify absolute diversity. It must be extended beyond the number of division into the Triad. Florensky reasons that if the 'I' is solely formed by the 'Thou', and the 'Thou' is formed by the 'I', there would be nothing to prevent them from dissolving into one another. Only a third Person, a 'He', can safeguard their distinct existences, and preserve a dynamic identity between them (Slesinski 113–14).

Florensky builds upon Fichte's Ich-philosophy, or, in Buber's words, upon "the idealistic discovery of I" ("What Is Man?" 148). It was Fichte who in his *Basis of the Entire Theory of Science* used the formal principle of identity *A is A* "as the first basic proposition of philosophy with variables substituted for definite values or content" (Copleston 49). Fichte takes for this content the transcendental self which he posits as the foundation of philosophy. Copleston thus depicts the difference between Fichte's transcendental self and the objectifiable self, the self "as object of introspection or of empirical psychology":

Fichte once said to his students: "Gentlemen, think the wall." He then proceeded: "Gentlemen, think him who thought the wall." Clearly, we could proceed indefinitely in this fashion. "Gentlemen, think him who thought him who thought the wall," and so on. In other words, however hard we may try to objectify the self, that is, to turn it into an object of consciousness, there always remains an I or ego which transcends objectification and is itself the condition of all objectifiability and the condition of the unity of consciousness. And it is this pure or transcendental ego which is the first principle of philosophy. (Copleston 40)

For Fichte, the I-subject or the transcendental self is not a thing, but an activity (Copleston 41) that posits nonself, or "the whole sphere of the objective including Nature and all selves in so far as they are objects" for an I-subject (Copleston 43). Since an individual self cannot posit the whole realm of objective reality, Fichte interprets the transcendental self as a supra-individual absolute self, or "a supra-individual productive activity which manifests itself in all finite consciousness" (Copleston 44). Thus, the I-subject, the absolute self, which is unlimited activity (Copleston 44), posits within itself a finite self and a finite nonself, "as reciprocally limiting and determining one another" (Copleston 46).

Fichte analyzes the principle of identity, A is A, in the light of the self-positing activity of the I-subject (Copleston 50) and discovers in this principle the triadic structure of subject, predicate, and the relation between the two. The principle of identity, according to Fichte, implies a necessary relation between A and itself. He reasons that if there is an A, it is necessarily self-identical. He then designates the necessary relation between A as subject and A as predicate as X (Copleston 49). Copleston emphasizes that for Fichte "this judgement is asserted or posited only in and through the I or self. Thus the existence of the self is affirmed in its activity of judging, even if no value has been assigned to A. "If the proposition A=A is certain, so also must the proposition *I am* be certain" (Copleston 49).[11]

Bulgakov carries Fichte's and Florensky's analysis further. In his work *The Tragedy of Philosophy* (*Tragediia filosofii*) he explores the German idealist notion that personality is revealed in the act of self-consciousness. The act of self-consciousness is expressed in a simple judgment: l am something, I am A. Bulgakov translates this into logical-grammatical terms, a sentence constituted by three necessary elements, subject, predicate, and linking verb ("Tragediia filosofii" 93). He uses Fichte's discovery that every judgment is related to the self. Thus, the act of judgment, expressed in a sentence, forms the foundation of consciousness, and this act is constituted by three necessary elements: (1) the pure hypostatic self which is the subject; (2) the nature of the self as it reveals itself in the self and for the self (we call this nature 'predicate'); and (3) the self-consciousness of the 'I', or the relationship of the self to its own nature, or the act of self-realization in one's nature, which is expressed in the copulative verb ("Tragediia filosofii" 98).

For Bulgakov the linking verb 'is' (to be), so common in grammar, becomes mysterious and significant in philosophy.[12] First, it serves as the main tool in the operations of thought; second, it joins together as identical that which is different ("Tragediia filosofii" 100). The copulative verb joins the hypostasis 'I' with its nature in the act of existence ("Tragediia filosofii" 103). For Bulgakov, the 'I' does not exist by itself. The 'I' as pure self is beyond existence, transcendent and absolute. It receives its existence, which is always contingent, through its predicate. Bulgakov, therefore, insists on the necessity of distinguishing the subject from subjectivity. For Bulgakov, the psychological subject of psychologists, the epistemological subject of Kant, and even the willing subject of Schopenhauer belong to the realm of subjectivity as distinguished from subject as such. These psychological, epistemological and willing 'selves' simply envelop the hypostatic 'self' that transcends them. Bulgakov defines this hypostatic self antinomically and apophatically. On the one hand, the self negates all definitions because its does not exist in the definable realm of thinghood. The self is *not* among things. On the other hand, the self possesses a superexistence, since everything can be predicated to it, and it can become everything. For this reason, all three elements of the I's self-determination in a sentence—subject, predicate, and linking verb—are necessary. They constitute a triunity. Any one of them implies the other two, but neither can be reduced to any one of the other two, nor to both of them ("Tragediia filosofii" 101).

Bulgakov agrees with Fichte that 'self' is absolute and free, that self is not given, but posits itself—by what Bulgakov calls *actus purus* ("Glavy o troichnosti" 33–34). Bulgakov maintains that the only boundary of the self is the nonself, which for Fichte is the world understood as an object for the 'self' ("Glavy o troichnosti" 33–34). Analyzing this proposition, Bulgakov argues that this nonself both posits a limit to the 'self' and is its mirror, so to speak. The 'self' cannot become aware of itself without this nonself. To deepen the analysis of nonself, Bulgakov uses Feuerbach's concept of 'Thou' According to Bulgakov, in this nonself, the self can see only itself, unless it discerns in it another self, which is 'thou'. Without the 'Thou', or without this 'self' in the other, the 'self' cannot understand or actualize itself in its own consciousness.

Thus, Bulgakov, in Florenskian fashion, corrects Fichte. He points out that the 'self' cannot exist, cannot even posit itself without another self, a 'Thou'. According to Bulgakov, there is no absolute, independent self as 'I'. The self-positing of 'I' necessarily implies a co-positing of 'Thou' as another 'I-subject', which in Fichte's terms is only the nonself. Bulgakov illustrates his point by addressing the grammar of the personal pronoun, which exists not only in the first but also in the second and the third person. Following Florensky, he points out that for its stability, this 'I-Thou' relationship needs a 'he' independent of both the 'I' and the 'thou', a 'he' that could take the place of each and of either 'I' and 'thou'. Thus, Bulgakov maintains, the triangle of personal pronouns actually reflects the mystery of a person's existence, the existence of self which needs for its own positing both the 'thou' and the 'he'. "The I," Bulgakov writes, "is not the only, but the first person to whom the second and the third are co-added. The self-consciousness, the self-positing of self is exhausted by these three" ("Glavy o troichnosti" 36).[13]

Bulgakov also makes use of Sergei Trubetskoi's teaching on the conciliar (*sobornyi*) nature of consciousness. For Trubetskoi, consciousness is neither impersonal nor unipersonal, but rather *sobornyi*. He maintains that in all cognitive and moral acts we "hold a conference [council] with all men within ourselves" (Zenkovsky 2:796). For Bulgakov, 'we' is not only a grammatical form but the true revelation of the *sobornyi* nature of self given to us in language. "I is not lonely, it is *sobornyi*, it is not one but 'multi-unitary' [*mnogoedino*], as the genius of language witnesses by fearlessly declining this personal pronoun in the plural" ("Glavy o troichnosti" 37). Bulgakov defines 'we' as the ontological love in 'I', which lives not only in oneself, but also in 'thou' and 'he', since love is precisely the life in another and by another. Regarding love as the very essence of relationality, Bulgakov corrects Descartes' cogito, replacing it with another metaphysical formula: *amo, ergo sum* ("Priroda v filosofii" 10).

Bulgakov makes a revealing comparison between human and divine selves. He considers that such comparison is possible because, following Feuerbach, he asserts that anthropology "is a necessary basis for theology," and "human spirit contains in itself the postulates of the triunity of God" ("Glavy o troichnosti" 31). The comparison of the finite human person and the infinite divine person, made by Bulgakov on the basis of his conviction that human and divine natures are commensurate, vividly illustrates his conception of personality. This comparison reveals the antinomian nature of the finite self. We have observed this antinomy already in Fichte. Bulgakov, however, underlines a different antinomy. He points out that the self which posits itself, and in this sense is *actus purus*, in fact cannot fulfill this self-positing, because it is not its own master. It is unable to co-posit the 'thou' and the 'he' by the act of self-positing. It can only postulate them. Thus the very self-positing of 'self' is conditional rather than absolute: the 'I' exists for itself inasmuch as both the 'Thou' and the 'He' also exist, but their existence or nonexistence does not depend on my finite self. Thus the very notion of self, of personality, transcends itself and points toward Absolute Subject, which, following Florensky (*Stolp* 48–49, 79–81), Bulgakov postulates as the absolute divine personality, one and unique because of its absoluteness, but also conciliar (*sobornyi*) in itself.

In postulating the triune personality, Bulgakov underlines the following antinomy: being absolute, the Absolute is one and unique. But being the Pantocrator (*Vsederzhitel'*), he holds all and everything in its multiplicity. The notion of the All-holding (*Vsederzhitel'*) Absolute must philosophically satisfy the requirements of both unity and manifoldness ("Glavy o troichnosti" 38). He next postulates that the Absolute subject must contain *in itself* the conditions that a finite subject has *outside of itself*. This is why the only way to understand the anthropological properties of human persons is to contemplate the properties of the absolute Personhood in God. As Bulgakov puts it, "the finite human 'I' cannot exist without 'Thou' and 'He'; it reveals itself only in 'We' and 'You'. It is *sobornyi* in its consciousness, and it is individual [*edinolichno*] in its existence. Therefore it necessarily needs to get out of itself and looks for its own foundation outside of itself. It is this very self-insufficiency that makes a finite subject relative. However, "this self-insufficiency and relativity must be overcome in the Absolute Subject, which must be wholly self-sufficient. The Absolute 'I' must be also the absolute 'Thou' and the absolute 'He' for Himself; it also must be absolute "We" and "You" in itself" ("Glavy o troichnosti" 43).

Thus, by analyzing the nature of personal consciousness within the Divine Personality, Bulgakov deduces from it the threeness of the Hypostases. "Personal consciousness," he maintains,

is not fully unfolded in a self-secluded, isolated *I*, but it postulates THOU, HE, WE, i.e., not a mono-, but multihypostaticity, the latter being both typologically and factually defined as three-hypostaticity. For its own self-affirmation the 'I' presupposes the 'Thou', or 'co-I' (with-I), and for its confirmation, the 'I' presupposes the 'He', being fully realized in 'We'. In the finite self, the 'I' is being posited not only in itself, but outside itself as well; it extrapolates itself and thus limits itself. Despite the finite self's feeling of its being absolute, it is unable to realize in itself its own selfness and must prove to itself its own existence by looking at the mirror of other 'selves'. Without such a mirror, it declines and loses its awareness of its own self. But in contrast to the finite 'I's', in the Divine Absolute Subject, united and truly unique, all alternative positings [*inopolozheniia*] of the 'I' cannot be realized outside of it, because there is no 'outside'. They must be contained within it, since the Absolute Subject is for itself all three at once—I, THOU, and HE, and therefore also We and You. ("Glavy o troichnosti" 66–67)

Bulgakov also clarifies his idea of personality by reworking the patristic notions of *ousia* (nature) and *hypostasis* (person). He observes that human self is not limited to naked self-consciousness, self-reflection. It has its own unfathomable depth, and its life is a continuous self-development of this depth and its inexhaustible possibilities. Whereas Fichte defines spirit as merely abstract self-consciousness, and the substance, the content of self, falls under the category of nonself, Bulgakov maintains that the substance of spirit cannot be nonself because it unfolds itself in the self ("Glavy o troichnosti" 55). The self-awareness of the self and its nature or content are united, are one. For Bulgakov, this unity is the very expression of personal spirit as a hypostatic substance. This hypostatic substance wills and creates. Therefore, in the substance of a spirit one discerns hypostasis and its nature (*ousia*), subject and its content, 'I' and 'mine'. "The *I* has its 'mine' as its own possession," argues Bulgakov. "But this 'mine' does not belong to the 'I' *in actu*, it only becomes 'mine' " ("Glavy o troichnosti" 56). I.e., the nature of the 'I' is a potentiality that actualizes itself in time. In Bulgakov's words, the nature of self "is not only an *act* of self but also a *fact* for self, a givenness."[14] The finite self is self-contradictory, because, on one hand, it posits itself by its own act, and, on the other hand, the self appears to itself as an external product and fact that is beyond the self's control ("Glavy o troichnosti" 57).

The life of the finite self is thus contradictory and incomprehensible in itself. The nature of the finite spirit, according to Bulgakov, could be understood only through one's understanding the Absolute Spirit. The limitations that have been detected in the existence of the finite spirit do not exist in the Absolute Spirit. One cannot apply to the Absolute Subject the definitions of life as development, becoming, and process. The life of the Absolute Subject, His self-consciousness, belongs to Him completely. His substance or nature does not appear to Him as a necessity, as something beyond His control. There is no potentiality in His substance, as opposed to the substance of the finite self.

This prompts Bulgakov to define the life of the Absolute Subject with the Thomist term *actus purissimus*. The Divine Person Himself is the only source of His own *ousia*, nature, life. The divine life is hypostatically transparent, and the Absolute Consciousness does not encounter any limitations in any givenness. Unlike the nature of the finite self, the nature of the absolute self is fully hypostatized, or personified. There is no subconscious, there is no 'It' or 'id', there is no darkness, or potentiality beyond awareness, there is no object that opposes the subject in deity ("Glavy o troichnosti" 59). Bulgakov states that "hypostasis and substance, so visibly distinct in a finite self, in God are united in one identical act of absolute positing: 'I am who I am' (Ex. 3:13)" ("Glavy o troichnosti" 60).

Thus Bulgakov's analysis of the Divine Personality unravels the mystery of human personality, the mystery that Berdiaev called the greatest riddle in the world. Berdiaev, an outspoken personalist, maintains that man is a riddle precisely as a person, "because he possesses personality." He explains man's agony by man's desire to know "who he is, where he comes from, and whither he is going" (*Slavery and Freedom* 20). Man may attempt to obtain this knowledge either "from above or from below," but the very consciousness of personality speaks of man's higher nature. As a personality man is not "a child of the world, he is of another origin," because "personality is like nothing else in the world, there is nothing with which it can be compared" (*Slavery and Freedom* 20–21). In the same essay on man, Berdiaev maintains that the Leibnizian concept of a monad cannot be applied to personality or explain it, since the monad is closed, and personality is open toward others and toward infinity, it is unfinalized. Or, in Berdiaev's words, in its self-revelation, personality "is directed toward an infinite content" (*Slavery and Freedom* 22).

What Berdiaev proclaimed in his affirmative style, Bulgakov elaborated in a systematic fashion, pointing to the infinite content of personality and its dependence in its very structure on the absolute divine personality. The riddle of personality is not abolished, its openness toward infinity, its "unfinalizability" to use Bakhtin's expression,[15] remains, and according to Berdiaev, Florensky, and Bulgakov, pertains to the very essence of personality.

Whereas Florensky sketched his concept of personality in a philosophical context relative to trinitarian theology (*Stolp* 73–84),[16] Bulgakov applied, reformulated, and developed it in his theological discourse on the Trinity. Both retrieved the Western theological and philosophical tradition, which pursued the reflection on the nature of *person*, "one of the most important concepts in the world today," to use the words of Leonardo Boff, a contemporary theologian of liberation (Boff 86–87).

The understanding of personality developed by Florensky and Bulgakov has several parallels in contemporary philosophy and theology. Among their philosophical kin we may list Martin Buber, a German Jewish thinker, Gabriel Marcel, a Frenchman, and John Macmurray,[17] an American; among theologians Jürgen Moltmann, a Lutheran, and Leonardo Boff, a Roman Catholic. Boff even maintains that the new concept of "person" as *"a being-for, a knot of relationships*, an identity formed and completed on the basis of relationships with others," which had been elaborated by modern philosophy, becomes the key notion in contemporary trinitarian theology (Boff 89). Bulgakov expanded this notion by his understanding of personality as an unfinalizable and *sobornyi* entity that stretches toward the divine triune personality as toward its ground, its unattainable limit and model.

Notes

1. Sobornost (*n*), *sobornyi* (*adj*) have been entered into English vocabulary. See Webster's *Third New International Dictionary of the English Language Unabridged*.

2. Bulgakov uses the Russian pun: *"Khoziastvo vedet khoziain"* ("It is a proprieter who manages property," to translate literally).

3. In "Religiia chelovekobozhiia u L. Feierbakha" (8), Bulgakov points out that Feuerbach was a student of Hegel, wrote his doctorate dissertation in the line of Hegelian thought, and later taught Hegel's philosophy at Erlangen University before he was fired.

4. The ideas that I am reconstructing as influential for Bulgakov's thought are so central for Feuerbach that they found their way even to an abridged translation, almost a digest of his book.

5. The development of Ivanov's relational personalism in which 'I-Thou' relations constitute the structure of personality is well traced by James West in *Russian Symbolism* (62–63).

6. Lidiia Ivanov (64) speaks about the close friendship between Viacheslav Ivanov and Bulgakov, who also was Ivanov's neighbor in Moscow.

7.   Askoldov, together with Bulgakov, was an active member of the Moscow Religious-Philosophical Society, and he published his book on his father's philosophy in *Put'* publishing house, which was intellectually managed by Evgeny Trubetskoi and Bulgakov.

8.   I owe the observation that Florensky's analysis of personality was a primary source that influenced both Bulgakov in theology and Bakhtin in literary criticism to Olga Meerson.

9.   Florensky makes the important distinction between identity as similarity (*homoiusia*), or generic and specific identity, and identity as sameness (*homousia*), or numeric identity, concepts introduced by Aristotle. Florensky accepts Aristotelian definitions of generic identity (*identitas generica*) as similarity according to generation, and specific identity (*identitas specifica*) as similarity according to sets of features, including even an infinite number of features and also all features. For Florensky, numeric identity, being as indefinable as personality itself, is a *symbol*, rather than a *concept* (*Stolp* 79, 647 n. 98, 78–83).

10.   In the interest of brevity we shall skip all Florensky's argumentation, and refer the reader to the second chapter of *Stolp* (15–50).

11.   Copleston quotes from Fichte's *Basis of the Entire Theory of Science*, in two editions: the edition of his *Works* by his son, I. H. Fichte, 1:95; and the edition of F. Medicus, 1:289.

12.   At this point, Bulgakov follows Vladimir Soloviev's argument. Soloviev makes three distinctions between his dialectic and that of Hegel which he formally accepts and uses. The second distinction is that whereas Hegel takes the notion of existence (being or *bytie*) as the logical subject and the departing point of dialectical development, Soloviev takes the notion of subsistence (*poniatie sushchago*, Solov'ev, "Filosofskie nachala" 1:343). Soloviev argues that "being" in general is an abstract concept and that the proposition "I am" or "it is" necessarily implies the question "who am I?" or "what is it?" In other words, real being implies subject as well as predicate that describes the content or the substance of the subject. "Thus," maintains Soloviev, "if the verb 'to be' links predicate to subject, then being correspondingly can be logically thought only as the relationship of subject to its objective substance or content, in which relationship the subject affirms, posits, or expresses this content one way or another" (Solov'ev, *Chteniia o bogochelovechestve* 3:83–84).

13.   This Florensky-Bulgakov analysis of the trinitarian pattern of self-consciousness finds a curious illustration in Vladimir Nabokov's *Speak, Memory*. In recollecting his first childhood memories, the author recalls that his first gleam of complete consciousness came together with his being conscious of his parents walking together with him and holding him by both hands. "The revelation that I was I and that my parents were my parents was directly associated with my discovering their age in relation to mine," states Nabokov, adding with some irony that probing of one's childhood "is the next best to probing one's eternity."

14.   Bulgakov apparently takes this expression from Florensky, who contrasts the dead identity of thinghood with living and open identity of

personality: "The identity dead in the case of fact can and certainly will be alive in the case of act" (*Stolp* 47).

15. In the West, this concept of personality became known primarily through Bakhtin's concept of unfinalizability (Morson and Emerson 36–40, 265). Florensky, however, following his friend Vladimir Ern who insisted on the "thorough personalism" of the Russian philosophic tradition (*vsestoronnii personalism*), speaks of the self-transcendence of personality as a "fundamental and distinctive proposition of Russian, and Eastern philosophy in general" (*Stolp* 73).

16. In this development, Florensky, among other authors, refers to Berdiaev's first philosophical book where he expressed these ideas (Berdiaev, *Filosofiia svobody* 97–127).

17. The relevance of Macmurray's relational concept of the person to the contemporary understanding of the Trinity is elaborated by Catherine Mowry LaCugna in her comprehensive study of contemporary trinitarian theology (255–60).

Works Cited

Bakhtin, Mikhail. *Problemy poetiki Dostoevskogo*. Moscow: Sovetskaia Rossiia, 1979.

Berdiaev, Nikolai. *Ekzistentsial'naia dialektika bozhestvennogo i chelovecheskogo*. Paris: YMCA Press, 1952.

Berdiaev, Nikolai. *Filosofiia svobody*. Moscow: Put', 1911.

Berdiaev, Nikolai. *Slavery and Freedom*. New York: C. Scribner's Sons, 1944.

Boff, Leonardo. *Trinity and Society*. Trans. Paul Burns. Maryknoll, N.Y.: Orbis, 1988.

Buber, Martin. "Believing Humanism." *A Believing Humanism: My Testament, 1902-1965*. Trans. Maurice Friedman. New York: Simon & Schuster, 1967.

Buber, Martin. "What Is Man?" *Between Man and Man*. New York: Macmillan, 1965.

Bulgakov, Sergei. *Filosofiia khoziaistva*. Moscow: Put', 1912; rpt. New York: Chalidze, 1982.

Bulgakov, Sergei. "Glavy o troichnosti," *Pravoslavnaia Mysl'* 1 (1928): 31–88; 2 (1929): 57–85.

Bulgakov, Sergei. *Ikona i ikonopochitanie*. Paris: YMCA Press, 1931.

Bulgakov, Sergei. *Karl Marx as a Religious Type*. Introd. Donald Treadgold. Belmont, Mass.: Nordland, 1979.

Bulgakov, Sergei. "Narodnoe khoziaistvo i religioznaia lichnost'." *Dva grada: issledovaniia o prirode obshchestvennykh idealov)*, vol. 1. Moscow: Put', 1911.

Bulgakov, Sergei. *Ot marksizma k idealizmu*. St. Petersburg, 1903.

Bulgakov, Sergei. "Priroda v filosofii Vl. Solov'eva." *Sbornik pervyi o Vladimire Solov'eve*. Moscow: Put' 1911.

Bulgakov, Sergei. "Religiia chelovekobozhiia u L. Feierbakha. " *Dva grada*, vol. 1. Moscow: Put', 1911.

Bulgakov, Sergei. *Svet nevechernii*. Moscow: Put', 1917.

Bulgakov, Sergei. "Tragediia filosofii. Gl. l. O prirode mysli." *Vestnik RSKhD* 3–4, nos. 101–2 (1971): 87–104.

Copleston, Frederick, S.J. *A History of Philosophy, Vol. VII*. New York: Doubleday, 1963, 66, 1994.

Ern, Vladimir. *G. S. Skovoroda*. Moscow: Put', 1912.

Feuerbach, Ludwig. *The Essence of Christianity*. Ed. and abridged E. Graham Waring and F. W. Strothmann. New York: Continuum, 1989.

Florenskii, P. A. *Stolp i utverzhdenie istiny*. Moscow: Put', 1914.

Ivanov, Lidiia. *Vospominaniia. Kniga ob ottse*. France: Atheneum, 1990.

Ivanov, Viacheslav. "Ty esi." *Works*, vol. 3. Brussels: Foyer Oriental Chretien, 1979.

LaCugna, Catherine Mowry. *God for Us: The Trinity and Christian Life*. San Francisco: Harper, 1992.

Macmurray, John. *Persons in Relation*. New York: Harper & Brothers, 1961.

Macmurray, John. *The Self as Agent*. New York: Harper & Brothers, 1957.

Morson, Gary Saul, and Caryl Emerson. *Mikhail Bakhtin: Creation of a Prosaics*. Stanford: Stanford University Press, 1990.

Nabokov, Vladimir. *Speak, Memory*. New York: Grosset & Dunlap, 1951.

Slesinski, Robert. *Pavel Florensky: A Metaphysics of Love*. Crestwood, N.Y.: St. Vladimir's Seminary Press, 1984.

Solov'ev, Vladimir. *Chteniia o bogochelovechestve. Sobranie sochinenii* Ed. S. M. Solov'ev and E. L. Radlov. 2d ed. 10 vols. St. Petersburg: Prosveshchenie, 1911–14. Reprinted with 2 additional volumes, Brussels: Zhizn' s Bogom, 1966–70. 3:83–84.

Solov'ev, Vladimir. "Filosofskie nachala tsel'nogo znaniia." *Sobranie sochinenii*. 1:343.

West, James. *Russian Symbolism: A Study of Vyacheslav Ivanov and the Russian Symbolist Aesthetic*. London: Methuen, 1970.

Zander, Leo. *Bog i mir. (Mirosozertsanie ottsa Sergeia Bulgakova), vol. 1*. Paris: YMCA Press, 1948.

Zenkovsky, V. V. *A History of Russian Philosophy*. Trans. George L. Kline. 2 vols. London: Routledge & Kegan Paul, 1953.

7

The Nature and Function of Sophia in Sergei Bulgakov's Prerevolutionary Thought

Bernice Glatzer Rosenthal

The art and thought of the religious renaissance is permeated with the idea and image of Sophia (Divine Wisdom), and with the related concepts of the "eternal feminine" and the World Soul. This essay will discuss why Sergei Bulgakov turned to the idea of Sophia and the functions she played in his prerevolutionary thought. A historical treatment of the origins and early development of his concept of Sophia will elucidate the roots of his mature sophiology (which will not be discussed in this essay) and explain to a degree (for every poet and thinker had his "own" Sophia) her appeal to an entire generation.

Bulgakov discovered Soloviev's philosophy in 1902, but Sophia did not become a major component of his thought until 1912—quite late compared with the symbolist poets who had been celebrating her for a decade. Moreover, Bulgakov came to Sophia by way of economics, a subject that the symbolists disdained and his fellow idealist philosophers ignored. The child of a poor priestly family, Bulgakov started out on the patrimonial path, but left the seminary and took his degree in economics. In the 1890s he was a Marxist and then an initiator of the "back to Kant" movement, but soon found Kant and neo-Kantianism unsatisfactory as well. He concluded that secular theories of progress, whether Kantian, Hegelian, Marxist, or positivist, were unconvincing and uninspiring, and lost interest in the neo-Kantians' endless debates on cognition, methodology, and proof. In this frame of mind, he discovered Soloviev, but only after a second, much more intensive reading of Soloviev's works did Bulgakov focus on Sophia. In *The Philosophy of Economy, Part I* (*Filosofiia khoziaistva*, 1912) and in *Unfading Light* (*Svet nevechernii*, 1917) Bulgakov tried to develop a specifically Orthodox worldview, an all-inclusive Orthodox cosmology, that would resolve the issues of modern life. Sophia became the axiom of this cosmology, the force that creates "positive all-unity" (*polozhitel'noe vseedinstvo*), but Sophia was not only an axiom. The image had a deeply personal meaning to him. Sophia served three distinct but interrelated functions in Bulgakov's prerevolutionary system: (1) the basis of an Orthodox economy and of an Orthodox eschatology (the two are related); (2) the sanctification of "the world," including the flesh; and (3) the exaltation of femininity, as distinct from feminism. Bulgakov's cosmology assumed masculine and feminine principles. Sophia is feminine; the Logos is masculine. Gender-inclusive language conceals this central aspect of his thought and will not be used.

Bulgakov regarded Sophia as the living link between God, man, and nature; she is that which endows the created world with divine force, gathers chaos into cosmos, and forms an organic, living whole. She is an ever-present idea, an image or model to be imitated, a moral-voluntarist element in the cosmic order, a real being that is operative in every area of human creativity. Through her, the wholeness of creation shattered by the Fall will be restored at the end of history, when the heavenly Sophia and the earthly Sophia will be reunited with one another, and with the Logos, Jesus Christ in a new heaven and a new earth. This eschatological process, however, is not foreordained, because the principle of Sophia is freedom. Sophia fell away from God (Bulgakov never went into detail as to why) and can choose to return to Him.

Bulgakov associated Sophia with the "eternal feminine" of the Romantics and with the World Soul of Schelling, but his primary referent was the biblical Sophia, present with God at the Creation, according to the apocryphal Wisdom of Solomon. He considered Aphrodite and Mary incarnations of Sophia, and also referred to Sophia herself as the "bride of the lamb" and as a mother. So important was Sophia to Bulgakov's cosmology that he called her a fourth hypostasis. It is this concept that provoked charges of heresy against him in the 1930s, even though he specifically stated that she is outside the Trinity (*Svet nevechernii* 212). The difference between Sophia as a force and Sophia as a person is somewhat blurred in his prerevolutionary writings, partly because Bulgakov believed that Sophia lies outside our possible knowledge and understanding (as does God). But it is very clear that Sophia is not an abstract idea, but a living, concrete, and tangible entity, and that life in Sophia is eternal.

Before going into the functions of Sophia in Bulgakov's cosmology, let us situate his discovery of Soloviev and, later on, of Sophia in the context of his changing concerns and the debates in which he was engaged. Bulgakov wrote several articles on Soloviev between 1902 and 1905, but they dealt with issues to which Sophia was not directly relevant.[1] As a result he barely mentioned her. In "What Does Soloviev Say to the Contemporary Consciousness?" ("Chto daet sovremennomu soznaniiu filofosiia Vladimira Solov'eva," 1903), he summarized Soloviev's views and contrasted Soloviev's ideal of "positive all-unity [*polozhitel'noe vseed-instvo*] . . . of whole knowledge, whole life, whole art," with the "inner disintegration and impotence" of contemporary thought (196). He noted Soloviev's desire for "animation and spiritualization of the world of substance" (214), in other words transfiguration, and described Soloviev's concepts of Godmanhood (*bogochelovechestvo*) and Sophia (for Sophia, see 222–26) but did not dwell on them, for he was intent on finding ways to apply the "living principle of Christianity" to practical political, social, and economic issues. Wishing to unify Christian theory and Christian practice, as he believed Soloviev had done, Bulgakov noted that Soloviev considered egoism the source of world-evil and described Soloviev's view of humanity as a universal organism, the incarnation of Sophia, the free and voluntary realization of the divine-human (*bo-gochelovecheskii*) idea in the world. But he did not grapple with the issue of how these metaphysical processes actually work. "Wholeness and the consequent development of a Christian worldview," he concluded, "this is what the philosophy of Soloviev gives to contemporaries" (262). He called Soloviev's thought a "colossal spiritual legacy," seconded Lev Lopatin's belief that Soloviev is to Russian philosophy what Pushkin was to Russian poetry, and stated that to "master and comprehend Soloviev is the primary and essential task for contemporary Russian thought." ("Po povodu" 361, 362, 367). In March 1905, he proclaimed Soloviev's significance for the "Russian Reformation" ("Bez plana" 394) and criticized the Merezhkovsky circle for ignoring social and political questions. Neither article mentioned Sophia.

Sophia did not even figure in a dispute (May–June 1905) with Georgy Chulkov on Soloviev's poetry. Chulkov declared that the "eternal feminine" is the Christian center of the cosmic process, the ultimate union of Christ and the world, and that it is impossible to reconcile "historical Christianity" (Merezhkovsky's term) with love of life. As a philosopher, Chulkov asserted, Soloviev did not reject the world, but as a poet he had contempt for it. Exalting Eros over Soloviev's "cold love," Chulkov bewailed the fatal division between body and soul in Christianity, and accused Christians of running from the world. ("Chulkov" 101–17). Bulgakov agreed that the World Soul or "eternal feminine" was Soloviev's basic metaphysical concept, but challenged Chulkov's other claims. Soloviev, Bulgakov asserted, taught love for life, "not in the vulgar sense like the Nietzschean positivists," but in the sense of life's higher religious meaning ("Bez plana" 295). Soloviev's "eternal feminine" or World Soul was not life-denying, claimed Bulgakov, and Soloviev did not reject the world—quite the contrary. Mystical idealism penetrates Soloviev's poetry, not only as "daydreaming" or "moralizing," but as revolt. "In the name of love for life, free and authentic, he preaches irreconcilability to ordinariness, winglessness [*bezkrylosti*], and limitedness," to all philistinism and voluntary slavery ("Bez plana" 298–99). This language is not typical for Bulgakov; it reflects his short-lived hope for liberation and the intensity of his disagreement with Chulkov's Nietzsche-influenced attack on Christianity. Unlike many of his fellow "God-seekers," Bulgakov was immune to Nietzsche, seeing him only as the advocate of the demonic man-god prophesied by Dostoevsky.[2]

For Bulgakov, the basic issue was the attitude of Christianity to the world, not Soloviev's "eternal feminine" or the World Soul. True, Christianity teaches that the world lies in evil, but it also teaches, he argued, that God made the world, found it good, and sent His only son to redeem it. That antinomy is fundamental to Christianity. The Christian theory of progress is a tragic one, but the "positivist eudaemonist" theory of endless progress is impossible and leads to moral absurdities as well. Christianity does not mandate passivity and quietism, but active struggle on behalf of its ideals. Challenging the secular epistemology of John Locke (and of the Enlightenment), Bulgakov asserted that "Man is not *tabula rasa*" ("Bez plana" 308), that he carries in himself a definite (divine) potential, a living force that creates culture. The motif of the historical process is not an ever-rising standard of living, but the self-definition of humanity, the self-revelation of the human soul in creativity. Bulgakov's subsequent attempts to sanctify the world and the flesh, including sex, were actually a continuation of this polemic, not only with Chulkov but, more broadly, with his fellow "God-seekers."

During the Revolution of 1905, Bulgakov was preoccupied with political issues, but in 1908 he returned to the Orthodox Church and took communion for the first time in many years; around the same time, he became friends with the philosopher-priest Pavel Florensky and began a second, intensive reading of Soloviev.[3] Both he and Florensky believed that overcoming secular ideologies entailed developing a renovated Orthodoxy that sanctified life in this world and endowed every human activity with religious meaning. This project required consideration of the ontological foundations and mystical nature of Orthodoxy, issues that led both of them to Sophia.

Bulgakov's first attempt to endow human activity with religious meaning centered on the most mundane subject of all—economics. In 1909, he called for studies of the spiritual sources of Russian industrial life (he had Old Believer entrepreneurs in mind) and for clarification of the economic potential of Orthodoxy. His goal was an Orthodox equivalent of the Protestant work ethic, one that would lead not to individualism and capitalism but to an economic version of the Slavophile ideal of sobornost'.[4] Two articles, both published in 1910, were way stations on his search for this Orthodox work ethic, which he expanded into a reconsideration of the nature and purpose of the economy per se. In "Problems of the Philosophy of Economy" ("Problemy filosofii khoziaistva"), an introduction to the subject of his doctoral dissertation, "The Philosophy of Economy," which was completed in 1912, Bulgakov argued that *the philosophy of economy is a part of general philosophy and therefore not some illegitimate daughter of political economy*" (514; emphasis in original). He distinguished between the ontology of the economy (its ethics and eschatology) and its axiology (practical activity), and he maintained that economics involves a definite attitude of man to the world, for economic activity is a process of interaction between man and the cosmos, and the subject of the economy is man.

In "Nature in the Philosophy of Soloviev" ("Priroda v filosofii Vl. Solov'eva," 1910) Bulgakov asserted that "religious materialism" was Soloviev's major epistemological innovation, and that Soloviev's concept of nature held the key to overcoming the "two nightmares" of contemporary philosophy—mechanical materialism (Marxism and liberalism) and idealistic subjectivism (abstract idealism, devoid of real life). In this context, he brought in Soloviev's concept of Sophia. Soloviev, he said, revealed the metaphysical reality of nature and treated man not as spirit imprisoned in matter, but as a spiritual-bodily natural essence, a real corporeal entity, whose metaphysical fate is inseparably connected to the natural world in which he lives and of which he is part, even while he struggles to subdue the forces of nature and bend them to his will. Soloviev considered matter not merely a "dead mechanism of atoms or a force with an ephemeral life" (4), but a part of living nature, a universal organism, the World Soul. In this universal organism, the central place belongs to man as a collective universal and an individual organism. To this unity (the universal organism), Soloviev gave the biblical name Sophia (18). Although Soloviev did not work his ideas into a complete system, he pointed the way to a "Christian nature philosophy, which senses the relationship of man to the cosmos" and poses metaphysical issues such as the limits of human will (16–17). At various times and in different ways, Soloviev came to the same idea. Everywhere, "before him was She, the Eternal Feminine, the Divine Sophia, the Soul of the World" (17). Bulgakov then went on to describe Soloviev's teaching on Sophia and her role in the historical process. Soloviev, he said, realized Nietzsche's "truth of the earth" in a Christian way; he teaches "sacred corporeality [*sviataia telesnost'*], the holiness of the flesh, forever connected with spirit" (24). Adam was the son of the earth, but not only of the earth, of the "divine earth" (*Bogozemlia*). Christ was the son of man, who was not only man, but the "God-man" (*Bogochelovek*). True humanism is faith in the God-man and true materialism is faith in divine matter. Bulgakov even reproached materialists for not paying sufficient attention to the nature of matter! In subsequent writings, he worked out the ideas of this article. Completing Soloviev's work, setting his ideas into a system, was the task Bulgakov set himself.

Orthodox Economy, Orthodox Eschatology

In his doctoral defense speech (1912) Bulgakov asserted that

> every principal problem is a mirror through which we look at the world [and which] to a certain degree colors the world for us with its own colored glasses. That which is revealed through a given window, or through various windows, is immeasurably broader and more significant than the window itself. . . . The role of such a window in my philosophizing is played by economism. (*Filosofiia khoziaistva* 78)

By "economism," he meant the view of life as only or primarily an economic process. Explicitly rejecting the "economic man" of classic liberalism (John Locke, Adam Smith) and of Marxism,[5] he argued that different philosophical systems "not only look at the world through different windows, they also assume the different dogmatic bases necessary for them, sometimes consciously, sometimes unconsciously" (79). To use Bulgakov's metaphor, through the "window" of "economism," he perceived the cosmic expanses of Sophia. In *The Philosophy of Economy*, he set forth a theology of labor as a joyful and creative task, and based not only labor but all creative and purposeful activity, including science and art, on Sophia.[6]

Sophia was Bulgakov's "dogmatic base," the axiom of an Orthodox cosmology slated to include every aspect of life, including economics, with each aspect subordinated to a higher goal. Economics, therefore, had a supra-economic goal, to be accomplished by Sophia. Bulgakov

still wanted to abolish poverty, but he broadened the concept of wealth
to include not only material goods, but culture, knowledge, and science;
and he defined labor as the expenditure of mental as well as physical energy. He rejected Enlightenment rationalism and its ontological base, the
Newtonian world-machine, and replaced rationalist historicism with a
view of history as a cosmic process. The laws of nature, the laws of
the market (Adam Smith's "invisible hand"), and the laws of history
(Hegelian or Marxist), Bulgakov claimed, are objective and impersonal.
History and labor are real; progress can be real, but there is no mechanical necessity or determinism at work. In place of such "laws," Bulgakov
postulated a subjective, personal, world-forming principle—Sophia—
who or which (it is not always clear) directs the economic process,
working through man. And the economic process has a suprahistorical
goal—the restoration of cosmic unity, the sophianization (my term) of
the world. Through Sophia, in a mystical version of Hegel's dialectic,
the world becomes a living organic whole.

> Sophia directs history, directs history as Providence, as its objective conformity
> with law, as the law of progress (which the positivist sociologists try unsuc-
> cessfully to ground empirically). . . . That history is not an eternal whirlwind,
> or a monotonous mechanism, or ultimately an absolute chaos yielding to no
> coordination, that history exists and is a single process pursuing the solution of
> a single creative task—of this we can be assured only by the metaphysical idea
> of sophianess [sofiinost'] with all the metaphysical presuppositions attendant
> to it. History is organized by a center that is beyond history and this world;
> earthly Sophia arises only because heavenly Sophia, her mother, exists to found
> and direct her. And if, instead of being a simple *bellum omnium contra omnes*,
> a beastly struggle for existence, the development of economy results in the
> subjugation of nature to the totality of humanity, then this will take place thanks
> to the suprapersonal power that Hegel called the "cunning of reason" and
> that has been designated as the sophianess [sofiinost'] of the economy. (*Filosofiia
> khoziaistva* 157)

Bulgakov barely mentioned the historical Jesus and the Orthodox concept of deification in this book; even the Logos was less prominent than
Sophia. Offering a metahistory of economics, Bulgakov stated that in
the Garden of Eden human labor was free, disinterested, and joyous.
Life was a gift from God and did not have to be earned. After the Fall,
labor became a curse and Adam and Eve became mortal. But labor is
also man's means of redemption.

> The defense and broadening of life, and to that extent its partial resurrection,
> compose the content of human economic activity. This is the active reaction of the
> life-creating principle against the death-dealing one. . . . The world as Sophia,
> which has fallen into a state of untruth, and hence of mortality, must enter into

the reason of truth [*istina*], and the means for this is labor or economy. . . . The economy is only the world's *path* to the realized Sophia, the transition from an untrue state to a true one; its final goal, beyond its own boundaries, is the restoration of the world by labor. (*Filosofiia khoziaistva* 155)

The economic process is sophian in nature, antisophian in its existence, because it contains elements of freedom and necessity, while the economy itself is sophian in its metaphysical base, but not in its product, not in the empirical casings of the economic process, with its mistakes, deviations, and failures (*Filosofiia khoziaistva* 142). The earthly world is potential Sophia, the body of Sophia interlaced with mechanism, ratio, necessity. The struggle for existence leads man to master nature, to animate and humanize it.[7] Sophia becomes apparent in experience and defeats "dark determinism" by acting in history as a quantitatively undefined multiplicity of separate independent centers of individual human consciousness and will.

Bulgakov praised individual activity and creativeness, but condemned egoistic individualism, which he considered a result of the Fall. In his view, man as essence precedes the individual; humanity is but one expression of an ontological category. He regarded the cosmos as one and used terms such as "communism of being" and "cosmic communism" to describe it. Sophia unites people by love; capitalist self-interest and Marxist class hatred are alien to her. The cosmic Sophia is eternal humanity, the unifying center of the world, but "only to the extent that she rejects her own *selfness* [*samost'*] can she posit her center in God." She is free to move that center, "to *want* herself" (in other words, to be selfish, to assert herself), "to reveal the selfness that is the dark basis of her being, her blind and chaotic will to life, which is all that Schopenhauer knows" (*Filosofiia khoziaistva* 149). In a footnote, Bulgakov stated that "Sophia has many aspects" and that he was paying attention to only one, the *cosmic*.

Sophia is the transcendental subject of the economy, its demiurge and moving force. Shining with the light of the divine Logos, reflecting a light not of this world, she enters the world of dark chaos, of inert matter, bridges the subject-object dichotomy, turns mechanism into organism, chaos into cosmos. She replaces "ratio" in Spinoza's *natura naturans*, literally nature naturing, as distinct from *natura naturata*, nature natured, the first active, the second passive. Though the empirical world is fragmented and broken, it cannot totally tear itself away from its cosmic harmony. "The person finds himself in Sophia and through her apprehends and reflects back to nature the intelligent [*umnye*] rays of the cosmos; through him and in him nature becomes sophian. Such is the metaphysical hierarchy" (*Filosofiia khoziaistva* 139).

Sophia is passive with respect to the Logos, but her rays activate and energize human beings. Since Bulgakov spoke much more of Sophia than he did of the Logos, the reader perceives Sophia as an active principle, despite her subordinate role in the cosmic hierarchy. Man is the potential all, the potential center of the anthropocosmos which, though incomplete, is in the process of being realized, and he is also a product of the empirical world. Human creativity, metaphysically grounded in man's participation in the Divine Sophia, is possible only because of man's participation in both worlds, the cosmic and the empirical. But man creates nothing that is metaphysically new. That is the province of the Creator. There are absolute limits on man as a creature; he is free only in the application of his powers. Human labor cannot create a new life, nor can it defeat death.

Bulgakov's treatment of science parallels his treatment of the economy, except that his argument is directed against "skeptical pragmatism and dogmatic positivism," not "economism." Science is connected to the economy, for it also arose in man's struggle for survival, and like the economy, is both sophian and antisophian. Through Sophia, science enters the dark force of inert matter, penetrates the chaos of phenomena, and organizes nature by positing general and rational laws, not as abstract deterministic theories, but as ideas. Science is a "child of this world" and, as such, alien to philosophical truth (*istina*) and blind to the prophetic and creative. "Ratio" is barren; unable to give birth to scientific ideas, it can only register and verify them. Truth is a matter neither of logical thinking nor of the accumulation of knowledge. It lies beyond knowledge and is not discovered, but revealed, in a "miraculous intuitive path" (*Filosofiia khoziaistva* 158). Nevertheless, by means of science, the Divine Sophia, the invisible sun that lights and warms man, leads the world to the truth that is beyond science, to the suprascientific, to life in Sophia, which is beyond our possible knowledge or understanding.

In all areas of creative human activity, Sophia works gradually and progressively, building up, not tearing down. Bulgakov's subtexts are "Wisdom hath built herself a house" (Proverbs 9: 1) and the original meaning of the Greek word for economy (*oikonomia*)—household management. Bulgakov described the economy as a function of life. "This divine fire, ignited by creative love, is the foundation of all *natura naturata*. . . . The task of the cosmic and historical process is to have this fire penetrate, warm, and enlighten all creation, all of nature" (*Filosofiia khoziaistva* 144). His language evokes the image of a domestic hearth, not the terrifying all-consuming fire of the Book of Revelation, Wagner's *Goetterdaemmerung*, and the catastrophic and bloody eschatological scenarios of Merezhkovsky or Blok. Bulgakov does not struggle with God;

implicitly, fire was God's gift to man—it was not stolen, as the Greeks believed. Bulgakov's eschatology was gentle and bloodless, for its agent, Sophia, is a mediator, bringing people together with one another, the created world, and the Logos.

Bulgakov ascribed to art a very special role in the redemptive process. Like Soloviev and like the symbolists, he attributed theurgical qualities to art and associated art with the transfiguration of the world, man included. According to Bulgakov, our present economic system was preceded hierarchically and cosmologically (and will be followed) by another economy, another type of labor, free, disinterested, and loving, which merges with artistic creativity. "Art has preserved in itself that first form [*obraz*] of economic labor." In a footnote he added that art has an economic side and economics has an artistic side; ultimately art will encompass the economy. "Art is the goal and limit of economy; economy has to return to its first form, to be transformed into art" (*Filosofiia khoziaistva* 156). Once again, this goal will be accomplished by Sophia, the demiurge of the economic process, who

transforms the world into an artistic production, in which every product is shining with its idea, and the entire world in its totality becomes cosmos, as conquerer, suppressor, and enlightener from within of chaos. Therefore, the victory of economy is expressed in the cosmic victory of beauty. From here comes the prophetic significance of art as a prototype: *"Beauty will save the world."* (*Filosofiia khoziaistva* 124)

Sanctification of "the World"

That Christianity was a life-affirming, world-affirming religion was one of the basic tenets of Bulgakov's faith. He believed that the dualisms of earth/heaven, matter/spirit, body/soul would be resolved, not by denying the material or corporeal half, but by transfiguring it. He attacked the gnostic contention that the redeemed world would be pure spirit and opposed the widespread assumption that Christianity forbade the "pleasures of the flesh." The *Philosophy of Economy* and *Unfading Light* were attempts to sanctify the world by, sophianizing it. But *Unfading Light*, written between 1911 and 1916, was in many respects a product of World War I. Bulgakov stated that although the war was a spiritual catastrophe from a humanistic point of view, it actually sharpened interest in religious questions, as if in a "spiritual mobilization for war in a higher spiritual area" (ii). Particularly important was the intellectual/spiritual collision of "Germanism" (*germanstvo*) with the Orthodox world.

In "Germanism," Bulgakov included not only abstract philosophy (by then Kant had become his bête noire), but German mysticism, which he denigrated as pantheism or "immanentism," and therefore unchristian. He claimed that Meister Eckhardt's acosmism was actually anticosmism, the Buddhist nirvana, and that Jacob Boehme expounded a special form of mystical rationalism, a "gnostic system," as Hegel did later on. Bulgakov particularly objected to the perpetual virginity of Boehme's "*Jungfrau* Sophia" (*Svet nevechernii* 270–76), an ideal that reveals the negative attitude to femininity, and to the flesh in general, that Bulgakov considered juridical, monophysite, and "typically Protestant." Half the German population was Catholic, but Bulgakov equated German thought with Protestantism, because most of the leading German philosophers and writers were sons of pastors and/or came from Pietist backgrounds.

From the "German West" (not the "Latin West," as Orthodox theologians, the Slavophiles, and the early Soloviev would have written), Bulgakov charged, came harmful spiritual influences that led Russians to view Christianity through the prism of the Germanic spirit. "Arian monophysitism" distorted the normal development of the Russian soul, this pernicious "Arian monophysitism always refining itself and assuming various forms of 'immantentism' and 'monism,' from Protestantism to the socialist man-god" (*Svet nevechernii* iii). Actually, the Arians denied the divinity of Christ, while the Monophysites denied His humanness, but Bulgakov lumped them together as allies against the tenet of the double nature of Christ, affirmed at the Council of Chalcedon. Despite its variety, German thought stems from a "common religious base"— "immanentism." "Luther, Bauer, A. Riehl, Harnack, Eckhardt, Hartman, Haeckel, Feuerbach, K. Marx, [and] H. S. Chamberlain" (author of the anti-Semitic tract *The Foundations of the Nineteenth Century*) represent "spurts of Germanism." It was this "immanentism" that weakened the tie between the Creator and the creature and led the Germans to make a fatal turn to this world, and to man-deification of various types. "And in order to oppose this it is first of all necessary to recognize and understand these threatening elements, so many-faced and creatively powerful" (*Svet nevechernii* iii). To Bulgakov, "immanentism" was a multiheaded hydra.

Nevertheless, Bulgakov continued, immanentism contains a pantheistic truth that must not be denied but absorbed into an all-enveloping Christian cosmology. "Orthodoxy is not in this—to deny the world in its authenticity—but in this: to make it the center of the human turn to God, prayerfully, with a flaming heart, and not autonomous thought or self-affirming will" (*Svet nevechernii* iv). Without that center, the world ceases to be cosmos, creation, and the revelation of God. Negation of the world is not Christianity, but ahistoricism, Monophysitism, or Manicheanism.

Bulgakov wanted to apprehend "God in the world and the world in God" by means of "living experience" (*Svet nevechernii* iv). To him the religious meaning of life was not some abstract idea, but concrete and revealed in flesh and form. The "great truth of the occult," he maintained, "is an animated world, not dead matter" (*Svet nevechernii* 230). Sophia, of course, is the force that animates and organizes the world, unites pantheism and gnoseological monism in a higher unity. The section of *Unfading Light* devoted to Sophia (210–34) was first published in article form as "The Sophianess of the Creature (Cosmodicy) ("Sofiinost' tvari [kosmoditseia]," 1916)." The term "cosmodicy" sets off Bulgakov's system from rationalistic theodicies and from pagan pantheism. The world is not outside Sophia and Sophia is not outside the world, but at the same time the world is not yet Sophia, because its own sophianess is still being created. "The World is becoming Sophia" (*Svet nevechernii* 222). As an entelechy of the world in its cosmic countenance, Sophia is the World Soul, *natura naturans*, the instinctive unconscious or supraconscious soul of the world, the *anima mundi* (*Svet nevechernii* 223).

The sophianess of the created world has various degrees and depths, for heaven and earth are parts of a hierarchical cosmos. In her highest aspect, Sophia is the Church, Motherhood, the Heavenly Jerusalem, the New Heaven and the New Earth. The earth is the body of Sophia. She is revealed to the world as beauty. Beauty is a sophian idea; it is man's sensation of the sophianess of the world. Ugliness (*bezobraznost'*, literally without form or image) is a property of the fallen world. Beauty in nature and beauty in art are phenomena of the Divine Sophia and have one essence. Therefore art, rather than philosophy, is the direct and immediate way to know her. Bulgakov's Sophia is not fallen. There is nothing negative about her; "she is only a *yes* to all" (*Svet nevechernii* 214). Bulgakov did not dwell on her lowest aspects, licentiousness or "Karamazovism," "a most indecent craving for life." Elsewhere, he stated that the Church is Christ's body; he had not yet sorted out the basic categories of his system.

"God as absolute is transcendental to the world, is NO-thing" (*Svet nevechernii* 210), i.e., not a "thing." But as Creator He brings to light the creature, giving it a place relative to Himself, by an unspoken act of love-humility. He posits it alongside Himself (*riadom s Soboi*) and outside Himself (*vne Sebia*), limiting Himself with His very creation (*Svet nevechernii* 210). Sophia is between the Creator and the creature, between God and the world, neither one nor the other, but something quite special, at once that which unites and that which separates God and the world. She is the "love of Love" (*liubov' Liubvi*, *Svet nevechernii* 212), a substantialization of God's love, and its eternal object, His "pleasure,"

His "joy," and His "play." Not an abstract idea or a dead mirror, Sophia is a living essence and has personhood (*lichnost'*) and an image (*lik*, the image on an icon); she is a subject, a face (*litso*), and, "so to say, a hypostasis," but not of the Trinity. The Divine Trinity, God-love (*Bog-liubov'*), is self-contained. She is "different [*otlichaetsia*] from the Trinity, special, of another order, a fourth hypostasis. She does not participate in life inside the divinity [*vnutribozhestvennoi*], is not God, and therefore does not turn the Trinity into a foursome [*chetveritsu*]" (*Svet nevechernii* 212). Rather she is the principle of a new creaturely multihypostasis; behind her follow many hypostases (people and angels), finding themselves in a sophian relation to God. But she remains outside the divine world and does not enter into its self-contained absolute fullness.

Even more than in *The Philosophy of Economy*, in *Unfading Light* Bulgakov subordinated economic activity to art. Economic activity, he declared in the latter work, is practical and utilitarian, technical and regular. Art, by contrast, is irregular and miraculous, erotic and inspired; it is a mysterious force, a voice from another world. The economy strives to expand, to incorporate everything, including art, while art through its special magic turns into an economic force, which strives to create a world of beauty, to become absolute, to transfigure the world. (Note the similarity to the symbolist concept of *zhiznetvorchestvo*, life-creation, the transfiguration of the world through art.) Opposed to mere aestheticism (art for art's sake) and the secularization of art, Bulgakov believed that the artist's work mirrors an already existing higher reality (a symbolist tenet), and that man cannot create by his own free will; his creative powers come from God, by way of Sophia (*Svet nevechernii* 370–74). Art becomes symbolic through its sophian ties with the cosmos; such art does not destroy the connection between the two worlds, but bridges them. It does not deny artistic canon or artistic form (he had futurism and cubism in mind). Bulgakov used the term "sophiurgy" (*sofiiurgiia*) to distinguish Christian creativity from theurgy, a mystical or magical act of transformation that is not necessarily Christian. His use of the term "sophiurgy" was not limited to art; he considered all creative activity, in which he included Church reform, sophiurgic. Art is the Old Testament of Beauty, because it leads humanity to the Comforter. The sophian thirst for beauty is a redeeming force.

Divine creation is not a passive outflow of the One, but a deliberate act.[8] In Christianity, the body is a primordial essence that was created by God. Matter is not the substance of the body as materialists think, but only its quality, the force that makes the body flesh. Life is not just flesh, but spirit; the materialization of the flesh is the source of its death (*Svet nevechernii* 254). Bulgakov referred to "spiritual corporeality" (*dukhovnaia telesnost'*), to the "transfiguration of the flesh" (*preobrazhenie ploti*), and to "holy flesh" (*sviataia plot'*, Merezhkovsky's term). He envisioned the entire world as "one corporeality and one body." Whether this body is that of Sophia, or of Christ, or of both united at the end of time, is not clear.

Bulgakov based this sanctification of the world, including the flesh, on the Bible. In the beginning was the creative "*let there be.*" God created the earth and "saw that *it was good*" (Genesis 1:10). "God saw everything that he had made and behold *it was* very good" (Genesis 1:31). God created Adam from the earth. The flesh is born from Mother Earth and in all its mystery became the flesh and blood of Christ and to the earth this holy flesh returns. (Genesis 3:19 in the Russian Bible reads "for earth thou art and to earth shalt thou return," rather than "from dust thou art. . . .") "From the earth," said Bulgakov, "from Great Mother Earth, was created everything that exists." "Matter-mother . . . is the necessary basis of existence, of birth and death." Bulgakov's tribute to Great Mother Earth reflects his belief in the pantheistic "truth of the earth."

> Great mother, grey earth! In you we are born, you feed us, we touch you with our feet, to you we return. Children of the earth love their mother, kiss her, wipe her tears, because they are her flesh and blood. For nothing perishes in her; she preserves everything in herself, the silent memory of the world that gives life and fruit to all. He who does not love the earth, does not feel her maternity, is a slave and an alien, a pitiful rebel against the mother, a fiend of nonexistence. . . . You silently preserve in yourself all the fullness and all the beauty of creation. (*Svet nevechernii* 188)

The above passage reflects his objection to Berdiaev's statement that in the new era "womanliness will be confirmed in the aspect of virginity rather than motherhood" (Berdiaev 204) and to Berdiaev's disdain for "the world" and "the flesh."[9] It may also express Bulgakov's love for his own mother; he dedicated *Unfading Light* to the memory of his parents, but did not say when they died. Moreover, Orthodoxy venerates Mary as the Mother of God (*Bogoroditsa*), placing less emphasis on Her virginity than does Roman Catholicism.

Obliquely, this same passage, and Bulgakov's exaltation of "femininity" generally, also articulate his reaction to contemporary events, especially to World War I. In effect he was invoking Mother Russia against the German Fatherland, and "feminine" qualities against "masculine" ones—love rather than force, mediation rather than conflict, and selflessness rather than self-assertion, aggressiveness, and war. The abstract rationalism he hated is conventionally linked with a "masculine" style of thought, and war has always been a "masculine" affair. Orthodoxy, he pointed out, stresses motherhood and the glory of the earth. The world rests in the bosom of God as a child in the womb of its mother (*Svet nevechernii* 178). His dead son was resting in Mother Earth.

Exaltation of the Feminine

Bulgakov's cosmology included a metaphysics of masculinity and femininity. In *Unfading Light*, "the eternal feminine," "femininity," and Sophia are almost interchangeable. "In femininity is the mystery of the world. The world in its feminine 'principle' was already conceived before it was created [*sotvoren*], and from this divine seed placed in it, the world by a process of unfolding was created [*sozdan*] out of nothing" (*Svet nevechernii* 213). The eternal feminine, Sophia, became the principle of the world. Sophia is the ideal intellectual comprehension of the world, the ALL, authentic all-unity. In its metaphysical essence, the eternal feminine is not a creature, because she is not created, but she is not nonexistence; never a no, always a yes, she is between God and the world. She is also unique in her relation to time, an eternal image (*obraz*), but at the same time not eternity but above time, free from time, and outside any process. Sophia cannot be separated from the world because without Sophia the world does not exist (*Svet nevechernii* 222).

It was Sophia that brought Bulgakov back to religion. His first encounter with her occurred when he was twenty-four. The sight of a beautiful sunset, with the outline of the Caucasus Mountains in the background, reawakened in him long-suppressed religious yearnings. In later years, he associated this glow with marital love. "A revelation of love spoke to me of another world, of much that had been lost" (*Svet nevechernii* 8). A second "sudden, unexpected, miraculous meeting" occurred four years later when he chanced upon Raphael's Sistine Madonna at an art gallery in Dresden. At the time he knew nothing of Western art.

The eyes of the Queen of Heaven, who holds the Eternal Infant in her arms, pierced my soul. In them was a *measureless force of purity and of sagacious sacrificialness*—the knowledge of suffering and the readiness for voluntary suffering, and that same prophetic sacrificialness was apparent in the unchildishly wise eyes of the Infant. They know what awaits them. . . . I forgot myself. My head spun. Joyous and at the same time bitter tears flowed from my eyes; the ice melted from my heart, and some sort of vital knot in me was loosened. (*Svet nevechernii* 8–9; emphasis in original)

He went to the gallery every day, early in the morning before anyone else arrived, and, although still an atheist, he was really praying. He returned to Russia, having lost the ground under his feet and with a diminished faith in his Marxist ideal. The experience made him realize, though not immediately, that he needed, "not a philosophical idea, but a living faith in God, Christ, and the Church" (*Svet nevechernii* 8). One wonders why a Western, Catholic holy picture had such an impact on Bulgakov, who must have been well acquainted with the icons of the Mother of God. Apparently it was the image rather than the formal qualities of the work that impressed him. Exactly what resonances did the Sistine Madonna set off in his soul? Was he homesick? Did the Madonna remind him of his mother? Of her sorrow at his abandoning his ancestral calling? Of some tragic event in childhood? Of a lost love? (He was not yet married—he got married in March 1898.) These questions cannot be answered: Bulgakov was very reticent about his personal life.

Bulgakov had an "essentialist" view of women, to use present-day feminist terminology, but he was not a misogynist. He did not use the "eternal feminine" to depersonalize real women, as is sometimes the case, or to deny female sexuality by exalting the Madonna over the Whore. We do know that he had an unusually happy marriage.[10] He had a positive attitude to women and to sex, and supported his views with biblical texts. Citing Genesis 1:17 ("In the image of God, created he him; male and female he created them"), Bulgakov maintained that "The full image of God in this sense is male and female" (*Svet nevechernii* 287). The Bible also states: "Be fruitful, and multiply, and replenish the earth, and subdue it" (Genesis 1:28). This, Bulgakov said, pertains to man and wife, father and mother of future children, the full image of man and woman in union in spiritual-bodily marriage (*Svet nevechernii* 295–303). Moreover, the Bible describes Sophia, in explicitly erotic language, as the "bride of the lamb" (Song of Songs). Flaming Eros, the experience of personal love, carries in itself endless revelations of the mystery of the world edifice. Bulgakov attacked "false spirituality" in love and called Tolstoy's "The Kreutzer Sonata" a sin against love and femininity. He claimed that Soloviev's poetic visions of Sophia (the occasion for his polemic with Chulkov) were based on concrete experience, and that without these visions, Soloviev's abstract philosophy was impossible. There are many singers of the "eternal feminine"—Dante, Petrarch, Boehme, Schelling, Goethe, Novalis—but the eroticism of Soloviev's vision is unique ("Stikhotvoreniia Vladimira Solov'eva," 1916).

Even in heaven, Bulgakov hinted in a later work, "intimacy" continues. His positive view of sex distinguishes Bulgakov from Fedorov and Berdiaev, who associated sex with the unredeemed natural order and hoped that by ceasing to procreate, man would break the endless cycle of birth-death. Berdiaev maintained that the new man would be a "youth-maiden," "an androgynous new Adam-Christ, in whom "there cannot be the differentiated and decadent life of sex." The "cult of the androgyne" will replace the "cult" of the eternal feminine (Berdiaev 203). Boehme and Soloviev also idealized the androgyne, but not to the same extent. Bulgakov, however, attacked androgyny as a gnostic idea, a function of the gnostics' hostility to matter and the flesh, a means of delivering humankind from sex. If Adam had been an androgyne, there would have been no need to create Eve (*Svet nevechernii* 293).

Bulgakov's treatment of Eve illustrates sympathy for woman, even though his gender stereotyping jolts feminist sensibilities. In Bulgakov's reading of Genesis, before the Fall Adam and Eve related to each other as man and woman, two in one flesh, and lived in a state of harmony and virginity. Sex was a result of the Fall, and not its cause. Adam and Eve were like married children, free from evil and burning lust. Then Satan introduced evil into the world. Why did Satan work through Eve? Not because woman is connected with sin, but as a consequence of the peculiarity of her sex, of its hierarchical significance for man. Woman is by nature passively receptive; she is birth-giving but not initiating. Her strength is her weakness. There was no need for Satan to demand the active opposition that is natural in the man; "it was enough to *deceive* woman" (*Svet nevechernii* 313; emphasis in original). Moreover, Eve did not have Adam's knowledge of the animal world, because she was created after him. Spiritually (and intellectually) younger, she was ignorant of the cunning of the serpent. For this reason, the serpent came to her when she was alone. Her sin was childish, but not intentionally evil. And Adam could have saved her. In *Unfading Light*, Bulgakov made God's curse gender-specific. Adam was condemned to labor; Eve's curse pertained to marriage and motherhood, activities that were free and joyous before the Fall (*Svet nevechernii* 317–18).

Bulgakov viewed Satan as the perpetual opponent of femininity, not in his capacity as a fallen angel (for the angelic nature does not oppose woman), but because of Satan's "monohypostatic egoism," which reduces marriage and sexual union to lust. Bulgakov did not view woman as only a sexual object. Indeed, he faulted Adam for referring to her as a thing, "the woman that thou gavest to be with me" (Genesis 3:12), attributing it to Adam's egoism, which resulted from the Fall. (Bulgakov considered gnosis, abstract knowledge, a product of egoism as well.) He ignored Genesis 3:15, "And I will put enmity between thee and the woman," and focused on the birth of Cain and Abel, augur of the fratricidal conflict that baptized the earth in blood, and continues unabated to the present day. Eve's fall, however, was not complete and final. Eve means life; she became the "mother of all living" (Genesis 3:20), making possible, through her descendants, the birth of Christ.

Bulgakov believed that male and female consciousness have their own distinctive traits, activism and passivity, for example. Man and woman, he stated, are not equal but distinctly different. Man is higher in the cosmic hierarchy. Bulgakov opposed "false equality," the blurring of gender distinctions, and considered feminism a cover for "sexual nihilism" (*Svet nevechernii* 304). He never resolved the ambiguity in his concept of Sophia, passive with respect to the Logos but an active world-forming principle all the same. From his holistic point of view, feminism was divisive. Moreover, the very concept of equal rights stemmed from social contract theory, which Bulgakov rejected. For Bulgakov egoistic self-assertion, which would include claiming one's "rights," was sinful, whether by men or by women. The Divine Sophia is selfless; she wants nothing for herself. He did not, however, invalidate or belittle the feminine consciousness, and he treated Anna Schmidt's "feminine mysticism" respectfully ("Vladimir Solov'ev i Anna Shmidt").

In his study *Medieval Misogyny*, R. Howard Bloch claims that the uniqueness of Christianity is in its gendering of the flesh as feminine, the aestheticizing of femininity, and theologizing of this aesthetic component (89). "The eternal feminine" works to keep woman "in her place," controls her by a double bind—"bride of Christ" and "the Devil's gateway." These remarks would have to be qualified for Orthodoxy, where the association of sex with sin is much weaker, among other reasons, but Bulgakov certainly associated woman with beauty. "In the beauty of Eve was revealed to Adam the beauty of the world" (*Svet nevechernii* 295). Venus, Aphrodite, and Mary are incarnations of Sophia. Bulgakov also associated beauty with cosmic wholeness, destroyed by the Fall, and with the transfigured flesh.

This is why he was so absolutely horrified by the distorted and dismembered female bodies of Picasso's paintings, which he saw at an exhibit in Moscow in 1914. To him, they purveyed a "demonic asceticism," the spirituality of a vampire or a demon, contempt and hatred for the flesh, a truly "diabolical evil" ("The Corpse of Beauty" ["Trup krasoty"] 5–36). If Dostoevsky's Stavrogin could paint, Bulgakov wrote, he would depict the flesh in a similar manner. He accused Picasso of blasphemy against Mother Earth, the soul of the world, the Divine Sophia, the eternal feminine in all its gradations, of blasphemy against the flesh in general and the body in particular. Unwittingly, Picasso has painted "The Corpse of Beauty"; his work reflects the horror of a world without God, its disintegration, decomposition, and inevitable death.

Conclusion

Bulgakov discovered Soloviev's concept of "positive all-unity" (*polozhitel'noe vseedinstvo*) at the very time that Russia lost its *axis mundi* and was coming apart, but only after he embarked on his attempt to develop an Orthodox cosmology did he turn to Sophia. She became the axiom of his system, the force by which "positive all-unity" is achieved. Mediating between God and man, earth and heaven, individual and society, Bulgakov's Sophia restores cosmic unity, lost in the Fall, by overcoming fragmentation and discord, and inspiring creativity in every area of human life. *The Philosophy of Economy*, Bulgakov's first venture in Orthodox cosmology, was an attempt to sanctify the mundane subject of economics, and expressed his hope for transfiguration without catastrophe, the sophianization of the world. In the much more mystical *Unfading Light*, Sophia is still a mediator, incorporating immanentism (pantheism) and gnoseological monism in a divine, cosmic unity of earth and heaven. Bulgakov's gradualist eschatology, pervaded by Sophia, was shattered by World War I and the Bolshevik Revolution. The concluding section of "At the Feast of the Gods" ("Na piru bogov"), Bulgakov's contribution to *From the Depths* (*Iz glubiny*, written 1918), opens with an epigram, " 'A Woman Enveloped in Sun'—The Apocalypse," but closes with the statement: "we must not fear for Russia in the final and only important ultimate sense, for Russia is saved—by the power of the Mother of God" (116, 118). In other words Russia is saved by a feminine power, Mary, whom he considered an incarnation of Sophia.

We have looked at Bulgakov's vision of Sophia from three angles: Orthodox economy and eschatology, sanctification of the world, and exaltation of femininity. In each case her face is unclear; she remains a sort of naive inspiration, an energy or a demiurge. But this very vagueness left room for subsequent definitions and interpretations. In emigration, Bulgakov returned to and developed the theme of Sophia, and made it the central idea of his dogmatic theology.

Notes

1.   To the best of my knowledge, "Paralleli. Vasnetsov, Dostoevskii, Solov'ev, Tolstoi," *Literaturnoe delo; sbornik* (1902), was his first article on Soloviev, but it is not available to me.

2.   Nietzsche was a major influence on Belyi, Berdiaev, Blok, Frank, Florensky, Ivanov, Merezhkovsky, and Rozanov. For details on the influence of

Nietzsche on the religious renaissance, see Rosenthal, *Nietzsche in Russia* 17–28, 69–145; Rosenthal, "New Religious Consciousness" 145–50; Clowes 15–72; Lane 125–486; and Swoboda 193–295, 359, 371–77, 458–71.

3. Bulgakov was a Christian Socialist. Having personally experienced the bitterness of poverty, he considered its abolition a moral obligation, but he objected to Marxist materialism, chiliasm, and class hatred. In 1906, he tried unsuccessfully to found a Christian political party and ran for the second Duma associated with the Cadet slate. He was elected and served, but the experience soured him on politics. Disappointment in the results of the Revolution was a factor in his return to Orthodoxy. He did not oppose political or social reform, but argued that real change occurred in the area of basic values and attitudes and for that religious renewal was required. The death of his young son on August 27, 1909 (he was born on Christmas Eve, 1906), intensified Bulgakov's religiousness. *Unfading Light* (*Svet nevechernii* 12–14) incorporates "intimate letters" in which Bulgakov described the child's "suffering and crucifixion" and the epiphany he and his wife experienced at the funeral.

4. Details in Rosenthal, "Search for an Orthodox Work Ethic."

5. Bulgakov rejected social contract theory on which the liberal concept of individual rights is based; he may have been a liberal theologically, but he was not one politically, in the sense that the word is used in the West.

6. The original title was *The Philosophy of Economy, Part I.* He never wrote part 2, but considered *Unfading Light* (1917) its continuation. Between writing these two books, he wrote "Basic Motifs in the Philosophy of Economy in Platonism and Early Christianity" ("Osnovnye motivy filosofii khoziaistva v platonizme i rannem khristianstve," 1916), but that article is not available to me.

7. Bulgakov's idea of an animated nature was indebted to Schelling and to the German mystics Baader and Boehme. Schelling's nature philosophy posited an animated universe, a kind of cosmic pantheism centered on the World Soul, and held that the individual is a microcosm of the macrocosm. Schelling turned out to be a way out of the Kantian bifurcation of subject and object, and out of rationalism generally, much as Kant had served Bulgakov as an exit from the amoral historicism of Hegel and Marx a few years before. And Bulgakov soon found Schelling deficient as well. In "Nature in the Philosophy of Soloviev," he stated that "after Schelling the word and the Word become flesh almost disappear" and "not accidentally" are expressed in the system of Soloviev and E. N. Trubetskoi, the first steps of Russian philosophy, "the doctrine of the Incarnation of the Word of the Orthodox East" (*Svet nevechernii* 30).

8. This is an allusion to Plotinus' conception of the soul as a monad. According to Plotinus, a Neoplatonist who lived in the third century B.C., the soul creates a body for itself and, as an organizing force, penetrates all the functions of the body but does not merge with it, for the soul is immortal and transcendental. According to Plotinus, the soul and the world possess a common substance, for both originated in the One; the disembodied soul connects the "upper" and the "lower" worlds, and sex is a distant mirror of a primal joining.

9. Berdiaev's book, *The Meaning of the Creative Act*, was published in 1916, but he completed it in 1914 and its contents were discussed at Religious-Philosophical Society meetings.

10. I am indebted to Philip Swoboda for this information.

Works Cited

Berdiaev, Nikolai. *The Meaning of the Creative Act*. Trans. Donald A. Lowrie. New York: Harper, 1954.

Bloch, R. Howard. *Medieval Misogyny*. Chicago: University of Chicago Press, 1991.

Bulgakov, Sergei. "At the Feast of the Gods." *From the Depths*, trans. and introd. by William Woehrlin, preface by Bernice Glatzer Rosenthal. Irvine, Ca.: Charles Schlacks, Jr., 1986. 65–118.

Bulgakov, Sergei. "Bez plana." *Voprosy Zhizni* (March 1905): 388–414; (June 1905): 293–317.

Bulgakov, Sergei. "Chto daet sovremennomu soznaniiu filosofiia Vladimira Solov'eva." *Ot Marksizma k idealizmu*. Moscow: Obshchestvennaia Pol'za, 1903. 195–262.

Bulgakov, Sergei. "Filosofiia khoziaistva" (doctoral defense speech, 1912). *Russkaia mysl'* 5 (1913): 70–79.

Bulgakov, Sergei. *Filosofiia khoziaistva; chast' pervaia, Mir kak khoziaistvo*. Moscow: Put', 1912. Rpt., Westmead, Eng.: Gregg, 1971.

Bulgakov, Sergei. "Po povodu vykhoda v svet shestogo toma sobraniia sochinenii Vladimira Sergeevicha Solov'eva." *Voprosy zhizni* (Feb. 1905): 361–68.

Bulgakov, Sergei. "Priroda v filosofii VI. Solov'eva." *Sbornik pervyi o Vladimire Solov'eve*. Moscow: Put', 1910. 1–31. First published in *Voprosy filosofii i psikhologii* 5 (Nov.–Dec. 1910): 661–96.

Bulgakov, Sergei. "Problemy filosofii khoziaistva." *Voprosv filosofii i psikhologii* 4 (Sept.–Oct. 1910): 504–27.

Bulgakov, Sergei. "Sofiinost' tvari (kosmoditseia)." *Voprosy filosofii i psikhologii* 2–3 (1916): 79–194.

Bulgakov, Sergei. "Stikhotvoreniia Vladimira Solov'eva." *Russkaia mysl'* 2 (1916): 14–17.

Bulgakov, Sergei. *Svet nevechernii*. Moscow: Put', 1917.

Bulgakov, Sergei. "Trup krasoty. Po povodu kartin Picasso" (written 1914). *Tikhie dumy*. Moscow, 1918. Rpt., Paris: YMCA Press, 1976. 32–52.

Bulgakov, Sergei. "Vladimir Solov'ev i Anna Shmidt." *Tikhie dumy*. 71–114.

Chulkov, Georgii. "Poeziia Solov'eva." *Voprosy zhizni* (May 1905): 101–17.

Clowes, Edith. *The Revolution of Moral Consciousness: Nietzsche in Russian Literature, 1890–1914*. DeKalb: Northern Illinois University Press, 1988.

Lane, Ann. "Nietzsche in Russian Thought. 1890–1917." Ph.D. diss. University of Wisconsin 1976.

Rosenthal, Bernice Glatzer. "The New Religious Consciousness: Pavel Florenskii's Path to a Revitalized Orthodoxy." *California Slavic Studies* 17: *Christianity and the Eastern Slavs* II, ed. Irina Paperno and Robert Hughes. Berkeley: University of California Press, 1994. 134–57.

Rosenthal, Bernice Glatzer. "The Search for an Orthodox Work Ethic." *Between Tsar and People*, ed. Edith W. Clowes, Samuel E. Kassow, James L. West. Princeton: Princeton University Press, 1991. 57–74.

Rosenthal, Bernice Glatzer, ed. *Nietzsche in Russia*. Princeton: Princeton University Press, 1986.

Swoboda, Philip. "The Philosophical Thought of S. L. Frank, 1902–1915." Ph.D. diss. Columbia University 1992.

8

Sophiology as the Dialogue of Orthodoxy with Modern Civilization

Paul Valliere

As everybody who works on Russian religious thought knows, the discussion of sophiology continues to be divisive and confused. The main cause of difficulty is lack of consensus as to what the sophiological enterprise was about. To ask what sophiology was about may seem straightforward enough, but the answers are legion. The contents that Sophia is made to bear are extremely diverse and, except for the name, lack a common term. Sophia is interpreted as a revisionist trinitarian doctrine, or as an expression of the feminine divine, or as a metaphysical concept, or as a gnostic or kabbalistic category. The interpretations have little if any connection with one another.

In this chapter I approach the question of what sophiology was about by relating sophiology to its practical context. My thesis is that Sophia, in the works of modern Russian sophiologists, is best seen as a conceptual representation of the dialogue between the Orthodox theological tradition and modern liberal civilization; sophiology, as a liberal Orthodox discipline of reflection "on Orthodoxy in relation to the modern world," as Archimandrite Feodor (Bukharev) phrased the problem in a book so titled (*O pravoslavii v otnoshenii k sovremennosti*, 1860). While most of this chapter is devoted to Sergei Bulgakov's thought, my aim is to shed light on Russian sophiology as such, which, I believe, has greater internal consistency than has sometimes been thought.

My thesis has the effect of relativizing, though not necessarily rejecting, speculative interpretations of Sophia by questioning the unacknowledged assumption they share: that Sophia was a concept answering first of all to certain theoretical or speculative concerns. If this was not the case, it is easy to see why no interpretation of sophiology in theoretical or speculative terms commands anything like a consensus. My approach rejects the rush to theoretical evaluation and calls for an examination of the intellectual and cultural problematics with which the sophiologists grappled.

It is not difficult to understand why sophiology has been viewed in speculative terms. The association of Sophia with the gnostic, kabbalistic, or theosophical underworld of theology prompts such an approach. Moreover, the concept of Sophia entered modern theology through the gate of German idealism, where it naturally wrapped itself in the mantle of philosophic speculation. The first Russian text to offer a sketch of sophiology, Vladimir Soloviev's highly abstract *Lectures on the Humanity of God* (*Chteniia o bogochelovechestve*), reinforced the image, including the self-image, of sophiology as a grand speculative enterprise.[1]

Yet speculative formulations of Sophia, while plausible when viewed in isolation, have relatively little explanatory power, and not just because there are so many of them. Even if we concede for argument's sake that sophiology was, let us say, an attempt to revise trinitarian doctrine, we remain in the dark about why its authors were interested in such a revision. If we concede that sophiology was about the feminine divine, we still learn nothing about why certain thinkers—individuals not otherwise noted for contributions to feminism—were interested in this matter, either. If we take it as a given that gnostic or kabbalistic literature was the primary source of sophiological vocabulary, we still remain in the dark about why Orthodox thinkers consulted this literature or why the terms they found there had the power to generate a continuous tradition of reflection in modern Russian theology.

An interpretation of sophiology in terms of received tradition will not do, either. The argument is sometimes made, especially by apologists for sophiology, that Soloviev, Florensky, Bulgakov, and the others were reviving an old Orthodox tradition in their work. To be sure, nobody disagrees that icons of the Wisdom of God, cathedrals dedicated to St. Sophia, the veneration of Christ as the Wisdom of God, and the Platonist wisdom vocabulary of Christian Hellenism provided rich grist for the sophiologists' mill. But it is also the case that the aforementioned monuments of Orthodox tradition were never implicated in anything resembling latter-day Russian sophiology. The construction of sophiologies is a purely modern phenomenon in Orthodox theology. That simple fact may be the surest clue to what was going on under the sophiological rubric.

My thesis presents sophiology as part of the larger, specifically modern phenomenon that I have described elsewhere as "liberal Orthodoxy" (see Works Cited). In a theological context liberal Orthodoxy refers to the work of nineteenth- and twentieth-century Russian Orthodox thinkers who sought a mutually productive synthesis of Orthodox theology and modern thought—a synthesis of dogma and freedom, Christian faith and modern "creativity," ecclesiastical tradition and contemporary culture. From the beginning the sophiologists belonged to this stream of thought. Florensky traced the roots of sophiology to the expositor of German idealism at Moscow Theological Seminary, F. A. Golubinsky (1797–1854), identifying Archimandrite Feodor and Soloviev as his heirs in the following generation.[2] The reference to Archimandrite Feodor (Bukharev) is particularly telling. Archimandrite Feodor was Orthodoxy's first liberal theologian. Unlike Soloviev he was not a philosopher, nor did he write a sophiology. What Bukharev took from Golubinsky was the deep conviction that modern humanist civilization contained untold treasures for Orthodoxy, and that serious dialogue between these two historical forces, which he felt called to initiate, promised a new level of insight into the mysteries of faith and the course of world history. A modernist pathos of this sort pervades all sophiology.

Soloviev's Witness

In *Lectures on the Humanity of God* (1877–81), sophiology took systematic form, although Soloviev's exposition of the concept there is laconic. Soloviev treated sophiology as a branch of christology. The eternal Word or Logos is Christ's "soul," i.e., the ideal-rational structure of his being; Sophia is Christ's "body," i.e., the material-positive contents of his being (3:114–15, 121). "Soul" and "body" together constitute the divine-human (*bogochelovecheskii*) organism: Christ the Word and Wisdom of God.

As one would expect, Sophia is strongly linked to the human nature of Christ. "Sophia is the ideal and perfect humanity which is eternally comprised in the integral divine being, or Christ." Christ as Logos is the self-manifestation of God; but "[this] manifestation presupposes another for which and in relation to which God manifests himself, i.e., it presupposes a human being" (3:121–22). Sophia is the humanity that God sees and loves in Christ from all eternity.

As a branch of christology, sophiology is necessarily concerned with the salvation and sanctification of human beings, not with theosophy in the usual sense of the word, i.e., esoteric speculation on the inner life of God. The sanctificationist motive is especially pertinent to the thesis of this chapter, and to this volume as a whole, because it concerns the issue of how the products of human wisdom should be regarded in the light of divine wisdom. The soteriological motive alone does not explain the term Sophia for the humanity of God in Christ. "Godman" and "second Adam" would have sufficed. So why Sophia?

The term becomes clear when we relate it to the general tasks of Soloviev's thought, i.e., the critique of abstract ideals, the justification of positive religion, and the advancement of liberal Orthodoxy. For Soloviev human beings are divinizable not as empty shells but as beings full of content—the content that makes them human in the first place. Now that which makes human beings human is above all creative human activity in its several spheres: ethics, politics, science, education, arts, crafts, technology, in other words, culture or civilization. Soloviev recognized that the humanity of God implies the sanctification of "wisdom." Christ as Sophia is the divinizer of human wisdom. The name fits the function. It also makes plain the connection between sophiology and the liberal Orthodox project of engagement with modern civilization. The practical-humanist, as distinct from speculative-theosophic, intentionality of Soloviev's sophiology appears plainly here.

Bulgakov's Philosophy of Economy

In Bulgakov's works sophiology undergoes extensive elaboration. The implications of Soloviev's project are drawn out and made explicit. This is particularly true of the humanist aspect of sophiology, which stands out clearly in Bulgakov's first sustained sophiological essay, *The Philosophy of Economy* (*Filosofiia khoziaistva*, 1912).

This book is one of Bulgakov's less known works and is often ignored in discussions of sophiology. But as the original statement of Bulgakov's sophiological position the text has tremendous significance. *The Philosophy of Economy* radically challenges assumptions about what sophiology is in that it sets the enterprise in the context of an analysis of economic activity. Sophiology and economics? We are not accustomed to thinking of them as related disciplines. Yet this linkage is the fundamental idea of Bulgakov's essay.

The Philosophy of Economy follows Soloviev's lead. One will recall that in *The Critique of Abstract Principles* (*Kritika otvlechennykh nachal*, 1880), the work that best reveals Soloviev's intellectual agenda, the author advanced three distinct, albeit interrelated, philosophical-theological enterprises: "free theosophy," "free theocracy," and "free theurgy." By the first Soloviev meant pure theoretical philosophy, the study of Being. He began such a work late in his career (*Theoretical Philosophy/Teoreticheskaia filosofiia*, 1899). By the second term he meant social and political philosophy informed by prophetic faith. The theocratic and ecumenical works that he produced in the 1880s and *The Justification of the Good* (*Opravdanie dobra*, 1897, rev. 1899) fall into this category. By "free theurgy" Soloviev meant the interpretation of culture as a divine-human creative process. He never wrote a "theurgy," although one may see some of his essays on literary and aesthetic topics as preliminary sketches. Bulgakov's *The Philosophy of Economy* fills the gap in Soloviev's project. Taking "economy" as the paradigm of cultural creativity, Bulgakov constructs a philosophy of culture as a divine-human process.

In the preface Bulgakov tells his readers that *The Philosophy of Economy* "has unique significance for the author, for it sums up the whole phase of his life colored by economic materialism and [so] represents the author's philosophical duty with regard to his own past" (i). The book does, in fact, occupy a special place among Bulgakov's works in that here, more than anywhere else, Bulgakov the economist and Bulgakov the religious thinker collaborate on a single task. *The Philosophy of Economy* may also be seen as a logical extension of some of the concerns raised in Bulgakov's 1909 *Signposts* (*Vekhi*) essay, "Heroism and Humility" ("Geroizm i podvizhnichestvo"). That essay, like so many others in the celebrated collection, summoned the Russian intelligentsia to disciplined professional work in the existing historical context, in other words, to concrete culture-building activities. *The Philosophy of Economy*, offering a theory of cultural creativity, underscored that appeal.

What is the fundamental question that the philosophy of economy tries to answer? Bulgakov states it in the idiom of post-Kantian idealism: "*How is economy possible?*" That is to say, what are the conditions and presuppositions that we must assume in order to account for the phenomenon? (*Filosofiia khoziaistva* 52). "Economy" here means the most essential aspect of the economic phenomenon, namely, labor, "the production or winning of vital goods, material or spiritual, as a result of *work*" (45–48). Now labor, as distinct from instinct or free gifts, manifests a complex interaction between human beings and the world in that every act of labor envisages, seeks to implement, and sometimes achieves a reshaping of the world. Another way to ask how economy is possible, then, is to ask: "*How is objective action possible?* How is it that [human] will becomes a force that transforms objects?" (69).[3]

It is obvious from the way in which Bulgakov poses the question of the philosophy of economy that he does not see economic activity as reducible to mechanical exploitation of material resources. He sees it as creative activity, "a continual modeling or projecting of reality," like art or science.

Philosophy of economy must do justice to all aspects of the phenomenon it studies: the embeddedness of human beings in nature, the creative freedom of human beings, and the responsiveness of nature to human will. Most philosophical approaches are too one-sided to meet this requirement. Dogmatic materialism does justice to the dependence of human beings on nature but not to freedom. Critical idealism does justice to freedom but cannot make sense of the involvement of free subjects in nature. Neither outlook accounts for the responsiveness of nature to human creativity. What is needed is a philosophical position beyond dogmatism and criticism, beyond one-sidedness and abstract ideals. This Bulgakov finds in the mediating approach of Schelling and Soloviev. Schelling's two revolutionary ideas, "the identity of subject and object, and the understanding of nature as a living, developing organism," make it possible to see "nature as unconscious spirit and spirit as nature that has become aware of itself" (59–60). This view is consistent with what we see happening at every moment in the economic process, namely, "the constant passage from I to not-I" and back again in an ongoing process of synthesis (95). The identity of subject and object is not itself the product of economic activity; rather, every economic act presupposes it. The identity of subject and object, of spirit and nature, is a cosmic fact, an aspect of the way things are.

Philosophy of economy thus forms part of what Schelling called *Naturphilosophie*, the philosophy of nature or cosmic process. "The problem of 'economic materialism'—the effect of economy and, in it, of nature on human beings, and of human beings in their turn on economy and, in it, on nature—is above all a problem of *Naturphilosophie*, and only as a result of a philosophical misunderstanding does the Marxian school take the idealist intellectualist Hegel for its godfather, not recognizing that the *Naturphilosoph* Schelling is incomparably more suitable for its purposes" (74).

Economic activity expresses a particular faith with respect to the destiny of nature and human beings, namely: "Nature is being humanized, it has the capacity to become the peripheral body of human beings, submitting to their consciousness and becoming conscious of itself in them" (105–6). This "eschatology of economy," as Bulgakov calls it, is a way of expressing Saint Paul's vision of the liberation of the cosmos from its bondage to futility through the revelation of the children of

God (Romans 8). Every productive act is a foreshadowing and partial consummation of that ultimate liberation. "In economy, in the conscious reproduction of nature, one can see a certain prototype, a prefiguration of that liberation of *natura naturans* from the fetters of *natura naturata* in its current state" (*Filosofiia khoziaistva* 108). The humanity that stands at the center of the eschatology of economy is the same humanity whose redemption in a divinized cosmos is promised by the Incarnation of Christ the Word of God in a concrete, fully human life. In other words, the eschatology of economy and the eschatology of the Incarnation agree with each other.

Wordsworth, in a famous poem, suggested that the contemplation of nature prompts "intimations of immortality." In *The Philosophy of Economy* Bulgakov may be said to suggest that the contemplation of "economy," i.e., human beings acting in nature and nature in human beings, prompts intimations of the Incarnation, or the humanity of God (*bogochelovechestvo*).

These connections lead directly to sophiology. Sophiology is reflection on the humanity of God as intimated in the cosmicizing, transformative works of human culture. The discipline starts from the concrete data of human creativity, for "*human creativity*—in science, economy, culture, art—is *sophianic*" (139). Sophiology responds to this fact, investigates it, seeks to relate it to theological truth in general and to Christian revelation in particular. Sophia herself is "the transcendental subject of economy," i.e., the ground of the unity of the cultural process.[4] Although the process is unfinished, its human agents must trust that it is fundamentally coherent, for without this faith they would be incapable of undertaking creative work. Sophia is the ground of this faith.

For all his interest in a general theory of culture, however, the author of *The Philosophy of Economy* evinces a special concern for modern culture. The sophiological faith wrestles first and foremost with the problematics of modernism, which Bulgakov views as a challenge without precedent in earlier times:

Our generation has been seized by this creative impulse especially forcefully, [and] all limits defining the possible are being lost. "The world is plastic," it may be recreated, and even in a variety of ways. Our children will live under different conditions than we do, and as for our grandchildren we cannot even begin to guess. . . . We live impressed by the growing might of an economy that opens up boundless perspectives for "the creation of culture." And so that we might relate with philosophical awareness to this doubtless grand and majestic fact which stands before the modern Oedipus as the riddle of the Sphinx— at times a sinister sign, at other times a prophetic augury—we must first of all answer for ourselves the question: what exactly is this human "creation" of culture and economy, how and by what power do human beings create here? (135)

Bulgakov weighs three responses to the question. The first is that modernism represents "the coming of age of humanity," the end of tutelage and superstitious awe. The second is that modernism and all its works are "wonders of the Antichrist," an attempt to usurp the power and prerogatives of the Creator. The third is that modernism is an evolutionary accident that will be superseded by another accident in the future, such as the emergence of a Superman (135–36).

Eliminating the last view as extremely dubious, Bulgakov divides his attention between the other two, which is to say he faces the classic predicament of liberal Orthodox theologians beginning with Archimandrite Feodor: how to reconcile an ecclesiastical culture that sees modern civilization as the work of Antichrist with a secular modernism that declares its majority, claiming rights without reverence for nature or God. Sophiology, a theory designed to affirm creativity in all fields of culture by relating it to its ground in the humanity of God, promises a way out of the standoff. Sophiology justifies the liberal Orthodox project of engagement with modern civilization.

It also justifies Bulgakov's Christian progressivism. In "Heroism and Humility" Bulgakov rejected utopianism but left room for a progressivism based on faith in Providence. As an Orthodox Christian, Bulgakov could scarcely be expected to find fulfillment in the abstract and severe providentialism of Calvinism. Sophiology, by lending human form and cultural content to Providence, concretizes and cosmicizes it. "Sophia directs history as Providence, as its objective conformity with law, as the law of progress (which the positivist sociologists try so unsuccessfully to ground empirically). Only in the sophianic character of history is there a guarantee that something will come of it, that it will give some sort of general result, that the integral of these endlessly differentiating series is a possibility." Sophia is what Hegel called "the cunning of reason" that lures all things to fulfillment (157).

By providing a theonomous (Soloviev's "theurgic") analysis of human creativity, sophiology enables the liberal Orthodox tradition to break the stalemate between autonomous secularism and heteronomous traditionalism. Like most solutions in philosophy, however, sophiology creates problems of its own. The most basic of these is the problem of reconciling the cosmism of sophiological faith with anticosmic phenomena such as disorder, evil, finitude, and sin. Sophia performs the "synthesizing function thanks to which unity is introduced in diversity and connectedness in multiplicity," yet the world is obviously not a unified and connected whole, not yet a true cosmos (121–22). Why not? Where does resistance to Sophia come from?

A second problem concerns the impact of anticosmic resistance on the integrity of Sophia herself. In order to shape the world-process Sophia must enter into it and "be 'subjected to the futility of decay' that hangs over all creation" (122). But since Sophia-in-bondage cannot be regarded as perfect Sophia, a distinction must be made between essential or "extratemporal, Heavenly Sophia and empirical Sophia, [between] metaphysical and historical humanity" (150). But then what is the connection between the two? In what sense are they one?

There is also the problem of Antichrist, or radical evil. Continuing the theme of "Heroism and Humility," Bulgakov is careful to distinguish between "two religions: the divinity of humanity [chelovekobozhie] for which the human being is not creature but creator, and Christianity, for which the human being is a creature but, as a child of God, receives the mission of re-creation, of stewardship in the creation of his Father." Yet Bulgakov recognizes that even the re-creative power of human beings "can be darkened by the spirit of satanism, can lose awareness of its true character and lead to human satanism, to Antichrist" (141–45). He promises to discuss this problem in a study of the eschatology of economy—a sequel he never completed. In The Philosophy of Economy, however, "creativity" remains an ambiguous category.

The ambiguity is inherent in the fundamental proposition of modernism: "the world is plastic." How far should this idea be pushed? In Bulgakov's day there were intellectuals who believed that even God was "plastic"—Nietzscheans, for example, and the "god-builders" (bogostroiteli) on the utopian fringe of the Bolshevik party. One could even argue that the Solovievian concept of "theurgy," reflecting willy-nilly its origin in magic, implies the plasticity of the divine, thereby guaranteeing the ambiguity of creativity in the sophiological tradition. In a world where Antichrist is at large, this indeterminacy is a dangerous thing, for the Adversary is the supreme theurgist, the consummate manipulator of divine things.

Bulgakov tries to address some of these problems by invoking Schelling's famous essay of 1809, Philosophical Inquiries into the Nature of Human Freedom (Philosophische Untersuchungen über das Wesen der menschlichen Freiheit und die damit zusammenhängenden Gegenstände), with its theory of the pretemporal fall or self-alienation of Sophia-Humanity from the divine ground of being. This metaphysical catastrophe gives rise to the world-process, which is conceived as alienated Sophia's struggle to return to her heavenly ground. Schelling's essay, an important source of both sophiological and existentialist ideas in Russia, helps

Bulgakov to be more precise about the nature of the problems confronting sophiology; but it solves none of them. The crucial question—how to bridge the gulf between "heavenly" and "earthly" Sophia—went unanswered by the masters, as Bulgakov has the courage to admit: "The question of the relation between the metaphysical fall of the World Soul and the fall of the first [historical] human being is one of the most difficult for religio-metaphysical speculation (it remained obscure in both Schelling and Vl. Soloviev)." His next sentence is less admirable: "For our discussion this question does not have independent and decisive significance, and consequently we prefer to leave it aside" (*Philosophy of Economy* 150 n. 1). But the question does have decisive significance for what Bulgakov is doing. If a convincing answer cannot be found, sophiology as a speculative project collapses.

Speculation and Faith

The shaky outcome of Bulgakov's first effort at sophiology raised the question of the direction his work should take after *The Philosophy of Economy*. The sophiological perspective was, as we have seen, too integral to Bulgakov's theology of culture for him to discard it. But how was he to proceed?

In the years immediately following *The Philosophy of Economy* Bulgakov directed his efforts to a reprise of speculative sophiology culminating in *The Unfading Light* (*Svet nevechernii*, 1917). The work was designed as a comprehensive "philosophy of revelation" (the term comes from Schelling) which proceeds from a phenomenology of religious consciousness to a theory of God, the world, humankind, and the meaning of history. All the main themes of Schellingian and Solovievian theological speculation, including the sophiological and theurgic motifs, find their way into the work. The book is an epitome of these themes, assembling them more architectonically than the masters did in *Philosophical Inquiries into the Nature of Human Freedom* or *Lectures on the Humanity of God*.

Unfortunately, the design of *The Unfading Light* limits the success of the work in an important way. While the book displays the sophiological themes on a large canvas, it does not offer solutions to the unanswered questions of *The Philosophy of Economy*. As we have seen, the theoretical problem threatening to undo sophiology is the difficulty of conceptualizing a mediating link between "heavenly" and "earthly" Sophia; or to put it in terms of the human aspect of Sophia, a link between actual human beings and the eternal humanity of God or unity of the human race in God.

This problem cannot be dismissed. But it may be approached in a different, less speculative way. The way of which we speak is also a kind of "philosophy of revelation," yet so homely and common that uncommon minds typically disregard it. Philosophy of revelation, whatever else it involves, means taking a serious look at the testimony of positive religion in the hope of shedding light on the problems of religious thought. It would not seem out of place, then, to ask how ordinary, "positively" religious people deal with the difficulty of conceiving, not to say explaining, the link between God and the world, Christ and the individual believer, the Church in heaven and the Church on earth; for they, too, wrestle with the problem.

The evidence from positive religion suggests an answer to this question: ordinary believers deal with the conceptual difficulty of religious propositions by means of *faith*, that is to say, by believing where they cannot prove, trusting where they do not see or understand, or see only "through a glass darkly." Empirically speaking, faith is the sturdiest mediator between heaven and earth in the middle world inhabited by human beings. It is far steadier than speculation. Admittedly, professing a faith is less than bathing in the divine light; on the other hand, it is more than lapsing into theoretical darkness. Moreover, the limits of faith's theoretical horizon do not necessarily vitiate its spiritual worth. Applying Bulgakov's famous distinction, one might say that while speculation is theology's "hero" (*geroi*), faith is its "humble witness" (*podvizhnik*).

Bulgakov always had a lively sense of the centrality of faith in positive religion, even though it took him a while to recast his systematic ambitions accordingly. As evidence, along with "Heroism and Humility," one may cite his long essay of 1908, "On Earliest Christianity" ("O pervokhristianstve"). The purpose of this essay was to lay to rest, at least to Bulgakov's satisfaction, the view that early Christianity was a rational ethical teaching that ecclesiastical guardians later mystified and turned into dogma. This view was common among the intellectuals of Bulgakov's day, including radicals like Karl Kautsky, who viewed Jesus as a protosocialist, and of course Lev Tolstoy. On the basis of his review of the New Testament sources and contemporary scholarship, however, Bulgakov concluded that earliest Christianity must in the end be appreciated as a positive religious phenomenon that is not reducible to theoretical philosophy, a matter of "living faith and devotion to God in simplicity, humility, and tears" (293).

The conclusion had systematic implications. If earliest as well as everyday Christianity is to be respected as a living faith and not reduced to something less than itself, presumably the concrete terms that Christians use to express their faith should be respected, too. The collective name for these terms is dogma, which—*pace* liberal and radical correctors of the Church—was an integral element of earliest Christianity. A philosophy of revelation that takes faith seriously will therefore leave plenty of room for dogmatic theology and may even find its fulfillment there.

Surely Bulgakov found his fulfillment there in the last two decades of his career during which he produced a large body of dogmatic theology crowned by the trilogy *On the Humanity of God* (*O bogochelovechestve*, 1933–45). By undertaking a dogmatics of the humanity of God Bulgakov embarked on a project that had not been attempted before in the liberal Orthodox tradition. He wove Solovievian, liberal Orthodox, and patristic strands together in new and complex ways. The general title of the trilogy acknowledges his debt to Soloviev. The title of the first volume, *The Lamb of God* (*Agnets bozhii*), bows to the pioneer of liberal Orthodox dogmatics, Archimandrite Feodor, whose kenotic christology was based on the theme of Christ the Lamb of God. The titles of the remaining volumes, *The Comforter* (*Uteshitel'*) and *The Bride of the Lamb* (*Nevesta agntsa*), underscore Bulgakov's trinitarian and ecclesiastical commitments.

Sophiology and Dogmatics in the Trilogy *On the Humanity of God*

The dogmatic turn of Bulgakov's late thought lends support to the interpretation of Sophia as the dialogue between Orthodoxy and modern civilization. For a dialogue to be substantive it has to be a flesh-and-blood encounter, not a clash of abstract ideals. For sophiology this means that religion must be dealt with just as concretely as the other activities with which Sophia has to do. Bulgakov achieves this concreteness by taking the sophiological enterprise into the orbit of dogmatic theology.

The contact between sophiology and Orthodox dogmatics challenges both disciplines. Dogmatics is forced to reckon with the culture-building activities with which Sophia has to do, such as science, art, and economics. Sophiology is forced to take seriously the positive religious concerns embedded in Orthodox dogmatics rather than spinning a cocoon of theosophical speculation. In the final analysis engagement with dogmatics fulfills the promise of sophiology. The issue underlying the sophiological project was never the either/or proposition: sophiology or traditional theology. From the start sophiology was a mediating discipline, a both/and conceptuality envisioning Orthodoxy and modern civilization speaking to each other, reflecting on each other, reflected in each other, walking through history together, confronting the eschatological horizon together.

A good way to approach the analysis of sophiology in Bulgakov's dogmatics is to ask what sophiology adds to dogmatics that would not be there otherwise. Would anything essential be lost if the sophiological aspect were discarded? This approach has the virtue of facing up to the criticism that sophiology, while perhaps not totally misguided, as conservative Orthodox tend to believe, is nonetheless superfluous. Frederick Copleston, for example, concludes his review of Russian sophiology by doubting "whether it is an essential element in the doctrine of Godmanhood" because it is not clear to Copleston that "in treating of the spiritualization of humanity the theologian cannot get on well enough with the doctrines of the Incarnation and the indwelling of the Holy Spirit" (98–99).

A close reading of the sophiological passages in Bulgakov's trilogy shows that sophiology is indispensable to Bulgakov's theological method. Sophia functions in Bulgakov's dogmatics as a benevolent fairy, rousing the discipline from its proverbial slumber by interjecting testimony from nature, history, and human experience. In particular the sophiological method refuses to regard dogma as a finished thing. This of course is exactly how many interpreters—Orthodox apologists and cultured despisers of dogma alike—often view dogma. If their view is correct, the liberal Orthodox project of dialogue with modern civilization falls apart, for a closed system excludes the dialogic principle.

But are they correct? Throughout the dogmatic trilogy Bulgakov says no. Bulgakov's evaluation of the Chalcedonian formula may serve as an example. The Chalcedonian definition—proclaiming two natures united in one person of Christ the Word—is the heart of the Orthodox Church's teaching about the Incarnation. As an Orthodox theologian Bulgakov reveres the formula, has no interest in altering it, and makes it the dogmatic cornerstone of the first (christological) volume of his trilogy, *The Lamb of God.* But as surely as a cornerstone is not a finished house the Chalcedonian formula is not, for Bulgakov, a finished christology. In fact, Bulgakov does not believe that an adequate, much less a complete, dogmatics of the Incarnation is to be found anywhere in the patristic tradition. "Having the force of a divinely inspired, *dogmatic* definition," Bulgakov observes, "the Chalcedonian formula is not, with respect to its content, a *theological* achievement. On the contrary, being theologically ahead of its time (and to some extent also of our own), it has remained unclarified and unrealized in theological thought—more an outline than a doctrine" (*O bogochelovechestve* 1:74).

Bulgakov's statement that the Chalcedonian formula was not a "theological" achievement may sound mysterious. What he means is, first, that the formula emerged from the actual life of the Church, not the rumination of theologians; second, that the formula received only limited development at the hands of patristic theologians. As Bulgakov sees it, the Chalcedonian definition served patristic theology mainly as a negative criterion. It fixed the boundaries of christological reflection by clarifying what could not be said about Christ, e.g., that he was not human, that he was not divine, that the Logos did not dwell in him without qualification, that the two natures were not distinguished. "But about the *positive* relationship of the two natures [in Christ], the dogma is silent" (1:221).

When later Church tradition spoke about the union of the two natures it tended to rely on notions of miracle and divine omnipotence. These categories all but rule out consideration of the ontological ground or positive contents of the divine-human relationship. Moreover, they are static, not dynamic ideas. A miracle, once proclaimed, can only be proclaimed again; it cannot be developed. But Bulgakov believes that without dogmatic development the Chalcedonian formula threatens to become "a clanging cymbal" or, just as bad, a pretext for "lazy obscurantism" (1:207). Reiteration substitutes for substance.

Dogmatic theology avoids this outcome—what we might call "abstract dogmatism"—by embracing the Incarnation as a positive religious ideal. This means investigating the contents of the Incarnation, finding, describing, and evaluating the concrete manifestations of the divine-human relationship in nature, history, and human experience. This is where sophiology enters the picture. Sophiology is the investigation of *sofiinost'*, the "sophianic" or divine-human character of reality, in all its manifestations. Applied to dogmatics sophiology is a method for elaborating dogmas as positive religious ideals, i.e., ideals rich in concrete cultural content. The historical context in which this elaboration proceeds is the dialogue between Orthodoxy and modern liberal civilization.

That Orthodox dogmatics is an unfinished business is the crucial assumption underlying this enterprise. Bulgakov applies the proposition to all branches of dogma. We have just examined the case of christology. What of mariology? "Orthodox dogmatic theology—partly because of hostility to Sophia [*sofieborstvo*] and partly because of polemical tendentiousness in the struggle against one-sided Roman Catholic positions— to this day has not realized the treasure of revelation concerning the Mother of God that is contained in the Church's veneration of Her" (1:232). Biblical theology? "While it is customary to think, or at least to pretend, that all is well in this area, that all the christological questions have essentially been resolved, this is in fact far from being the case, and at the key point no less—namely, how to view the image of Jesus Christ in the Gospels in the light of the fundamental dogmatic definitions accepted by the Church" (1:232). *Communicatio idiomatum?* Bulgakov believes that this doctrine was the closest patristic theology ever came to a positive understanding of the humanity of God; but close was not close enough for him. "When applied to support the concept of theosis, [*communicatio idiomatum*] is kept within bounds and correctly interpreted only if it is also made to show the influence of human nature on the divine. But here we see a total lack of clarity [in patristic theology]" (1:237–38). Kenosis? "[The idea] is stated—that's the important thing— but not elaborated in patristic theology" (1:239). At these and many other points in his dogmatics Bulgakov stresses the need for dogmatic development, a need generated by actual religious life and Church history. Sophiology is a method that enables dogmatic theology to generate fresh constructions. Of course the defining limits of sophiology must be observed. Sophiology is a discipline for elaborating positive religious ideals. This means first of all that there can be no final "system" of sophiology, since new content is at all times being produced by the world-process. A system of sophiology would inevitably turn Sophia into an abstract ideal. A sophiology that is true to itself, a constructive sophiology, will be forever in process.

Another constraint is that constructive sophiology does not and cannot generate dogma. Sophia is the Lilac Fairy, not Sleeping Beauty. Sophiology works on dogmas in all sorts of wonderful ways—galvanizing, crystallizing, illuminating, extending, elaborating; but it does not discard dogmas or invent new ones. It catalyzes new relationships within dogma and between dogma and culture. Its job is to guide theologians on the terrain, mostly uncharted, where dogma meets experience, Church meets world, Christianity meets culture, Orthodoxy meets modernity.

A final observation. If my thesis about sophiology as a representation of the dialogue between Orthodox theology and modern liberal civilization is right, it clarifies the most notorious chapter of Bulgakov's career, namely, the attacks on his sophiology by the Moscow Patriarchate and the Synod of the Russian Orthodox Church Abroad. On my reading this conflict turns out to have been a substantive matter, not a peripheral squabble that threatened to obscure Bulgakov's lasting achievements. Archenemies on most issues of the day, the Moscow Patriarchate of the Stalin era and the emigré Synod were similar in one respect: neither was interested in a dialogue with modern liberal civilization. If sophiology was a device for promoting such a dialogue at the heart of Orthodox dogmatic theology, then the patriarchal and synodal bishops, given their perspective, were right to attack it. They knew, however vaguely, what many of Bulgakov's friends seemed not to know: that sophiology was not an accidental feature of his theology, but the heart of the matter.

Notes

1. I translate *bogochelovechestvo* as "the humanity of God." Besides being more graceful in English than "Godmanhood," my translation may be recommended on theological grounds. "Godmanhood" encourages the misconception that *bogochelovechestvo* represents a synthesis of commensurate or complementary entities: Godhood + Manhood = Godmanhood. But the proposition that divinity and humanity are commensurate or complementary is a theological absurdity, at least for any monotheist, because divinity intrinsically transcends humanity. The Christian doctrine of the Incarnation, on which the Russian concept *bogochelovechestvo* is based, does not imply that God and humanity are, so to speak, two halves of a whole. On the contrary, it assumes that humanity can never reach God, that the human can never be joined to the divine on the basis of equality; but that God condescends to the human condition, "taking the form of a slave" (Phil. 2:7) for the salvation of humankind. True, the doctrine of the Incarnation implies that humanity in some sense must have nestled in the bosom of God from all eternity, a proposition borne out by the veneration of the Son as the second Person of the Trinity. But the Son of Christian dogma is not a Superman or goal of human ambition. The human may be engulfed in the divine, but not the divine in the human. One may therefore speak of the humanity of God or of the divinity of God, but not of the divinity of man. Indeed, the latter was regarded by Russian religious thinkers as the demonic perversion of the humanity of God: *chelovekobozhie* as opposed to *bogochelovechestvo*.

"Humanity of God" has the added virtue of distinguishing *bogochelovechestvo* from theosis. Theosis may be seen as the consummation of *bogochelovechestvo* in the world to come. But when the two concepts are melded together prematurely the creative tension that is the whole point of *bogochelovechestvo* is lost: either the ultimate overwhelms the penultimate, abolishing the human by redeeming it too abruptly (the tendency of patristic and neopatristic theology); or empirical-historical humanity claims divinization here and now, legitimating various sorts of utopianism. The aim of the liberal Orthodox theologians from Bukharev to Bulgakov was to steer a middle course between these extremes, affirming the human but at the same time keeping the human open to Christ and the Church.

2. See Florensky's letter to Luk'ianov, Luk'ianov 1:344 n. 662, quoted in S. M. Solov'ev 90.

3. Bulgakov is in dialogue and to a considerable extent in continuity with the Marxist views of his youth throughout *The Philosophy of Economy*. He equates the concept of "objective action" (*ob"ektivnoe deistvie*) with Marx's "Praxis" (49–50) and owes an obvious debt to Marx when he writes that labor (*trud*) is "the supreme principle of economic life" (105).

4. "The Transcendental Subject of Economy" ("O transtsendental'nom sub"ekte khoziaistva") is the title of chapter 4 of *The Philosophy of Economy*. From the start (109–10) Bulgakov makes it clear that he is not talking about "economy" in a restricted sense, for he views the "transcendental subject" as the ground of all knowledge (*znanie*) and all history. In other words, "economy" stands for culture as a whole.

Works Cited

Bulgakov, Sergei. *Filosofiia khoziaistva*. Moscow: Put', 1912; rpt., New York: Chalidze, 1982.

Bulgakov, Sergei [Nikolaevich]. "Geroizm i podvizhnichestvo." *Vekhi: sbornik statei o russkoi intelligentsii*. 2d ed. Moscow: Tipografiia V. N. Sablina, 1909. 23–69. Rpt., Frankfurt am Main: Posev, 1967.

Bulgakov, Sergei [Sergii]. *O bogochelovechestve*. 3 vols. Paris: YMCA Press, 1933–45.

Bulgakov, Sergei. "O pervokhristianstve: o tom, chto bylo v nem i chego ne bylo.—Opyt kharakteristiki." *Dva grada: issledovaniia o prirode obshchestvennykh idealov*. 2 vols. Moscow: Tovarishchestvo tipografii A. I. Mamontova, 1911. 1:234–303.

Bulgakov, Sergei. *Svet nevechernii: sozertsaniia i umozreniia*. Moscow: Put', 1917.

Copleston, Frederick C. *Russian Religious Philosophy: Selected Aspects*. Notre Dame, Ind.: University of Notre Dame Press, 1988.

Feodor, Archimandrite [Aleksandr Matveevich Bukharev]. *O pravoslavii v otnoshenii k sovremennosti, v raznykh stat'iakh*. Izdanie "Strannika." St. Petersburg: V Tipografii Torgovogo Doma S. Strugovshchikova, G. Pokhitonova, N. Vodova i Ko., 1860.

Luk'ianov, S. M. *Materialy k biografii V. S. Solov'eva*. Petrograd, 1916–21.

Solov'ev, Vladimir. *Chteniia o bogochelovechestve*. *Sobranie sochinenii*. Ed. S. M. Solov'ev and E. L. Radlov. 2d ed. 10 vols. St. Petersburg, 1911–1914. 3:1–181.

Solov'ev, Sergei. *Zhizn' i tvorcheskaia evoliutsiia Vladimira Solov'eva*. Brussels: Zhizn' s Bogom, 1977.

Valliere, Paul. "The Liberal Tradition in Russian Orthodox Theology." In *The Legacy of St. Vladimir*, ed. J. Breck, J. Meyendorff, and E. Silk. Crestwood, N.Y.: St. Vladimir's Seminary Press, 1990. 93–106.

Valliere, Paul. "Theological Liberalism and Church Reform in Imperial Russia." In *Church, Nation and State in Russia and Ukraine*, ed. Geoffrey A. Hosking. London: Macmillan Academic and Professional, 1991. 108–30.

FRANK

Background

Semën Liudvigovich Frank (1877–1950) occupies a special place in the history of Russian religious thought. Frank was one of the few professionally trained philosophers of the Russian religious renaissance, and his thought is as complex and systematic as that of any Western thinker (indeed it seems to anticipate several facets of more recent European epistemology and ontology), but remains steeped in the general vocabulary of Soloviev and his heirs.

At the time of the Polish rebellion of 1863, Frank's Jewish family moved from Poland to Moscow. Liudvig Frank died when the future philosopher was still quite young, and Frank's upbringing was entrusted to his maternal grandfather, an Orthodox Jew who was prominent in the local synagogue, and who became one of the major influences in Frank's life. The other great influence of Frank's youth was his stepfather, V. I. Zaek, who introduced Frank to populism, from which the future philosopher moved on to revolutionary Marxism, the scientific form of which attracted Frank's attention in secondary school and remained his major interest when he began to study law at Moscow University in 1894.

In 1896, however, Frank professed dissatisfaction with Marxist solutions to social problems and began to turn away from the study of law. For the next three years, Frank studied political economics, while remaining involved in socialist activities. In 1899, he was exiled from Moscow for writing a revolutionary pamphlet and went to Berlin, where he continued to study political economics and took up philosophy. In 1901, having returned to Russia, Frank was asked by the publicist Pëtr Struve to contribute to *The Problems of Idealism* (*Problemy idealizma*, 1902), a volume of essays by major intellectuals that preceded *Signposts* (*Vekhi*, 1909). From this time forward, Frank devoted himself almost exclusively to philosophy.

In the years leading up to the Revolution and Civil War, Frank held a variety of academic and editorial positions, continued his collaboration with Struve, and passed several major milestones in his life. In 1908 he married Tat'iana Bartseva, with whom he had three sons and one daughter, and in 1912 he converted to Orthodoxy, although scholars continue to question his adherence to the totality of Christian dogma. In 1913–14, Frank wrote his first major work, *The Subject of Knowledge* (*Predmet znaniia*), for which he was awarded a master's degree in philosophy in 1916. During this time, Frank also contributed to both *Signposts* (a famous essay on the "Ethics of Nihilism") and its successor volume, *From the Depths* (*Iz glubiny*, 1918).

In 1922, Frank, along with a number of other leading intellectuals, was exiled from Russia, never to return. He lived in Germany until 1937, when Nazi persecution forced him to flee to France. In 1945, he moved from France to England, where he lived until his death. Frank left the world a wealth of materials in the diverse fields of epistemology, logic, metaphysics, literature, anthropology, and ethics. Despite his interest in such vastly differing philosophical and critical areas, Frank's works are unified by several major themes, the most prominent being his concept of total-, all-, or pan-unity (*vseedinstvo*).

About himself, Frank wrote the following:

My philosophical worldview is based on ideal realism or (as I prefer to call it) "absolute realism," combined with the teachings (similar to "negative theology") about superrational metaphysical knowledge, by virtue of which it is based on the principle of the antinomial juxtaposition of opposites. Platonism had the greatest influence on me, together with Plotinus and Nicholas of Cusa. In terms of religious-philosophical thought, I am a panentheist. I call my religious-social outlook "Christian realism." I recognize a divine base to that outlook, and thus attribute a positive religious value to all concrete being, combined with a judgment about the fatal imperfection of being's empirical condition and thus the limitedness of possibilities for purely human perfectibility. (*Iz istorii russkoi filosofskoi mysli* 265)

Many scholars have correctly noted the basically Germanic heritage of Frank's thought in its reliance on synthetic a priori knowledge, rigorous terminology, and a roughly phenomenological approach to the act of cognition. As the above passage suggests, however, there is another side to Frank's work, more closely related to the holistic or integral metaphysics of modern Russian religious thought. Frank attempts to speak of the mystical union of human and divine existence, or of each individual truth as simultaneously expressing and participating in one greater Truth, without falling into the trap of monism (i.e., by declaring that such propositions are essentially and necessarily prior to any analytical deduction about them, and hence to logic itself). Tendencies such as these, contrary as they are to post-Kantian Western epistemology, make it clear that although an understanding of the systematic nature of Frank's thought is important, it is also insufficient, and that Frank should be studied as a part of the specifically Russian intellectual tradition.

—Peyton Engel

Bibliography

Major Works

Predmet znaniia. Ob osnovakh i predelakh otvlechennogo znaniia, 1915.
Dusha cheloveka. Opyt v filosofskuiu psikhologiiu, 1917.
Smysl zhizni, 1925.
Dukhovnye osnovy obshchestva, 1930.
Nepostizhimoe, 1939.
S nami Bog, 1946.
Svet vo t'me, 1949.
Real'nost' i chelovek, 1956.

Collections edited by Frank

Iz istorii russkoi filosofskoi mysli kontsa XIX i nachala XX veka. Antologiia. Ed. V. S. Frank. Washington., D.C., and New York: Inter-Language Literary Associates, 1965. (This collection, published posthumously by Frank's son, Viktor, is one of the best concise anthologies of Russian religious thought in any language.)
A Solovyov Anthology. Trans. Natalie Duddington. New York: Scribner, 1950.

English Translations

"The Essence of Logical Connection." In *Readings in Russian Philosophical Thought: Logic and Aesthetics*, ed. and trans. Louis J. Shein. The Hague, Paris: Mouton, 1973. 177–91.
"The Ethic of Nihilism: A Characterization of the Russian Intelligentsia's Moral Outlook." In *Landmarks: A Collection of Essays on the Russian Intelligentsia*,

ed. Boris Shragin and Albert Todd, trans. Marian Schwartz. New York: Karz Howard, 1977. 155–84.

God with Us: Three Meditations. Trans. Natalie Duddington. New Haven: Yale University Press, 1946.

The Light Shineth in Darkness: An Essay in Christian Ethics and Social Philosophy. Trans. Boris Jakim. Athens: Ohio University Press, 1989.

Man's Soul: An Introductory Essay in Philosophical Psychology. Trans. Boris Jakim. Athens: Ohio University Press, 1993.

"Of the Two Natures in Man." In *Russian Philosophy,* vol. 3; *Pre-Revolutionary Philosophy and Theology—Philosophers in Exile—Marxists and Communists,* ed. J. M. Edie, J. P. Scanlan, Mary-Barbara Zeldin, with the collaboration of George L. Kline. Knoxville: University of Tennessee Press, 1965. 306–314.

"Reality and Man." In *Russian Philosophy,* vol. 3; *Pre-Revolutionary Philosophy and Theology— Philosophers in Exile—Marxists and Communists,* ed. J. M. Edie, J. P. Scanlan, Mary-Barbara Zeldin, with the collaboration of George L. Kline. Knoxville: University of Tennessee Press, 1965. 281–305.

Reality and Man: An Essay in the Metaphysics of Human Nature. Trans. Natalie Duddington. Forward by Georges Florovsky. New York: Taplinger, 1966.

The Spiritual Foundations of Society: An Introduction to Social Philosophy. Trans. Boris Jakim. Athens: Ohio University Press, 1987.

The Unknowable: An Ontological Introduction to the Philosophy of Religion. Trans. Boris Jakim. Athens: Ohio University Press, 1983.

Secondary Sources in English, Selected

Boll, Michael Mitchell. "The Social and Political Philosophy of Semen L. Frank A Study in Prerevolutionary Russian Liberalism." Ph.D. diss. University of Wisconsin-Madison 1970.

Edie, J. M. J. P. Scanlan, Mary-Barbara Zeldin, eds., with the collaboration of George L. Kline. "S. L. Frank." *Russian Philosophy,* vol. 3: *Pre-Revolutionary Philosophy and Theology—Philosophers in Exile—Marxists and Communists.* Knoxville: University of Tennessee Press, 1965, 1976. 55–61.

Lossky, N. O. "S. Frank." *History of Russian Philosophy.* New York: International Universities Press, 1951. 277–80.

Swoboda, Philip James. "The Philosophical Thought of S. L. Frank 1902–1915: A Study in the Metaphysical Impulse in Early Twentieth Century Russia." Ph.D. diss., Columbia University 1992.

Zenkovsky, V. V. [Zen'kovskii]. *A History of Russian Philosophy.* Trans. George L. Kline. 2 vols. London: Routledge & Kegan Paul, 1953. 2:852–72.

Zernov, Nicolas. *The Russian Religious Renaissance of the Twentieth Century.* London: Darton, Longman & Todd, 1963. 158–63.

9

S. L. Frank's Intuition of Pan-Unity

Robert Slesinski

Although Semën Liudvigovich Frank (1877–1950) is generally acknowledged to be one of Russia's most articulate philosophers, it does not follow that his exact approach to philosophy is itself readily graspable and appreciated. What is philosophy for Frank? A consideration of this question is not extraneous to an analysis of particular aspects of Frank's philosophical thought and worldview. Indeed, it is worth noting that Frederick C. Copleston, S.J., the famed historian of philosophy, in his own treatment of Frank's philosophy (*Philosophy in Russia* 358) comments, although without much elaboration, that his conception of philosophy would not be acceptable to most academic philosophers in the English-speaking world, not to mention the Marxist-Leninists of the then Soviet Union. Fr. Copleston, of course, conspicuously omits mention of continental Europe, but his observation still has merit. When we think of the positivist and analytical strains that have prevailed in the modern English-speaking world, much of what Frank affirms must simply sound unintelligible. Ever since the time of Kant and his distinction between synthetic and analytic a priori knowledge, classical metaphysics, which has primarily sought to lay bare the synthetic a priori of experience, has trenchantly been dismissed by the multiform variants of positivism, which for their part have been, at once, united in their rejection of the validity of synthetic a priori knowledge and in their acceptance of only synthetic a posteriori knowledge along with analytical a priori knowledge.

Certainly for Frank philosophy is an exercise in concrescent insight whereby real truths about being and existence accrue to man that inextricably link his personal meaning to the meaning of reality as such. Synthetic a priori knowledge is thus at the heart of Frank's conception of philosophy. At the same time, Frank does not hold that being is accessible to man's cognitive grasp in its full plenitude and depth. To the contrary, the truth of being, its essential meaning for human life— the very quest of man's philosophic striving—ultimately eludes man's rational understanding. The meaning of being, according to Frank, transcends rational categories and in the last analysis is achieved only though the act of communion with being itself. It is thus in this context that his own paradoxical definition of philosophy as *"the rational transcendence of the limitations of rational thought"* (*Real'nost' i chelovek* 90/44; emphasis in original)[1] must be understood. What follows for Frank is that philosophy is little more than "indirect knowledge" or "knowledge through ignorance" (90/44), appealing, of course, to the thought of Nicholas of Cusa. With this description of the philosophical task, Frank endeavors to disclose how a genuine, yet essentially inadequate, grasp of the real is given to man in experience.

The future study of Russian philosophy may well hinge to a large extent on an acceptance or, at least, an appreciation of Frank's own approach to philosophy. This is especially true if we agree with the judgment of V. V. Zenkovsky that Frank is the most outstanding representative of Russian philosophy to date (Zenkovsky 2:871). If the efforts of one of Frank's stature are in vain, then one must openly wonder whether a serious study of Russian philosophy is worthwhile. Although every author must be evaluated on his own merits, it must be noted that the most original philosophy coming from Russian pens shares in the general tradition in which Frank writes. This is the line of intuitional philosophy, which finds various expression at the hand of Soloviev, in the antinomical thought of Florensky and Bulgakov, in the concrete ideal-realism of N. O. Lossky, and in Nikolai Berdiaev's programmatic critique of all "objectification" in knowledge.

Given Frank's importance in the history of Russian philosophy, it is only natural that Russian philosophers themselves have devoted much attention to his thought. However, the focus of this consideration has largely been Frank's metaphysical ideas and not the epistemological foundations of his worldview. Frank is, indeed, best-known as a leading representative of the school of pan-unity (*vseedinstvo*) metaphysics. The governing insight of his life was explicitly metaphysical in character, affirming as it did the metalogical unity of being in Being or the pan-unity of Being. Frank's entire philosophic corpus is nothing but an articulation of this metaphysical insight. Considering that his scholarly output spanned an over-forty-year period, it is remarkable how faithful Frank remained to his primordial intuition, first elaborated in *The Object of Knowledge* (*Predmet znaniia*). It is this book that will be the focus of this essay. Not surprisingly, criticism of Frank has largely been centered on the metaphysical problems that get highlighted in the debate over pan-unity. Chief among these is, of course, pantheism. In its affirmation of the essential correlativity of all contingent being with Absolute Being, pan-unity metaphysics has tended to appear to favor a monistic interpretation of being. Specifically, in its doctrine of God as the metalogical unity at the basis of the manifold diversity in being, pan-unity metaphysics can, at least, appear to favor the view of God as being the one reality. If we grant this thesis, a whole host of other metaphysical difficulties readily comes to the fore. These include the relation of God to created being or, more radically, the very meaning itself of creation, the exact nature of personal being, the reality of human freedom, the nature of sin, and the origin of evil. The chief critics of the metaphysics of pan-unity have all underscored these difficulties and have pointed to the inadequacy of the stated pan-unity formulations in elucidating, let alone resolving, these problems. The names from Russian philosophy that we meet here include N. O. Lossky, Nikolai Berdiaev, and V. V. Zenkovsky.

As for Frank himself, it must be noted that he was not unaware of these difficulties and did not in any way wish to minimize them. Indeed, he does proffer solutions to them in line with his pan-unity metaphysics. The point to be made, however, is that in spite of the inherent problems of pan-unity metaphysics, Frank never veers from his primordial intuition and never tires of savoring what he sees as its fundamental truth for man. Given this fact, it behooves present-day analysts to return to Frank's fundamental intuition and reassess it at its genesis before any further attempt is made to discuss its potential dangers. The true originality of Frank's thought can be more properly appraised as well as more productively critiqued *in ovo*. Apart from a few brief words in Berdiaev ("Two Types of Worldviews" ["Dva tipa mirosozertsaniia"]), only Nicholas Lossky ("The Metaphysical Grounding of Intuition by S. L. Frank" ["Metafizicheskoe obosnovanie intuitsii S. L. Frankom"] and "The Theory of Knowledge of Frank" ["Teoriia znaniia Franka"]) seems to dwell on this matter to any significant degree. But even he stresses the attendant metaphysical difficulties that seem to flow from the premises of pan-unity metaphysics.

If the focus of Frank's lifework is on the articulation of a specifically metaphysical thesis, namely, the pan-unity of all being in Being, the impulse for this thesis is found in a more properly epistemological insight concerning the nature of identity as evidenced in the synthetic judgment. Thus, it can be seen that from an initial epistemological query, Frank comes to an ontological discovery about the nature of being and existence. The best starting point for a penetration into the metaphysical worldview of Frank would thus seem to be an analysis of his more foundational epistemological ideas whence his metaphysics flows.

Frank's point of departure is an analysis of the act of judgment through which we come to know the world around us. We, of course, live in the world, are a part of it, before we come to any specific knowledge of it. This "blunt" fact becomes for Frank later a fundamental metaphysical insight a priori: We can know being because we belong to being (*Predmet znaniia* 154, 158–59). But this primary ontological truth about man's being can be consciously appropriated only in an act of understanding. Thus, knowledge does enjoy a certain priority over being. This fact explains Frank's course of investigation. What is it that we are given in our acts of knowledge? What does it mean to know? To answer these fundamental questions, Frank turns to the most elemental of all human acts, the act of affirmation, and specifically to how it is encountered in the synthetic judgment. What do we intend by affirming any particular "A" of "B"? How is it that "A is B"? No obvious answer springs forward; an element of mystery remains. But what we do find as an undeniable given is a clear duality between the "object" of our knowledge and its "content" for us (1). On the one hand, we have an object which is the focus of our physical or intellectual gaze, and, on the other, we have the "that which" we speak about the object, its specific "contents" for us. Knowing is thus seen to be a process. From "that about which we speak," we arrive at "that which we speak about it." In other words, the act of knowing gives rise to *meaning*. From an object "out there," we grasp an inner content that makes it intelligible to us and, thus, founds our knowledge of it.

The relation between an object and its content for us, the very locus of meaning, thus becomes the specific focus of Frank's attention. This relation finds expression in the synthetic judgment in which we affirm specific attributes or content "B" to any given object "A." The meaning of any judgment is determined by an object and its content, which of themselves are never identical. It is thus in their relation to one another that meaning arises. The standard formulation of the synthetic judgment, "A is B," is, according to Frank, not fully adequate, since it fails to account for that element of linkage that conjoins the two. Without this element, we can readily affirm only "A is A," and thus we remain in the realm of the tautological. It is the added dimension of linkage that brings us to the level of synthesis in which we can rightfully affirm that "A" really is "B. " To express this insight, Frank resorts to the formula "Ax is B" whereby "x" is that "added something" or "surplus" (16) of being which expresses the note of connection. The symbol "Ax" itself denotes only "A's" connection with something unknown. It stands, in other words, against a background of indeterminateness, which is its necessary correlative insofar as the initial determinateness of "A" in and of itself is yet incomplete. Only once we can affirm "B" or "C" of "A" does it become fully intelligible to us. Still, even as "Ax," "A" is never an empty content; it is here graspable in its necessary relation to the dark, indeterminate background from which it first arises. There is, in other words, no "A" without an attending "non-A." The two are simply correlative entities that constitute the dynamic, and not empty, identity of any "A" with itself. As Frank later expresses this insight in *The Unknowable* (*Nepostizhimoe*): "The known content of 'A' is delineated . . . on its dark background, but it is not detached from it. On the contrary, it is known precisely on this background, on this basis, as something inseparably belonging to it" (23/3–4).[2] If this is true and, indeed, a *necessary* correlation exists between them, then, Frank argues, a *unity* transcending the opposition between "A" and "non-A" must also obtain. This unity must be a *metalogical* unity, since the indeterminate background to all determinate knowledge precedes all logical determination (*Predmet znaniia* 235–40). In all this Frank appears to formulate in his own original fashion the key insights of Fr. Pavel Florensky on dynamic identity as first expressed in *The Pillar and Foundation of Truth* (*Stolp i utverzhdenie istiny* 25–30, 47–49, 483–88). In contradistinction to Florensky who heads out in the direction of sophiology with this insight, Frank is drawn to an explicit metaphysics of pan-unity, pan-unity (*vseedinstvo*) being the absolute or metalogical unity at the basis of all the determinations of conceptual knowledge.

Before Frank gets to the point of laying bare all the groundwork that evinces the intuition of pan-unity, he has a more fundamental point to make. The specific aim of the first part of his investigation is to show that the act of knowing is necessarily an act of knowing an object existing independently of the knowing subject, but still immediately capable of being known as such. His crucial distinction between the object of knowledge and its content should not obscure this end. Frank specifically aims to refute all copy or representational theories of knowledge in which what we are held to know is only the "copy" of reality as given to our mind (*Predmet znaniia* 50–51). At the same time, he also wishes to indicate the inadequacies of Kantian idealism with its key distinction between phenomena or reality as it presents itself to consciousness according to the forms of space and time, and the noumena or things-in-themselves that constitute transexperiential reality, that is, reality as inaccessible to immediate apprehension (56–57). Both the one and the other, whatever their variation, deny an immediate contact with reality itself. It is precisely the contrary position that Frank strives to disclose as the true state of affairs in cognition.

This discussion is nothing but an elaboration of the problematic of transcendence in knowledge. Is knowledge directed toward a transcendent object or not? And then—and this is the dilemma Frank confronts—even if it is, is not the *content* of any given perception merely the immanent material of our knowledge and not the object in itself? What we stand before, in other words, is the problem of the relation between the object of knowledge and a knowing subject or consciousness (47). In order to address the fundamental queries of this problematic, Frank directs the discussion to the phenomenon of consciousness itself as a datum of experience and points out the key fact that consciousness is never the self-contained or closed receptacle the theories he holds up for critical review would make it out to be (79). The insight that needs to be conveyed is twofold. First, consciousness itself enjoys a nonspatial character, and second, but strictly linked to the first, consciousness enjoys an essentially bipolar nature. It is *relational*; it is marked by what Frank generally calls "directionality" (*napravlennost'*) (79, 82, 84, 150, 153, 259), employing the proper phenomenological term "intentionality" (*intentsional'nost'*) (150) only once apart from a passage referring to its variant "intentionalism" (*intentsionalizm*) (79–83). Thus, the primary datum of consciousness, *correlativity*, comes to the fore. "Consciousness," Frank writes, "is nothing but a general designation of the functional correlation, the coordination, between a knowing 'I' . . . and a known thing, the 'object itself' " (79). In this way, being is grasped as immanent to consciousness, and the very marvel of knowledge discloses itself as the "immanency of the transcendent" (81). But the problematic of transcendence in knowledge, Frank insists, is still not fully resolved, as the question of the real being of the object prescinding from the act of consciousness has yet to be adequately addressed (83).

Before getting to this all-important question, Frank backs up and notes how one condition of the possibility of any knowledge has to be a prior unfamiliarity or state of being unknown already present in anything that would be the object of our knowledge. He thus harks back to the enigmatic surplus of being "x" of any inchoate affirmation that "Ax is B" (100–102). At the same time, he is in the position to make his breakthrough discovery regarding the composition of the data of human cognition that enables him legitimately to posit the real independent existence of the transcendent object of knowledge. Frank observes: "The examinable or the known is immediately recognized as a part of an available, though not given, boundless whole" (115). In grasping any given datum, in other words, we also notice that we perceive it against a background that is not fully given to us. Thus, we can rightfully distinguish between the "given" (*dannoe*), properly speaking, and the "nongiven given" (*dano ne-dannoe*) or "unknown known" (*izvestno neizvestnoe*), which, for reasons of clarity, he prefers simply to call the "available" (*imeiusheetsia*) (112). In this fashion, Frank discloses that there are two distinctly different levels of givenness accessible to human cognition. The first level of givenness immediately presents itself to our intuitive grasp, whereby we perceive the essences of things and thereupon form our "concepts" about reality, concepts that are not contained, Frank remarks, in the immanent material of knowledge, but rather represent an "expansion" into the sphere of extratemporal being (103).

But the more vexing question is how we are to account for the second level since it is not an immediate presence and is thus not open to our perception. We can do so, Frank elaborates, by way of reflexive understanding. When we focus our gaze on a determinate object we always extract it, as it were, from an indeterminate background. What itself was once indeterminate becomes determinate for us in our conscious gaze and in our act of conscious appropriation. Moreover, in the very process of fixing our gaze on a determinate object, we have to filter out other contents, we have to concentrate our attention, we have possibly to sift through a myriad of other competing data. We thus fully realize that reality itself is truly a sheer totality of contents that can never be fully and immediately accessible to us in their fullness (104). But the exact insight Frank wishes to convey is that even though reality is such an ungraspable immensity, it is, nonetheless, in principle accessible to an infinite number of separate cognitive acts and is, thus, essentially "available" to us. While this domain of the available is itself strictly speaking not subject to intuition since it is, in its infinite possibility of givenness, necessarily also a nondeterminate givenness, the fact of its necessary existence is itself graspable a priori by insight. It is thus paradoxically a givenness even in its nongivenness. We can "see" or rather "have" this truth, as Frank himself subtly clarifies his own position (115).

At this point, Frank also embarks upon a new reflection that greatly deepens our appreciation of his insight concerning the division in the composition of the immediately evident between the "given" and the "available." This properly ontological distinction he now casts in spatial and temporal terms. The former he notes is encountered in the "here and now," while the latter presents itself at a distance in the "there and then" (106, 120). The full force of the implications of these commonsense designations only gradually shows itself in the remaining pages of Frank's epistemological volume. What becomes evident, however, is that the moment of temporality is undeniably a constitutive factor in all human experience and, indeed, uniquely opens the door for an intuition of pan-unity in which the fullness of being in all its unity and multiplicity, however indirectly perceived, is found to be at one with the experience of time itself.

On the level of givenness in its proper sense, it would appear, at first glance, that we have only an experience of the present moment in the experience of the immediately given. After all, the very notion of immediacy seems to entail presentness. But if this is so, how do we then found our notions of the past and the future which we know, however unthematically, to be part and parcel of our experience of time? This is no vain question if we are in true search of an ontological foundation for the standard division of time into the present, the past, and the future. How do we experience the past as an immediate givenness subject to intuition, if such a givenness must needs be an experience of the present? In the same line, how can we affirm the future which is not yet and, therefore, is in principle not subject to experience? Clearly there must be an approach to the given that is not exhausted by its immediate accessibility. If we ask whether our understanding of the past and the future is only a mediated given, we must wonder whether we merely conclude the existence of the past and the future through logical deduction. Against this view, we do seem to fashion our concepts of the past and the future on the basis of experience. So we still must persist in our search for an experiential ground for our knowledge of the full reality of time as it manifests itself in the past and in the future. Certainly without an understanding of the past and the future we can have no concept of duration, and—more to the point, Frank adds—we cannot really have any experience of "being-in-time" either, let alone a concept of it (119).

Already an answer suggests itself in our very experience of the present, indeed, of the instantaneous present that immediately begins to disappear once attention fades or is focused elsewhere and we become oblivious to the problem itself. The immediateness of the moment as a conscious given simply begins to fade away into the immense, indeterminate background of being. The objects of our immediate perception thus, in this sense, become indefinite again. But, more important, we would never think that in their fading away from consciousness they cease to exist. They simply remain "out there" with no link to our consciousness. With conscious effort and attention, in fact, they can once again explicitly return to our conscious grasp. So where do we turn for a solution to this problem? Frank's response is forthright: in the available for us, that is, in the indefinite background of being that must of itself entail the infinite dimensions of space and time. What else could we conclude from the definiteness of the moment in which a restricted given is the focus of our attention? After all, as Frank says, "everything restricted is thinkable only as restricted by something other, i.e., it presupposes the limitless" (115). For its part, the limitless must entail the dimensions of both space and time. This state of affairs exists independently of our acts of consciousness.

And thus, for Frank, it is immediately evident that we have an indubitable knowledge a priori of the indefinite, yet infinitely complex, matrix of the domain of the available for us. The title of his later masterwork, *The Unknowable*, most felicitously captures the reality, or metareality, of this realm. The givenness of the available, in fact, Frank continues, presents itself in any and all acts of consciousness. Any given or datum of experience cannot but be given as part of a greater whole, indeed of an infinitely greater whole understood both spatially and temporally (*Predmet znaniia* 120). The data of experience necessarily present themselves as finite magnitudes, or slices, in other words, of an infinitely larger whole. Another essential aspect of reality is also given at the same time in our grasp of the necessary link that obtains between any concrete given and its boundless background in being, namely, the phenomenon of continuity (*nepreryvnost'*) of being, as it presents itself not only in space and time, but also intensively in infinitely divisible parts in the very instance of so-called atomistic reality (121).

It might, of course, still be objected that Frank has not yet fully justified his position since he has not yet refuted the standpoint of solipsism and subjectivism, which could be cited, however inconsistently, to argue for the ultimate illusoriness of any presumed objective existence of the realm of the available, or even shown how his position can be exonerated from the charge of being merely an instance of blind faith alone. The resolution to these remaining difficulties in regard to the truth-value of his position that there indeed exists an infinite reality behind the immediate object of any given act of knowledge Frank finds in the order of intelligibility. There may well be no empirical verification of his thesis that is in principle possible, and there may well also be no possible ratiocination or logical deduction that could be cited without begging the question, but even in the would-be stance of solipsism and subjective idealism we meet, at least, a solipsism of the "moment," the concept of which, Frank dryly adds, itself necessarily presupposes a *relation*, both in space and time, given that no moment can be grasped in and of itself apart from the greater whole of which it is necessarily a part. Specifically as regards time, the denial of relations between the immediate moment and extratemporality or "eternity" beyond our conscious perception is in Frank's view simply unthinkable (138–39).

In this process of reflection, Frank tries to convey the intrinsic structure of reality as entailing the moments of temporality and extratemporality as a priori givens of experience. Frank holds that the condition of the accessibility of all that is not yet given to us is the very examinability of time itself (137). Thus, on the one hand, "insofar as 'consciousness' is a totality of the 'given,' it is subordinate to time—it is a flow of changing images," but on the other hand, "insofar as the 'given' does not exhaust all that is accessible to us . . . consciousness is not subordinate to time, but on the contrary *time is subordinate to consciousness*" (137f.; emphasis in original). Expressed otherwise, while it is unmistakably true that consciousness and time are linked together insofar as consciousness is necessarily a temporal flow, they are not to be identified with one another since from consciousness also emerges the background voice of the timeless or extratemporal in the sheer available that exceeds our experience of time. Thus, we come to grasp how in our very experience of temporal flux, we discover not only time, but also the nontemporal moment lying at the foundation of all experience in the order of timelessness or extratemporality (138–39).

This latter insight conveys a key development in Frank's analysis. It is precisely in the experience of temporal flux that we grasp how time is also a constitutive factor in the accompanying intuition of timelessness or extratemporality and, with ever-deepening insight, in the intuition of pan-unity itself or that higher unity enveloping the unifying activity of consciousness in time. To quote Frank, "outside of consciousness of time, i.e., outside of the rising *above* time, there is in general no consciousness, even of 'the instant.' Consciousness, as a temporal flow, is indivisible from its 'riverbed,' from its extratemporal foundation: it is by its very essence a flow enveloping its very self; its movement not only is linked with an enveloping unity and constancy, but also is possible only in the one, on the ground of a higher unity" (148). In this fashion, timelessness and time are nothing but the warp and woof of the intuition of reality. Frank repeats this idea in another passage, this time going so far as to identify timelessness with eternity, remarking how even the instantaneous moment of time is not just surrounded by eternity, but even filled by eternity (129).

At this point in his reflection on temporality as an a priori given of reality, Frank is nearing the apex of this insight into the all-embracing character of reality itself or absolute being as pan-unity. A fully thematic awareness of the givenness of consciousness opens up to us the very ontological groundedness of consciousness in the experience of consciousness as necessarily a relation. "Consciousness," Frank once again notes, "is a flow of actual experiences in its very self containing a relation to its own beyond, a fixation on the cognized" (152). Thus, the essential mark of consciousness as intentionality once again returns to center stage. But this time we are in the position to affirm, even more than the phenomenon of intentionality, the fact that consciousness is necessarily a consciousness *of* being, that is, an act in relation to being. More primordially, we can now grasp that consciousness, being itself a member of a relation, presupposes the existence of something over and beyond its bounds, but still available to it, that constitutes it, that makes it possible, indeed, that envelopes it in a supratemporal unity (153). Frank writes that this "supratemporal unity, in which we have perceived the ground of the relation of consciousness to the 'object,' is given to us as such not in the form of consciousness, but in the form of *being*" (154). In other words, it is in the very perception of the objects of knowledge that we first perceive ourselves as being and then precisely as *being in relation*. This being, however, is not of the order of the blunt object of our knowledge; that is, it is not an "objectified" or "transcendent" being, but rather it is that being that is the immanent foundation of any possible transcendence. It is, in other words, primary being or "absolute being," in the words of Frank. It is the being in which we exist and which is in us, and, as such, it is being before objectification, that is, it is antecedent to conceptual or abstract knowledge. It is also, Frank observes, a supratemporal unity that must needs be a continuous unity, the very grasping of which cannot but elicit the intuition of pan-unity or integral being itself (241).

These insights cannot be savored enough. Of special note is the division of the types of knowledge that follows from Frank's search for the ontological foundations of knowledge. First, there is the objectivized knowledge that seeks determinate knowledge out of the full range of the available for us. It is the knowledge that ferrets out the extratemporal content of our knowledge as expressed in conceptual or abstract-logical knowledge. It comes to us under the form of both empiricism and rationalism and is otherwise known as "knowledge-thought" (240–42, 419f.). It is what we can say is the more common approach to the world of being. In his posthumously published anthropological study, Frank speaks of this type of knowledge as approaching its object "from without" (*Real'nost' i chelovek* 39–40/16–17). It is detached, scientific knowledge that puts us into contact with only the "outer layer" of reality.

Contrasted to this type of knowledge is that "from within," knowledge that is essentially a living experience and, thus, that is never detached in its approach. It is the knowledge of being and not of mere "having." This deeper dimension of knowledge, which is, in truth, the primary form of knowledge, comes only in what Frank calls "living knowledge." It is the knowledge of being that precedes the analysis of knowledge into distinct determinations and extratemporal contents. Unlike knowledge-thought, which is the abstract-logical knowledge of extratemporal content and which as such prescinds from the experience of temporality, even if it is had only in time, living knowledge is nothing other than *experiential* knowledge, which cannot but be a moment in time. Here intuition comes under the form of "life." In living knowledge, we do not just contemplate an object, but live with it and grow with it as it partakes of the source of all being. Thus, the ultimate foundation of all knowledge unmistakably discloses itself. It is the pan-unity or metalogical unity of all being in Being. What is transcendent to us in knowledge is immanent to us in being. We know being, in other words, because we *are* being. We *belong* to being, and it is being that unveils itself to us (*Predmet znaniia* 419, 424, 429–33; see also *Nepostizhimoe* 43–47/23–28).

With so much of a positive nature in Frank's epistemological inquiry, we might be tempted to forget the fundamental metaphysical objections that have been lodged against his metaphysics of pan-unity. Can the latter find their resolution in the former? Or does Frank's epistemology need supplanting or correction in order for it to take into account these difficulties of a metaphysical order? If there is a common root to the various metaphysical objections to Frank's developed system, it has to be its tendency toward monism and, thus, pantheism. Frank does, of course, speak of the gift-character of being, which would seem to belie any monism, but his language of correlativity, on the other hand, can lead to a monist view. Is there any way to resolve this tension? (See Slesinski 217–35, where this problem is discussed.) Frank offers a searching analysis of what he deems the two strata of knowledge: knowledge-thought and knowledge-life. There is, however, one grand lacuna in his discussion of the experience of knowledge, namely, the fact of its *analogicity*. His own division, of course, *presupposes* this aspect of knowledge, but by failing to give it a specific treatment, he is not in the position to see its full ramifications. Analogicity emphasizes the similarity in diversity in knowledge, which, for its part, only reflects the primary mode of analogicity *in being*. Being is one; yet it is also diverse. Different relationships occur among beings, and different proportions of being arise among them. Since one of the chief apparent weaknesses of Frank's system is its too close approximation between God and the world (Lossky, *History of Russian Philosophy* 282), an explicit doctrine of analogy could help to overcome this difficulty. The same would be true in regard to the other related difficulties as to the nature of creation, freedom, sin, and evil, since these too are all problematical in monistic worldviews.

Another related difficulty has to do with Frank's equivocal use of terms. Are timelessness, extratemporality, supratemporal unity, absolute being, and eternity all the same thing? An understanding of analogy could show how they are not, even if they are linked together. In Frank, however, depending on the passage, one could argue that they are. Of course, at times, the notions seem to be different. For example, in one instance he speaks of the temporal (*vremennoe*) and the timeless (*vnevremennoe*) forming "one concrete supratemporal being" (*edinoe konkretno-sverkhvremennoe bytie*), implying their distinction (*Predmet znaniia* 385). Further along, he introduces a new difficulty in understanding them when he adds that together they constitute the supratemporal unity (*sverkhvremennoe edinstvo*) that is eternal life (*vechnaia zhizn'*) (430). The question arises as to what is correlative to what. His basic thesis is that time and the extratemporal are correlative. But in one place, correlativity obtains between time and eternity (129). In still another, it is time and timelessness or extratemporality that are correlative, with a clear indication that eternity and the absolute pan-unity that is at one with it are of a completely different order (371f.). Obviously, no final judgment on Frank's thought here can be rendered until this ambiguity is eliminated. What is more significant, however, is that the fact that there is this confusion at work in Frank clearly indicates that Frank himself never fully grasped the full import of the traditional viewpoint of Christian metaphysics that eternity absolutely transcends time such that *no relation at all* is to be found between them apart from the freedom of God to create the cosmic order ex nihilo. From the standpoint of Christian metaphysics, the central task is to show how eternity envelopes time without there being any temporal relationship. Frank does try to address this challenge, but falters in his notion of supratemporality as a kind of supra-unity between time and timelessness that brings us to eternity. Between time and timelessness, on the one hand, and eternity, on the other, there is a chasm. True, time and eternity are "analogically" one, but the link between them is not being, but the absolute freedom of creation.

These critical observations notwithstanding, the true richness of Frank's thought is in no way compromised. They only challenge us to pick up the discussion where Frank left off. It is also difficult to see how anyone could hold that his metaphysics of pan-unity is a mere period piece. Itself reminiscent of Vladimir Soloviev's *Critique of Abstract*

Principles (*Kritika otvlechennykh nachal*) and its affirmation of pan-unity as the ontological condition of knowledge, *The Object of Knowledge* at the same time seems to be a forerunner of sorts to Martin Heidegger's *Being and Time*, which has so influenced the course of Western philosophical reflection. For Heidegger, man's knowing is nothing but the unveiling of being. Man as *Dasein*, as the there of being, is, indeed, the being through which being is revealed. Does not this idea also resonate in Frank's position on the priority of being over thinking? We know being, after all, as Frank is wont to stress, because we *are* being.

Notes

1. Citations of this volume refer to the YMCA Press edition and the Duddington translation.
2. Citations of this volume refer to the Munich edition and the Jakim translation.

Works Cited

Berdiaev, Nikolai. "*Dva tipa mirosozertsaniia.*" *Tipy religioznoi mysli v Rossii.* Paris: YMCA-Press, 1989. 635–49. Originally published in *Voprosy filosofii i psikhologii* no. 134 [1916].)

Copleston, Frederick C., S.J. *Philosophy in Russia.* Notre Dame: University of Notre Dame Press, 1986.

Florenskii, P. A. *Stolp i utverzhdenie istiny.* Moscow: Put', 1914.

Frank, S. L. *Nepostizhimoe.* Paris, 1939; rpt., Munich: Wilhelm Fink Verlag, 1971. *The Unknowable.* Trans. Boris Jakim. Athens: Ohio University Press, 1983.

Frank, S. L. *Predmet znaniia.* Petrograd, 1915.

Frank, S. L. *Real'nost' i chelovek.* Paris: YMCA Press, 1956. *Reality and Man.* Trans. Natalie Duddington. New York: Taplinger, 1966.

Heidegger, Martin. *Being and Time.* New York: Harper & Row, 1962.

Lossky, N. O. *History of Russian Philosophy.* New York: International Universities Press, 1951.

Lossky, N. O. "Metafizicheskoe obosnovanie intuitsii S. L. Frankom." *Osnovnye voprosy gnoseologii.* Petrograd: Nauka i Shkola, 1919. 225–47.

Lossky, N. O. "Teoriia znaniia Franka." In *Sbornik pamiati Semëna Liudvigovicha Franka.* Munich, 1954. 133–44.

Slesinski, Robert. "The Relationship of God and Man in Russian Religious Philosophy from Florensky to Frank." *St. Vladimir's Theological Quarterly* 36 (1992): 217–35.

Solov'ev, Vladimir. *Kritika otvlechennvkh nachal.* In *Sobranie sochinenii,* ed. S. M. Solov'ev and E. L. Radlov. St. Petersburg: Prosveshchenie, 1911–14. Reprinted with 2 additional volumes, Brussels: Zhizn' s Bogom, 1966–70. 2:xiii–397.

Zenkovsky, V. V. [Zen'kovskii]. *A History of Russian Philosophy.* Trans. George L. Kline. 2 vols. London: Routledge & Kegan Paul, 1953.

10

The Religious Roots of S. L. Frank's Ethics and Social Philosophy

George L. Kline

In our efforts to understand the unique aspects of Russian religious philosophy (e.g., its relation to Eastern Orthodoxy, and the latter's emphasis on salvation as deification), we often ignore those aspects that suggest similarity to Western philosophers, some of which point toward a lack of unity among the Russian thinkers themselves. Although an ontological and theological focus on the doctrines of total-unity (*vseedinstvo*)[1] and conciliarity or "organic religious togetherness" (*sobornost'*) is indeed characteristic of many Russian religious thinkers, certain of them, including S. L. Frank,[2] devote a good deal of space and much thoughtful discussion to law, the state—including the "rule-of-law or law-governed state"—and civil society, as well as individual rights and obligations. It will be a central claim of this essay that Frank is much closer to Hegel in his treatment of these topics—especially such questions as the right to property, the right of inheritance, and freedom of conscience—than to the position of most Russian philosophers to whom total-unity and conciliarity are central. Moreover, Frank's stress on the religious roots of the social and political order is characteristically and decisively Hegelian. The following exploration of Hegel's influence on Frank's thought, beginning with a brief examination of Frank's use of specifically Hegelian terminology, will prepare the way for a closer examination of Frank's ethics and social philosophy, one that will reveal a certain combination and reconciliation of Hegelian and uniquely Russian motifs.

In a late letter to Nikolai Berdiaev, Frank made two revealing Hegelian points: "I do not (and this is essential) agree with you in what you reject and in general I tend to replace your 'either/or' with a 'both/and'." Frank continues: "Your rebellion against objectification is a denial of the idea of incarnation, which, when carried to the extreme, leads to a kind of abstract [in the Hegelian sense: 'one-sided, detached, unrelated'] idealism."[3] For the anti-Hegelian, quasi-anarchist Berdiaev, law, the state, and civil society are all hated forms of alienating objectification. In contrast, for the Hegelian Frank they are necessary and positive forms of human interaction, embodied in indispensable institutions. (Frank's sensitivity to the positive function of law may have been in part a result of his years as a law student at Moscow University, 1894–98.)

I

The powerful influence on Frank's philosophy of the thought of Plato, Plotinus, Nicholas of Cusa, and Vladimir Soloviev has been adequately documented.[4] Frank himself has repeatedly stressed the influence of Platonism in general and of the thought of Plotinus and Nicholas of Cusa in particular on his philosophical position (*Real'nost'* 8/xvii).[5] In one place he even calls Nicholas of Cusa "in a certain sense" his "*only* teacher of philosophy" (*Nepostizhimoe* 184/xi; emphasis added). However, the influence—in some respects no less powerful—of *Hegel's* thought, an influence that Frank absorbed both directly and through the mediation of Soloviev,[6] has been much less noticed. In my judgment, it deserves equally close examination.

To begin with, there are a number of widely used Hegelian terms that Frank shares with other Russian thinkers of his generation and indeed of earlier generations (going back to Herzen and the Slavophiles). Among them one finds the adjective *vsemirno-istoricheskii* (*welthistorisch*, "world-historical"), and such nouns as *samosoznanie* (*Selbstbewusstsein*, "self-consciousness" in the sense of the socially constituted self that is a subject of awareness, experience, and knowledge) and *durnaia beskonechnost'* (*schlechte Unendlichkeit*, "bad infinity" in the sense of a merely reiterative, unending series of elements or stages, without dialectical development or enrichment). And one finds the key expressions *bytie-v-sebe* (*Ansichsein*, "being-in-itself"), *bytie-dlia-sebia* (*Fürsichsein*, "being-for-itself"), and *samost'* (*Selbstheit*, "selfhood"). Frank approves of Hegel's definition of freedom as *bei-sich-selbst-sein*, but renders the German somewhat

lamely into Russian as *bytie-u-sebia-samogo*. (The English renderings—
Duddington's "being at one's own self" [*Real'nost'* 308/167] and Jakim's
"being-in-one's-own-self" [*Nepostizhimoe* 337/115]—are even less sat-
isfactory. "Being-at-home-with-oneself" perhaps renders this difficult
German expression a bit more adequately.) Finally, Frank explicitly mentions that his much used expression *neposredstvennoe samobytie* (immediate self-being) is a rendering of the German—and he might have added,
Hegelian—expression *unmittelbares Selbstsein* (*Nepostizhimoe* 318/100; cf.
Nepostizhimoe chap. 5 [317–346/100–123] passim; 403/170, 484/239).

Some of these terms are difficult to interpret and to translate into
Russian or English, but they are not equivocal; that is, they do not have
both a special Hegelian sense and a general non-Hegelian sense. Three
key terms *are* thus equivocal, and Frank gives little sign that he is aware
of the equivocity or that he considers it important to alert his readers to
the distinct and even opposed senses in which he is using these terms.
The first is *moment*, a term widely used by other Russian thinkers; the
other two are *konkretnyi/konkretnost'* and *organizm*, where the special
senses are characteristic only of Russian thinkers strongly influenced
by Hegel. I have traced Frank's use of these three terms through four of
his most important works: *The Spiritual Foundations of Society* (*Dukhovnye
osnovy obshchestva*), *The Unknowable* (*Nepostizhimoe*), *The Light Shineth in
Darkness* (*Svet vo t'me*), and *Reality and Man* (*Real'nost' i chelovek*).

Hegel was the first German thinker to make a clear distinction between the grammatically neuter term *das Moment* ([dialectical] phase,
element, aspect, component [of a larger whole]) and the grammatically
masculine term *der Moment* (a brief interval of time). It is only the former
that is a technical term in Hegel's speculative thought. As it happens, in
Russian as in English there is no way to distinguish these two senses: in
Russian the word *moment* is necessarily masculine; in English 'moment'
is genderless. I deplore the practice of most English translators of Hegel,
and indeed of many Hegel commentators, who tend to use "moment"
to render both *das Moment* and *der Moment*, leaving only context to
suggest the specific meaning in any given case. I shall here resort to an
awkward but effective device to specify Hegelian and "ordinary" non-
Hegelian meanings, putting 'moment$_h$' for *das Moment* and 'moment$_o$'
for *der Moment*. In an earlier essay I did something similar with the terms
'concrete$_h$' and 'concrete$_o$' (see Kline, "Some Recent Reinterpretations
of Hegel's Philosophy" 40–44).

Both Duddington and Jakim have improved on most Hegel translators by rendering *moment* in the Hegelian sense as 'element' and
sometimes 'aspect'. But the first rendering creates another problem,
since Frank himself uses the Russian word *element* almost as frequently

and in roughly the same sense as *moment*. When both *element* and *moment* are translated as 'element', whatever subtle distinction Frank may have intended when he used the two different terms is entirely lost.

Typical uses of *moment* in the Hegelian sense include the distinction, within society, between the *moment prava* (element of law) and the *moment vlasti* (element of [political] power). Frank refers to the *moment zakona v nravstvennoi zhizni* (element of law in moral [Hegel's *sittlich*] life). He sees the state as one of the *momenty obshchestva* (elements of society) and civil society as a *neustranimyi moment integral'noi prirody obshchestva* (uneliminable element of the integral nature of society) (*Dukhovnye osnovy* 309/175). He speaks of the *moment sluzheniia* (element of service),[7] the *moment stanovleniia* (element of becoming), . . . *svobody* (. . . of freedom), . . . *bezuslovnoi . . . neobkhodimosti* (. . . of unconditional . . . necessity), . . . *neposredstvennogo samobytiia* (. . . of immediate self-being), . . . *samosti* (. . . of selfhood), and . . . *dukhovnosti* (. . . of spirituality).[8]

Frank, much more often than Hegel, uses both Hegelian and non-Hegelian senses of a given term, sometimes on the same page or in the same passage. He could, I think, have prevented a certain amount of confusion and misunderstanding if he had taken the trouble to avoid, or at least minimize, cases such as the following, where *moment* in both senses appears in a single passage: *Moment absoliutnogo bvtiia* (element of absolute being) occurs in close proximity to *lovi moment* (seize the moment) (*Dukhovnye osnovy* 29/13), and *moment dolzhnogo* (element of the obligatory) occurs only a page before *v dannyi moment* (at the present moment) (*Dukhovnye osnovy* 206/116, 207/117). *Moment stanovleniia* (element of becoming) stands close to the phrase *vo vsiakii moment nashei . . . budnichnoi zhizni* (at every moment of our . . . everyday lives) (*Nepostizhimoe* 247/41).[9]

One wonders whether Frank, who is often very careful about conceptual distinctions, and even introduces such neologisms as *sub"ektnyi* to distinguish a second, more positive sense of 'subjective' from the standard *sub"ektivnyi* (see *Real'nost'* 49/21), was not conscious of the equivocity of such terms. Perhaps he thought of 'moment$_h$' and 'moment$_o$' as homonyms, morphologically identical but semantically distinct, and thus in need of no special treatment. Another much-used term appears to be subject to the same usage, namely *vechnyi* (eternal). In ontological and theological contexts it means "timeless" or "having no relation to temporality," roughly, what Frank calls *sverkhvremennoi* (supratemporal). But in social and political contexts it means something quite different, namely, "permanent" or "long-lasting." Note that the first sense is "all or none": a given entity is either eternal in the sense of timeless or it is temporal; the second sense is "more or less": here one "eternal" entity may last longer than another "eternal" entity, e.g., the Holy Roman Empire than the French Republic. For this reason, I have suggested calling the first sense 'absolute' and the second 'relative'. But the main point is that the meanings are distinct, even opposed.

Frank uses *vechnyi* in the absolute sense to modify *real'nost'* (reality) (*Nepostizhimoe* 528/276), *realnost'* . . . *kak* . . . *edinstvo* (reality . . . as . . . unity) (*Nepostizhimoe* 525/273), *ontologicheskaia neobkhodimost'* (ontological necessity) (*Dukhovnye osnovy* 55/28), and the *iskonnoe nachalo mirovogo bytiia* (primordial principle of the world's being) (*Nepostizhimoe* 525/273). He uses *vechnyi* in the relative sense to modify the *osnovy* (foundations) (*Dukhovnye osnovy* 13/4), *normy* (norms) (*Dukhovnye osnovy* 51–52/25–27), and *usloviia* (conditions) (*Dukhovnye osnovy* 52/27, 58/32) of social life; *protivoborstvo* (antagonism) between "I" and "thou" (*Dukhovnye osnovy* 91/50) and among individuals (*Dukhovnye osnovy* 98/54); *kolebanie* (oscillation) between anarchy and despotism (*Dukhovnye osnovy* 229/130). It seems clear that all of these are "permanent" or "long-lasting" but by no means "timeless" or "supratemporal." As it happens, in this usage Frank has good, or at least distinguished, company. Spinoza used *aeternum* in the absolute sense to modify *Deus*, *Substantia*, and *Natura*, and in the relative sense to modify authorities, commonwealths, councils, and decrees.[10]

Puzzlingly, in at least one place Frank admits that although mathematical truths are timeless or *vnevremennye* (extratemporal), "a given law, social relation, or form of government does not have such extratemporal being. Instead, these forms appear, exist for a while, and disappear in time . . ." (*Dukhovnye osnovy* 138/77). Fair enough! But then why call them *vechnye*, since they are only eternal$_r$ (the relative sense) not eternal$_a$ (the absolute sense)?

The two other terms which, in contrast to many Russian thinkers of his generation, Frank uses in Hegel's special senses are 'concrete$_h$' and 'organism$_h$'. The first he took from Hegel directly, the second both from Hegel and, more immediately, from Soloviev. It is likely that Frank was inspired to use 'concrete' in Hegel's speculative sense by Ivan Il'in's magisterial study of 1918.[11] We know that he had some familiarity with Il'in's book and also that he was critical of certain aspects of the latter's interpretation of Hegel's system.[12] But it appears that Frank fully appropriated the Hegelian speculative sense of 'concrete' first adequately clarified by Il'in. 'Concrete$_h$' (Hegel's speculative sense) means "many-sided, adequately related, complexly mediated."[13] As Il'in stressed, Hegel contrasted it to the *sinnlich-Konkrete* (sensuously concrete). The latter is close to the use of 'concrete' by most thinkers in the empiricist Anglo-American tradition, beginning with Locke and Hume, for whom only the sense-particular is concrete$_e$ in the full sense. Thus, a concept or universal can quite sensibly be characterized as concrete$_h$ and, at the same time, without paradox, as abstract$_e$. A sense-particular, or what Hegel calls *sinnliche Gewissheit* (sense certainty), is necessarily abstract$_h$ and, at the same time, unparadoxically, concrete$_e$. It is significant that 'concrete$_e$' (like 'eternal$_a$') is an "all-or-none" predicate; a given entity either is or is not concrete$_e$. In contrast, 'concrete$_h$' is a "more-or-less" predicate; it admits of degrees. A given entity or process can be or become "more concrete$_h$" than another entity or process.

'Concrete' in the "ordinary" sense differs from both of these, meaning, roughly, "particular, specific, down-to-earth." In one key passage Frank appears to use *konkretnyi* in all three of these senses, when he castigates

a misunderstanding that is common to limited, narrow minds, incapable of perceiving reality in all its depth and fullness [one that involves] the assertion that philosophy leads thought away from knowledge of concrete$_o$ reality . . . into the domain of abstractions. Only the individual, that which is present *here* and *now*, that which is accessible to our senses . . . is considered to be concrete$_e$. And everything that is universal, eternal, and all-embracing is considered to be an . . . impoverishing abstraction$_h$. But in fact the opposite is true for anyone who knows how to see reality genuinely. The universal . . . is not an abstraction$_h$; rather it is the whole, and precisely the whole is what concretely$_h$ is. (*Dukhovnye osnovy* 13–14/5; trans. revised, subscripts added)

Aside from this remarkable passage, 'concrete$_e$' occurs infrequently in Frank's writings, and is always linked with such terms as 'empirical' and 'sensuous'. Thus we find *konkretno-empiricheskii* (concretely$_e$- empirical), *konkretnyi empiricheskii mir* (concrete$_e$ empirical world), and *konkretnyi empiricheskii material* (concrete$_e$ empirical material).[14]

As Hegel was well aware—and Frank must have known, since he had an excellent command of Latin—etymology favors Hegel's speculative sense of 'concrete', since *concretum* is the past participle of the verb *con-crescere* (to grow together), suggesting the unification of a manifold. Both the empiricist and the "ordinary" sense of 'concrete' may be considered aberrations from this semantic core.

Frank uses 'concrete$_h$' to modify a number of terms designating entities or processes that Hegel himself considered concrete$_h$. To begin with, Frank's privileged term *vseedinstvo* (total-unity) has a strongly Hegelian flavor. Although it was Schelling, Hegel's youthful friend and younger fellow student at the theological *Stift* in Tübingen, who made the terms *All-Einheit* and *All-Einigkeit* current in German, Hegel no less than Schelling emphasized the *hen kai pan* (one and all) of Plato and the Neoplatonists. Frank speaks repeatedly of *konkretnoe vseedinstvo* (concrete$_h$ total-unity)[15] and occasionally of *zhivoe konkretnoe vseedinstvo* (living concrete$_h$ total-unity).

Among the other terms that are regularly characterized as 'concrete$_h$' are *polnota* (fullness), *real'nost'* (reality), *tsel'nost'* (wholeness), *vseobshchnost'* (universality), and *zhiznennost'* (vitality, aliveness).[16] Typical expressions include *konkretnaia real'nost' vo vsei ee polnote* (concrete$_h$ reality in all of its fullness) and *real'nost' v ee zhivoi konkretnosti* (reality in its living concreteness$_h$).[17]

In the light of Frank's statement quoted above, it seems fairly clear that he was aware that the term 'concrete' can be used equivocally; still, he sometimes, confusingly, used more than one sense in a single passage. In the following examples I have substituted "specific"[18] or "particular" for what I take to be 'concrete$_o$' and have identified 'concrete$_h$' as such. Thus, the expression *konkretnoe vseedinstvo* (concrete$_h$ total-unity) appears on the same page with the expression *chetyre konkretnykh predmeta* (four specific objects), and *konkretnaia vseobshchnost'* (concrete$_h$ universality) stands close to *konkretnaia tochka* (a particular point).[19]

In Hegel's speculative system an *Organismus* is not a living being but something like "an organized, self-constituting, inwardly articulated whole." It is in this speculative sense ('organism$_h$') that Hegel calls the state an *Organismus* (*Philosophy of Right*, sections 267, 269, and 302). But he also calls the state a *lebendiger Geist* (living spirit) and an *organisiertes . . . Ganzes* (organized whole) (*Enzyklopädie*, section 539). Frank, following Soloviev, often says that a society, a community, or a Church—as a manifestation of positive or inclusive total-unity—is a *konkretnyi dukhovnyi organizm* (concrete$_h$ spiritual/cultural organism$_h$), i.e., an "organized, self-constituting, inwardly articulated whole of a spiritual or cultural kind in which the individual members are adequately related to one another and mediated in and through the whole."

When Frank uses *organizm* in this sense he applies to it such adjectives as *blagodatnyi* (marked by Grace), *dukhovnyi* (spiritual/cultural), *kollektivnyi* (collective), *nezrimyi* (invisible, unseen), *obshchestvennyi* (social), and *sobornyi* (conciliar). In contrast *organizm* in the "ordinary" sense is modified by such adjectives as *biologicheskii* (biological), *psikhofizicheskii* (psychophysical), and *telesnyi* (bodily).[20]

In the case of *organizm*, no less than in the cases of *moment* and *konkretnyi*, Frank sometimes uses both Hegelian and non-Hegelian ("ordinary") senses in a given passage, without alerting his readers to what he is doing. Thus, a single sentence contains both the expression *obshchestvennyi . . . organizm* (social . . . organism$_h$) and *biologicheskii organizm* (biological organism$_o$) (*Dukhovnve osnovy* 78/43). Another passage refers both to the *obshchestvennyi organizm* and to the *rozhdenie novykh kletok organizma* (birth of new cells of an organism$_o$) (*Svet vo t'me* 340/198).[21]

Frank makes a valid distinction between complex wholes that are organized by an *external* agent, such as machines, and those that develop *inwardly* in an organic way, such as persons and communities (*Dukhovnye osnovy* 102–3/57). It might be objected that Hegel's "organized . . . whole" would fall into the former category, something that Hegel himself would obviously resist. I think the key is the expression "*self*-constituting," which is included in the definition I have given for 'organism$_h$'. A machine, after all, cannot be said to be *self*-constituting.

Another Hegelian term, *opredelennost'* (*Bestimmtheit*, "determinateness")—often in the plural, *opredelennosti* (*Bestimmtheiten*, "determinatenesses")—is central in Frank's epistemological and ontological discussions.[22] However, the focus and the limits of the present essay preclude our saying anything further about it here.

There is one important term that Frank, for no clear reason that I have been able to discover, uses in a markedly un-Hegelian way. The term is *deistvitel'nyi* (*wirklich*, "real" or "actual"), with noun *deistvitel'nost'* (*Wirklichkeit*, "reality" or "actuality"). For Hegel, as for most of his Russian followers—from Belinsky, Herzen, and the Slavophiles to Soloviev— the term has the strong and honorific sense of "that which has been actualized [in the course of the dialectical process]" and "that which is both active and efficacious." However, Frank uses it, in contrast to his own honorific term *real'nost'*, in the thin and pejorative sense of the "merely empirical or factual," frequently applying to it such predicates as "external," "superficial," and "objective" or "objectified."[23] He seems to have adopted this idiosyncratic usage as early as 1904, at which period he was concerned to condemn the "moral indifference" of what he called *slepaia deistvitel'nost'* (blind reality). However, the contrasting honorific use of *real'nost'* did not appear in his writings until after 1927.[24] In this un-Hegelian usage Frank is—to the best of my knowledge—unique among Russian thinkers.

II

So much for *terminology*. What are the main *doctrinal* influences of Hegel on Frank, especially in the area of ethics and social philosophy? It is clear, to begin with, that Frank had not only absorbed a great deal of Hegelian terminology, but was also well acquainted with Hegel's work, even though he wrote only three relatively short pieces directly focused on Hegel: "The Philosophy of Hegel" ("Filosofiia Gegelia," published belatedly in 1932 for the 1931 centennial of Hegel's death); a review of Debol'sky's translation of Hegel's *Science of Logic* (1916); and a review of the book on Hegel among the Slavs edited by Chizhevsky (1935). However, there is fairly frequent mention of Hegel, and even more frequent reference to Hegelian terms, concepts, and doctrines— sometimes with mention of Hegel, sometimes without such mention— in all four of the books considered in this essay.

It is clear that Frank has the greatest respect for Hegel as one of the towering speculative thinkers of the Western tradition, and that he is in agreement with Hegel on many specific points (some of which have been indicated in section I above). Examples of such specific points of agreement include: the way that Hegel by a deft remark "decisively undermined" a certain Kantian argument (*Real'nost'* 197/102; trans. revised); Hegel's discussion of teleology and his "true" assertion that "the end is the beginning" (*Real'nost'* 155/79); the claim that "rational proofs" of God's existence are only "secondary, derivative interpretations of this experiential apprehension of God; they are, as Hegel aptly remarks, 'movements of thought accompanying the soul's ascent to God' " (*Real'nost'* 206/117).

But Frank's most important agreement with Hegel is on the major theme of reconciliation (*primirenie, Versöhnung*). I entirely agree with Vladimir Zielinsky's claim that Frank's life project was one of reconciliation: of reason and faith, of philosophy and religion, of the "Russian, Jewish, and Western philosophical traditions, of truth as logical necessity and truth as gift and miracle, of abstract knowledge and mystical life, . . . of God as concept, rationally comprehensible and common to all, and God as unfathomable mystery, as my inner 'Thou' open only for me."[25] In this project of reconciliation Frank is following both Hegel and Soloviev, while adding his own characteristic stress on the dimension of the "unfathomable" and mysterious. This is perhaps what he has in mind when he says that Hegelian reconciliation is only "rational" whereas his own is "transrational" (*Nepostizhimoe* 316/98). I shall come back to this point in section IV below.

On another key point Frank is highly appreciative of Hegel, seeing him as coming close to a doctrine of living concrete$_h$ total-unity, that is, as coming close to Frank's own central insistence that the universal "living total-unity" is many-sided, is adequately related to its many constituents, and involves the complex mediation and self-mediation of these constituents. However, for Frank Hegel in the end fails to arrive at such a doctrine because of his "pantheistic tendencies" and his consequent failure to acknowledge the profoundly irrational and personal nature of the deepest stratum of reality ("Filosofiia Gegelia" 42, 47, 48). In the past, Hegel was often accused of "pantheistic tendencies," but more recent scholarship has shown this charge to have been misplaced.[26] Hegel's theological position is not a pantheism, but a *panentheism*; that is, his claim is not that the world taken as a whole is identical with God's being, but rather that the world constitutes a part or aspect, but *not* the whole, of that being. It seems to me that Frank's own theological position, while certainly remote from pantheism, is quite close to panentheism.[27]

III

Frank's ethics and social philosophy, as well as his political philosophy, are massively influenced by Hegel's *Philosophy of Right*. This is especially evident, as I have already suggested, in his treatment of the role of law (or "the system of law"), individual human rights and obligations, the state, and civil society.

According to Frank, the need to follow the "way of law is, as it were, a tribute paid to *human sinfulness*" (*Dukhovnye osnovy* 176/99; emphasis modified). I take this to mean that if human beings were not aggressive, acquisitive, and deceptive, if they were instead entirely peaceable, unselfish, and cooperative, then law as an institution would be unnecessary. It is clear that Frank (like Hegel) rejects the anarchist claim that human beings "in the state of nature," before they are corrupted by repressive institutions, are precisely such peaceable, unselfish, and cooperative creatures. As a good Hegelian, Frank stresses the function of law in peaceably reconciling opposing needs and interests. He even speaks of the "*supreme* reconciling and harmonizing function of law" (*Dukhovnve osnovy* 313/177; emphasis added). And he notes that political power can be "substantially *limited in its effect* by law (as in a law-governed state [*pravovoe gosudarstvo* = *Rechtsstaat*],[28] or it can be *independent* of law (as in a despotic form of government)" (*Dukhovnye osnovy* 154/86; trans. revised).

Frank goes on to identify, in order to reject, two unacceptable extremes:

1. law regarded as the unlimited and arbitrary will of the ruler(s) of the state, where the state power has clear priority over civil society, and

2. the opposed view of law as only an "expression of the free intersection of the wills of the separate participants in [civil] society," where civil society has clear priority over the state.

The first situation, Frank aptly notes, leads to *despotism*, the second to *anarchy*. Both of these are forms of the "*destruction* of society as an organically integral unity the separate members of which are harmoniously ordered" (*Dukhovnye osnovy* 313/177; emphasis added; the last nine words in this quotation represent a very free but, I think, adequate rendering of Frank's highly compressed expression *raschlenenno-uporiadochennogo edinstva*).

Frank defines the *"system of law"*—pregnantly—as the "totality of *public subjective rights"* (*Dukhovnye osnovy* 311/176–77) and makes a central place for the individual person (*lichnost'*) as a subject of rights— but also of obligations, including the ultimate obligation of serving a spiritually grounded good or ideal of truth-justice (*pravda*). Since—like the Latin *jus*, French *droit*, German *Recht*, etc.—the Russian word *pravo* means both "law" and "right," there are cases in which only context will identify the intended meaning.[29]

Like Hegel, Frank sees the right to private property as fundamental, but limited. It is not "an absolute individual right; . . . it does not signify the *absolute power* over some definite sphere of goods [*blag*], it does not signify the right to 'use and misuse things' (*jus utendi et abutendi*) according to one's own arbitrary will" (*Dukhovnye osnovy* 305–6/173; trans. revised). The right to property is what Frank calls "functional and subservient"—what we might more accurately call "instrumental"— since property is a means to the end of cooperation in the service of the good. A property owner is not an absolute master but something like an "empowered steward or manager" of his (or her) property, which "in its ultimate ground, 'belongs to God', and is ultimately under the control of the social whole." In Hegelian terms, it is subject both to state regulation and to the regulation of civil society and its various institutions. In Frank's words, "Objective law normalizes [*normiruet*, i.e., establishes norms that regulate] private property, setting limits to it and imposing specific obligations on the owner" (*Dukhovnye osnovy* 306/173–74).

Frank concisely summarizes his main point in the following words:

The system of property relations, like the structure of civil society in general, is formulated in a *system of law*, . . . which insures the subjective rights of every participant in civil society. . . . But law as the totality of norms decreed or at least defended by state power is the reflection . . . of the state principle in civil society. Civil society as the system of the free interaction and agreement of particular wills is itself based on the planned [*planomernyi*], systematic organization of the whole. . . . (*Dukhovnye osnovy* 309–10/175–76)

Again like Hegel, Frank sees the right to bequeath and inherit property as an "ontologically grounded" (*Dukhovnye osnovy* 287/162) expression of the "supratemporal solidarity and connection between [past and present] generations" (*Dukhovnye osnovy* 289/163).

As for freedom of conscience, Frank makes the essential point in mainly negative terms, rejecting the suggestion that any state has a right to impose a religion, ideology, or philosophy on its citizens. Here Frank differs slightly from Hegel, who held that, because religion is a unifying and integrating factor in society, the state has a right to "require all of its citizens to belong to a [C]hurch," but does *not* have the right to specify *which* Church, since the "content of a man's faith depends on his private ideas" (*Philosophy of Right*, section 270). In any case, Frank, quite in the spirit of Hegel, views the attempt to impose a religion or ideology by totalitarian states, whether communist (Stalin's Russia) or fascist (Mussolini's Italy), as "a blasphemous and essentially impotent [presumably, in the long run] effort to substitute the mechanical for the organic, which is tantamount in practice to the destruction of the substantial foundation of society." Frank's example is vivid and down-to-earth:

A policeman carrying out his proper function is not only necessary but is even performing a sacred duty [a form of service of the good and ultimately of divine truth-justice]. But a policeman who controls ideas and beliefs, whose job is not to catch criminals but to drag people into church (be it the Church of God or the Church of atheism) is an "abomination of desolation." (*Dukhovnye osnovy* 301/171; trans. revised)[30]

More generally, according to Frank, civil society is the "empirical substrate of social culture," ultimately rooted in a deeper *sobornost'*; thus, it cannot be legitimately controlled or organized by the state, any more than spiritual life as such can be. The proper task of the state is to "defend the freedom of [the society's] inwardly growing life," to *"organize freedom,"* giving form, allowing space, and setting limits to free spontaneous cooperation. He summarizes the relation between the state and civil society in the following concise passage: "The state is inconceivable without its natural foundation [namely] civil society with its spontaneously woven fabric, as civil society is inconceivable except as shaped by the planning [*planomernyi*] and unifying activity of the state principle [*gosudarstvennost'*]" (*Dukhovnye osnovy* 302/171; trans. revised).

In all of this Frank shows himself to be both close to Hegel and close to the truth—as I see it—concerning the role of law, individual human rights and obligations, the state, and civil society. It is quite understandable that he should have placed "spontaneity" (*spontannost'*) on the side of civil society, and it is notable that he should have recognized that one of the most destructive aspects of Bolshevism in Russian was its suppression of that spontaneity and the virtual annihilation of civil society (cf. *Dukhovnye osnovy* 303/172). But it is regrettable that in 1930, almost halfway through Stalin's first five-year plan, he should have used the term *planomernost'* (roughly, "the activity and policy of planning"), a term that he had used quite innocently in writings dating from 1905–6, to characterize the legitimate organizing and regulating activity of the state power, directed at society generally and civil society in particular (cf. *Dukhovnye osnovy* 313–14/177–78). The rather sinister ring of such words as *planomernyi* and *planomernost'* to our post-Stalinist ears is something that at that time Frank presumably *did* not, or perhaps *could* not, detect, despite his pointed critical remarks about revolutionary movements in general and Bolshevism in particular scattered throughout *The Spiritual Foundations of Society*. In later writings, fortunately, he exhibited a greater sensitivity on this terminological point and, especially in "The Heresy of Utopianism" (1946), offered a trenchant critique of the inhumanity of state planning for "paradise on earth," which leads instead to an inferno of desolation, destruction, and suffering.

IV

The above examination of Frank's views on individual rights and obligations, civil society, and the state is not intended to deny Frank's place within the specifically Russian tradition of religious and speculative thought, but only to point out the significant parallels between that tradition and Hegel's thought, which is no less firmly grounded in religious values and theological principles. Hegel insists that "true philosophy" leads to both God and the state, whereas what he calls "half philosophy" leads away from both (*Philosophy of Right*, Preface 17/12). Furthermore, it is the philosopher's insight (*Einsicht*) that "while the [C]hurch and state differ in form, they do not stand opposed in content, for truth and rationality are the content of both" (*Philosophy of Right*, section 270).

This claim is a special case of Hegel's more general claim that religion and speculative philosophy have the same content or object (*Gegenstand*), namely, God or the Absolute. The two differ only in their mode of appropriation of that object. The religious mode of appropriation is "receptivity and worship," which is a mode of feeling and representation (*Vorstellung*); the philosophical mode is conceptualization, a mode of thought.

On three specific points I see the positions of Hegel and Frank as essentially parallel, with Frank's position being influenced more powerfully by Hegel in some cases and more powerfully by the tradition of Russian religious thought in others. The three points—all, I think, central to Frank's account of the "spiritual foundations of society"[31]— are: (1) the claim that *obshchestvennost'* (sociality, the social structure) is grounded or "rooted" (a favorite metaphor of Frank's) in *sobornost'*;

(2) the claim that the "principle of service" is more fundamental than either individual rights or obligations; and (3) the special place that Frank assigns to the "metalogical," "transrational," and mystical in his metaphysics and epistemology.

1. It is evident enough that Frank's ethics and social philosophy is a theory of *sobornost'* (see Levitskii 129). *Sobornost'* is the abstract form of *sobor*, which is a kind of calque on the Greek *ekklēsia*. *Sobor* means both "council" and "cathredral" and, like *ekklēsia*, is derived from a verb meaning "to call together" or "to assemble" (*sobirat'*), as the Greek term is derived from the verb *ekkalein* (to call out [citizens to the assembly]). A *sobornost'* is a spiritual community. But spiritual community is also a central concept in Hegel, expressed repeatedly in the term *Gemeinde* (commune, community, congregation) and occasionally in the more abstract term *Gemeinschaftlichkeit* (roughly, "commonalty") (see *Philosophy of Right*, section 270).

As a recent commentator has put it: "[T]he freely contracted *Gesellschaft* [society] is the ideal of Rousseau; but the freely willed *Gemeinschaft* [community] is the ideal of Hegel" (Luft 1). Moreover, Hegel's ideal of the state, based on "the unified will of free individuals, instead of on 'contract,' compromise, or majority rule, is modeled after the *ekklēsia* of the New Testament. . . . The *Sittlichkeit* [cohesive social morality] of the state is a theonomy, in which divinely inspired law and right permeate the entire established order" (Luft 1).

This strikes me as entirely true to the spirit of Hegel's social and political thought. And I see nothing in it with which Frank would disagree.

2. Hegel, no less than Frank, emphasizes the interconnectedness and reciprocity of rights and obligations or duties (*Pflichte*). He insists that "by being in the ethical order [*das Sittliche*], a man [or "person," *Mensch*] has rights in so far as he has duties, and duties in so far as he has rights" (*Philosophy of Right*, section 155). This applies in the realm of the family and civil society; in the political realm "individuals have duties to the state in proportion as they have rights against it" (*Philosophy of Right*, section 261).

To be sure, Hegel does not make Frank's characteristic transition from rights to obligations to *service*. But he sees *Gottesdienst* ("divine worship," lit. "service of God") as fundamental at two levels: (a) because of the identity of the object of religion and philosophy, noted above, Hegel claims, "philosophy is theology" and its activity is "worship" (*Gottesdienst*) (*Vorlesungen* 1:30); and (b) "reverence for the law" springs from the "inner worship of God [*Gottesdienst*]" (*Philosophy of Right*, Preface 10/6). This strikes me as close to Frank's implicit derivation of the "principle of service" (*nachalo sluzheniia*) from a more general "worship of God" [*Bogosluzhenie*], since what is served is a set of values higher than the social or political, values that are ultimately spiritual. As Frank often says, this involves a "service of divine Truth-Justice" (*sluzhenie bozhestvennoi Pravdy*).

In Hegel's social and political philosophy the principle of service is less pervasive than in Frank's, but it appears in connection with what Hegel calls the "universal class," the class that dedicates itself to the service [*Dienst*] of the government." This class, which in sociopolitical terms is "the class of civil servants," must, Hegel insists, "have the universal as the end or purpose [*Zweck*] of its essential activity" (*Philosophy of Right*, section 303; trans. revised). Although Hegel does not in such discussions refer to *Gottesdienst*, I think that it may be seen as a tacit subtext in such passages. In any case, Frank and Hegel agree that such service is unselfish, directed toward a higher and more inclusive good, and ultimately has a religious foundation and motivation.

3. It is no doubt the influence of Nicholas of Cusa and other Neoplatonists, as well as that of Soloviev, which leads Frank to place such a central emphasis on the "metalogical," "transrational," and mystical in his metaphysics and epistemology. Echoes of this resound in his social and political philosophy, in his references to the "supratemporal" unity of past, present, and future generations, and in the claim (noted above) that his own kind of reconciliation is "transrational," whereas that of Hegel is merely "rational." This may be a significant residual difference between the two thinkers. But we should not forget, as some of the passages already quoted suggest, that Hegel is sensitive to the "inner" and even the "mysterious. " He refers to the "mystery" (*Mysterium*) of freedom (*Philosophy of Right*, section 139). More generally, as an acute commentator has noted, there are philosophies that, though "rationalistic in principle," are "filled to overflowing with purely mystical enthusiasm [*pod"em*]." Among them are the philosophies, precisely, of the Neoplatonists and of Hegel. The "mystical overtones" of these philosophies are not mere "chance accompaniments." Rather, they are "necessary complements, which, like a kind of inspiration, accompany the subtlest analyses and most exalted flights of the purest and most perfect work of *reason* alone" (Shpet 155).

These words of Gustav Shpet apply, I would suggest, no less directly to Frank than to Hegel. *Both* are rationalists for whom the mystical or "transrational" is a kind of "overtone" and "inspiration." This means that Frank's difference from Hegel on the central question of philosophical, social, and political "reconciliation" may not be as deep as he took it to be.

Notes

1. *Vseedinstvo* has sometimes been rendered as "pan-unity," e.g., in Lossky's *History of Russian Philosophy* and in Robert Slesinski's contribution to the present volume. But this term is of mixed etymology: half Greek and half Latin. The term I prefer (and have used in translating Zenkovsky's *History of Russian Philosophy*) is of entirely Latin roots: "total-unity." I have similar reservations about "all-unity" since the term is half-Anglo-Saxon and half-Latin. The purely Anglo-Saxon variant, "all-oneness" strikes me as dubious on other grounds.

2. We should also include Frank's mentor, Vladimir Soloviev, and the legal theorist Pavel Novgorodtsev among philosophers of *vseedinstvo* who paid close and positive attention to questions of law, the state, and civil society.

3. S. L. Frank to N. A. Berdiaev, London, 1948, Frank Collection, Bakhmeteff Archives, Columbia University, New York.

4. See the discussion of Frank's philosophical sources in Zenkovsky 2:852–72, Lossky 266–92; and V. N. Il'in 85–116. Philip Swoboda, a leading American authority on Frank's philosophy, claimed in his Columbia University dissertation that such commentators as Zenkovsky and Lossky had overstated Soloviev's influence on Frank. However, more recently he has modified his earlier skeptical stance on this question (private communication, October 15, 1994).

5. Citations to Frank consist of page numbers of Russian text, a diagonal, and page numbers of the English translation.

6. For an account of the Hegelian influence on Soloviev's philosophy as well as his "metaphilosophy" (i.e., his position on the development of, and the relationships among, various philosophical movements), see Kline, "Hegel and Solovyov."

7. In one passage Frank uses both *nachalo sluzheniia* (principle of service) and *moment sluzheniia*. The former expression occurs several times between *Dukhovnye osnovy* 223/126 and 234/132, as well as at *Dukhovnye osnovy* 305/173. Thus Jakim may be justified in eliding the two terms, putting simply "the supreme principle of *service* determines the entire structure of rights and obligations . . ." for Frank's syntactically more elaborate: *Momentom sluzheniia opredelena, kak verkhovnym nachalom, vsia struktura prav i obiazannostei . . . (Dukhovnye osnovy* 227/129).

8. For further examples of Frank's use of 'moment$_h$', with detailed references to his texts, see "Hegelian Roots" 199–200.

9. For further examples of Frank's use of both 'moment$_h$' and 'moment$_o$' in a single passage, and an indication of the relative proportion of occurrences of 'moment$_h$' and 'moment$_o$' in the four works discussed, see Kline, "Hegeiian Roots" 200.

10. See Kline, "Absolute and Relative Senses of *Liberum* and *Libertas* in Spinoza," esp. sec. 2 (263–65). The use of the term *aeternum* in the "relative" sense goes back at least to Cicero, who spoke of the founding of a city (*civitas*) in such a way as to make it *aeterna*, i.e., long lasting (see *De re publica*, bk. 3, chap. 23).

11. See I. A. Il'in, *Filosofiia Gegelia*. An annotated reprint of this important book is planned for the final volumes of Il'in, *Sobranie sochinenii v desiati tomakh* (Collected Works in Ten Volumes), the first four volumes of which, edited by Iu. T. Lisitsa, were published by Russkaia Kniga in Moscow in 1993 and 1994. In 1994 a reset one-volume edition of Il'in's Hegel book, with a preface by I. I. Evlamp'ev, was published by Nauka in St. Petersburg. See Grier, "The Speculative Concrete."

12. In 1932 Frank declared that two Hegel scholars, Ivan Il'in and Richard Kroner, had for the first time adequately assessed Hegel's "striving for concrete-ness$_h$, for a coincidence of thought with the wholly exhaustive fullness of being" ("Filosofiia Gegelia" 45–46). Iury Lisitsa is my source for the claim that Frank disagreed with certain of Il'in's Hegel interpretations; I have not yet found a text in which that disagreement is explicitly stated.

13. See Kline, "Some Recent Reinterpretations of Hegel's Philosophy," esp. 40–44, and Grier, "Abstract and Concrete in Hegel's Logic," esp. 60–65.

14. For further examples of Frank's use of 'concrete$_e$', with detailed references to his texts, see Kline, "Hegelian Roots" 201.

15. Frank had used the expression *konkretnoe vseedinstvo* as early as 1915, in the title of part 3 of his book *Predmet znaniia*.

16. See Kline, "Life as Ontological Category," for a discussion of what Hegel called *das logische Leben*, something close to what Frank refers to as the *konkretnaia polnota i zhiznennost'* . . . *real'nosti* (concrete$_h$ fullness and vitality [or "aliveness"] . . . of reality) ("Filosofiia Gegelia" 42) and the *konkretnaia polnota zhivoi real'nosti* (concrete$_h$ fullness of living reality) (*Real'nost'* 72/33).

17. For further examples of Frank's use of 'concrete$_h$', with detailed references to his texts, see Kline, "Hegelian Roots" 202–3.

18. In a few places Frank uses the Latinate Russian word *spetsificheskii* as an apparent synonym for 'concrete$_o$'. See *Nepostizhimoe* 207/8, 244/39, 333/112, 358/133.

19. For further examples of Frank's use of both 'concrete$_h$' and 'concrete$_o$' in a single passage, and an indication of the relative proportion of occurrences of 'concrete$_h$' and 'concrete$_o$' in the four works, see Kline, "Hegelian Roots" 202, 203.

20. For further examples of Frank's use of 'organism$_h$', with detailed references to his texts, see Kline, "Hegelian Roots" 204.

21. For further examples of Frank's use of both 'organism$_h$' and 'organism$_o$' in a single passage, and an indication of the relative proportion of occurrences of 'organism$_h$' and 'organism$_o$' in the four works, see Kline, "Hegelian Roots" 204.

22. The Hegelian flavor of the term *opredelennost'* is somewhat obscured by Jakim's rendering of it as "definiteness" rather than the more usual "determinateness" (see *Nepostizhimoe* 222/22, 224/23, 226/25, 227/26, 241/37, 243/38, 270/60, 271/61, 272/61, 276/65, 277/66, 305/89, 414/178). Jakim also translates *opredelennost'* as "determination," which may be less awkward than

"determinateness" (especially in the plural), but which blurs the distinction between *opredelennost'* and *opredelenie* (*Bestimmung*, "determination") (see *Nepostizhimoe* 222/21, 224/23, 227/26, 240/36, 261/52, 262/53, 271/61, 272/61, 411/176).

23. Although it is *deistvitel'nost'* that Frank standardly characterizes as empirical (e.g., *Nepostizhimoe* 272/63, 273/63), he sometimes applies this predicate, confusingly and I think carelessly, to *real'nost'* (e.g., *Dukhovnye osnovy* 206–7/116, 210/118). This would appear to be an uncharacteristic downgrading of the usual status of *real'nost'*. An equally uncharacteristic upgrading of the status of *deistvitel'nost'* occurs in a quotation from Hegel in which Frank renders the Hegelian *wirklich* as *deistvitel'nyi* ("Filosofiia Gegelia" 43). Earlier in the same work Frank had used *deistvitel'nost'* in his usual pejorative and un-Hegelian way, qualifying it as *vneshniaia* (external) ("Filosofiia Gegelia" 41).

24. My thanks to Philip Swoboda for helpful references and clarifying comments concerning the history of Frank's use of the term *deistvitel'nost'*.

25. V. Zielinsky, "The 'God of the Philosophers' or the 'Other' God? Some Reflections of the Religious Philosophy of Semën Frank," conference proceedings, Conference on Russian Religious Thought, 1993.

26. An impressive recent study of Hegel's thought emphasizes the rejection of the charge of pantheism by several recent commentators, including Ivan Il'in, whose Hegel commentary the author consulted in the abridged German edition: *Die Philosophie Hegels als kontemplative Gotteslehre*. The author accepts, with appropriate qualifications, the characterization of Hegel's position as a panentheism. See O'Regan, esp. 172–74 and 296–98, 446–47 n. 6, and 448 n. 13. One of O'Regan's principal claims is that the mystical tradition was a much more powerful influence on Hegel's thought than has generally been recognized. This claim, which O'Regan presents in a highly convincing way, supports my contention that Frank is close to Hegel on essential points of philosophical theology.

27. On one point Frank got Hegel wrong, but here he was following Marx (in *The Poverty of Philosophy*, 1846) and certain popularizers of Hegel, who claimed that Hegel's triad involves "thesis, antithesis, and synthesis" ("Filosofiia Gegelia" 43). This was a common error at the time; but it is now widely recognized that Hegel in fact *never* used this formulation to state his own position, but only to criticize the positions of Kant and Fichte. There is, to be sure, a triadic (sometimes tetradic) structure to his thought, and he *did* speak of the "negation of the negation." But he did *not* speak of "thesis-antithesis-synthesis."

28. Boris Jakim's generally readable and accurate translation of *The Spiritual Foundations of Society*, widely quoted in the present chapter, fails at this point, putting "legitimate state" rather than "rule-of-law state" or "law-governed state." Although the term "legitimate" suggests the general sense of *pravovoi*, it fails to convey the intended specific reference to the Hegelian *Rechtsstaat* (standardly translated into Russian as *pravovoe gosudarstvo*), and thus fails to suggest that in such a state a central place is assigned to both law (*Recht*) and rights (*Rechte*).

29.   A generally reliable clue is the use of *pravo* in the singular to mean "law" and in the plural to mean "rights." But this clue is not infallible. In two cases where *pravo* in the singular means "right" Jakim has gotten it wrong. (1) Where Frank has *vysshei . . . kategoriei nravstvenno-obshchestvennoi zhizni iavliaetsia . . . obiazannost', a ne* pravo; *vsiakoe pravo mozhet byt' lish' . . . proizvodnym otrazheniem obiazannosti,* Jakim has "the highest . . . category of the sociomoral life is not *law* but *obligation*; all law is only a . . . derivative reflection of obligation" (*Dukhovnye osnovy* 226/128). But clearly, in this context, Frank means, "not *right* but obligation," and "every *right* is only a . . . derivative reflection." (2) Where Frank has *Element grazhdanskogo obshchestva (sub"ekt prava)* Jakim puts, "The element of civil society (the subject of law)" (*Dukhovnye osnovy* 310/176). Here again, Frank means, "the subject of a *right* [or *rights*]."

30.   "Abomination of desolation" is the rendering in the King James Version of the Koine *bdelugma tes erēmōseōs,* which the Russian Bible, here quoted by Frank, renders as *merzosti zapusteniia* (see Mt 24:15, Mk 13:14). The sense of this rather odd expression appears to be "sacrilegious object causing the desecration (of a sacred place)"—a meaning that fits nicely with Frank's intention in this passage.

31.   The very title of Frank's main work in social and political philosophy—*Dukhovnye osnovy obshchestva*—has, as Vladimir Golstein has pointed out, a distinctly German ring to it. And the German counterpart—*Die geistigen Grundlagen der Gesellschaft*—has a no less distinctly Hegelian ring. Note that *geistig,* like *dukhovnyi,* means both "spiritual" (in a narrowly religious sense) and "cultural" (in a broader, more inclusive sense). Frank, like Hegel, sometimes notes this second sense explicitly, as when he refers to the *dukhovnoe (nravstvennoe, religioznoe, umstvennoe) sostoianie obshchestva* (spiritual [moral, religious, and intellectual] state of a socety) (*Dukhovnye osnovy* 216/123).

Works Cited

Frank, S. L. *Dukhovnye osnovy obshchestva.* Paris: YMCA Press, 1930; rpt., New York: Posev, 1988. *The Spiritual Foundations of Society.* Trans. Boris Jakim Athens: Ohio University Press, 1987.

Frank, S. L. "Eres' utopizma" (1946). In *Po tu storonu levogo i pravogo,* ed. V. S. Frank. Paris: YMCA Press, 1972. 83–106.

Frank, S. L. "Filosofiia Gegella (K stoletiiu dnia smerti)." *Put',* no. 34 (1932): 39–51.

Frank, S. L. *Nepostizhimoe: Ontologicheskoe vvedenie v filosofiiu religii.* Paris: YMCA Press, 1939; rpt. in Frank, *Sochineniia.* Moscow: Pravda, 1990. 181–559. Page references will be to the Moscow edition. *The Unknowable: An Ontological Introduction to the Philosophy of Religion.* Trans. Boris Jakim. Athens: Ohio University Press, 1983. (This title is sometimes given, e.g., in the *Histories* of Lossky and Zenkovsky, as *The Unfathomable*.)

Frank, S. L. *Real'nost' i chelovek: Metafizika chelovecheskogo bytiia.* Paris: YMCA Press, 1956. *Reality and Man: An Essay in the Metaphysics of Human Nature.* Trans. Natalie Duddington. New York: Taplinger, 1966.

Frank, S. L. Review of *Gegel'*. *Nauka logiki. Perev. s nem. N. G. Debol'skogo* [Hegel. *Wissenschaft der Logik*, trans. N. G. Debol'skii]. "Kriticheskoe obozrenie." *Russkaia mysl'*, no. 5 (1916): 1–2.

Frank S. L. Review of *Hegel bei den Slaven*, ed. Dmitrii Tschižewski. *Zeitschrift für slawische Philologie* 12 (1935): 435–40.

Frank, S. L. *Svet vo t'me: Opyt khristianskoi etiki i sotsial'noi filosofii*. Paris: YMCA Press, 1949. *The Light Shineth in Darkness: An Essay in Christian Ethics and Social Philosophy*. Trans. Boris Jakim. Athens: Ohio University Press, 1989.

Grier, Philip T. "Abstract and Concrete in Hegel's Logic." In *Essays in Hegel's Logic*, ed. George di Giovanni. Albany: State University of New York Press, 1990. 59–75.

Grier, Philip T. "The Speculative Concrete: I. A. Il'in's Interpretation of Hegel." In *Hegel, Interpretation, and History*, ed. Shaun Gallagher. Albany: State University of New York Press, forthcoming.

Hegel, G. W. F. *Enzyklopädie der philosophischen Wissenschaften im Grundrisse* (1830). Ed. Friedhelm Nicolin and Otto Pöggeler. Hamburg: Meiner, 1969.

Hegel, G. W. F. *Grundlinien der Philosophie des Rechts* (1821). Ed. Johannes Hoffmeister. Hamburg: Meiner, 1955. *Philosophy of Right*. Trans. T. M. Knox. Oxford: Oxford University Press, 1952.

Hegel, G. W. F. *Vorlesungen über die Philosophie der Religion*. Ed. Georg Lasson. 2 vols. Hamburg: Meiner, 1966.

Il'in, I. A. *Filosofiia Gegelia kak uchenie o kondretnosti Boga i cheloveka*. 2 vols. Moscow: Leman & Sakharov, 1918.

Il'in, I. A. *Die Philosophie Hegels als kontemplative Gotteslehre*. Bern, 1946.

Il'in, V. N. "Nikolai Kuzanskii i S. L. Frank." In *Sbornik pamiati Semёna Liudvigovicha Franka*, ed. V. V. Zen'kovskii. Munich: n.p., 1954. 85–116.

Kline, George L. "Absolute and Relative Senses of *Liberum* and *Libertas* in Spinoza." In *Spinoza nel 350 anniversario della nascita*, ed. Emilia Giancotti. Naples: Bibliopolis, 1985. 259–80.

Kline, George L. "Hegel and Solovyov." In *Hegel and the History of Philosophy*, ed. Keith W. Algozin, Joseph J. O'Malley, and Frederick G. Weiss. The Hague: Nijhoff, 1974. 159–70.

Kline, George L. "The Hegelian Roots of S. L. Frank's Ethics and Social Philosophy." *Owl of Minerva* 25 (1994): 195–208. (This is an earlier, quite different, and only partly overlapping version of the present chapter.)

Kline, George L. "Life as Ontological Category: A Whiteheadian Note on Hegel." In *Art and Logic in Hegel's Philosophy*, ed. Kenneth L. Schmitz and Warren E. Steinkraus. New York: Humanities Press, 1980. 158–62.

Kline, George L. "Some Recent Reinterpretations of Hegel's Philosophy." *Monist* 48 (1964): 34–75.

Levitskii, S. A. "Etika Franka." In *Sbornik pamiati Semёna Liudvigovicha Franka*, ed. V. V. Zen'kovskii. Munich: n.p., 1954. 117–32.

Lossky, N. O. *History of Russian Philosophy*. New York: International Universities Press, 1951.

Luft, Eric von der. "On the Religious Roots of Hegel's *Rechtsphilosophie*." M. A. thesis Bryn Mawr College 1977.

O'Regan, Cyril. *The Heterodox Hegel*. Albany: State University of New York Press, 1994.

Shpet, Gustav G. *Vnutrenniaia forma slova: Etiudy i variatsii na temy Gumbol'ta*. Moscow, 1927.

Zenkovsky, V. V. *A History of Russian Philosophy*. Trans. George L. Kline. 2 vols., New York: Columbia University Press; London: Routledge & Kegan Paul, 1953.

11

"Spiritual Life" versus Life in Christ
S. L. Frank and the Patristic Doctrine of Deification

Philip J. Swoboda

Unlike some other leading representatives of twentieth-century Russian religious philosophy, Semën Frank did not choose to present himself to the world as an "Orthodox thinker," or to portray his thought as a creative elaboration in philosophical form of ideas or themes distinctive to the Orthodox theological tradition. In the major works he produced after his expulsion from Soviet Russia in 1922, Frank did come forward as the advocate of what he conceived to be a "Christian" interpretation of human existence, but in so doing, he only rarely alluded to distinctively Orthodox doctrines or practices, paid little attention to the points of controversy dividing the Orthodox from other branches of the Christian Church, and quoted Orthodox, Catholic, and Protestant writers indifferently as authorities on matters of Christian belief and Christian living. The tradition of thought with which, as a philosopher, he was most eager to associate himself was that of late antique and Renaissance Neoplatonism: his acknowledged "masters" in philosophy were the pagan sage Plotinus and the Roman Catholic cardinal Nicholas of Cusa (see *Predmet znaniia* vii; *Unknowable* x–xi; *Reality* xvii). Although he is often described as a "disciple" of Vladimir Soloviev, Frank did not in fact accord Soloviev recognition as a precursor of his own manner of thinking until quite late in his career (*Reality* xvi–xvii) .

What a given thinker has to say about his own intellectual affiliations is rarely the final word on the subject: his statements are almost always subject to amendment or amplification by later students of his thought. In the present case, one might conceivably argue that Frank, a practicing Orthodox Christian for most of his adult life, was more affected by the assumptions of his Orthodox milieu than he recognized, or that he owed greater debts to the Orthodox writers whose works he had studied than he was prepared to acknowledge. As evidence of this, one might seek to identify features of his thought which can be seen as characteristic of the Orthodox tradition in general, or as reminiscent of the views of particular Orthodox thinkers with whose writings it is reasonable to believe Frank was familiar.

The problem of Frank's intellectual relationship to Orthodoxy is clearly an important one. It has a direct bearing on the question of the unity of the religious-philosophical movement in twentieth-century Russia, and on the kindred question of this movement's ultimate sources of inspiration. But while the present chapter seeks to contribute to the elucidation of this problem, the approach to the problem I shall be taking is one that appears to me more fruitful than a long, involved, and, in the end, quite possibly inconclusive inquiry devoted to identifying unacknowledged points of contact between Frank's thought and the doctrines of this or that spokesman of a normative "Orthodoxy." The point of departure for this alternative approach is a group of passages in Frank's later writings in which the philosopher, departing from his usual custom, does make overt claims regarding the kinship of his own ideas with traditional Orthodox teaching—specifically, with the thought of the Greek Fathers of the Church, whose writings have served as a standard of "right belief" for all subsequent generations of Orthodox Christians.

In the major treatises Frank produced during the last two decades of his life—the series of books that includes *The Unfathomable* (*Nepostizhimoe*, 1939; translated into English as *The Unknowable*), *The Light Shineth in Darkness* (*Svet vo t'me*, 1949), *God with Us* (*S nami Bog*, 1946), and the posthumously published *Reality and Man* (*Real'nost' i chelovek*, 1956)—we find him making fairly frequent reference to the patristic doctrine of salvation as deification. These references generally appear in contexts where Frank is engaged in expounding what he himself considered the central notion of his mature philosophy of religion—the concept of "Godmanhood" (*bogochelovechestvo*). In several of the passages where the doctrine of deification is evoked, Frank asserts that the two conceptions are closely akin, or even identical in their ultimate content (*Unknowable* 257–58; *Reality* 141; *God with Us* 162). Given that both notions are pivotal elements of the systems of thought to which they respectively belong, the question whether they are in fact identical would appear well worth asking. Either a positive or a negative answer to this question would have weighty implications for an inquiry into the relationship between Frank's thought and classical Orthodox theology—if not the "Orthodox tradition" as such.

The thesis of this chapter is that Frank's claims regarding the kinship of the two conceptions prove, upon scrutiny, quite unfounded. The philosopher may have been sincerely convinced that the essential content of the patristic doctrine of deification was captured by his own conception of "Godmanhood"; but, in actuality, the whole cast of his thought was such as to inhibit him from endorsing the basic theological axioms upon which the patristic doctrine rests. Between even the most Orthodox-sounding of Frank's formulations of his conception of "Godmanhood," and the doctrine of the Fathers, there gapes a narrow but profound conceptual fissure.

The explanation of this state of affairs, I shall argue, is to be sought in Frank's intellectual biography. Frank was a philosopher before he was a Christian. A Jew by family origin, he abandoned the practices of Judaism in adolescence; at roughly the same time, he accepted the atheistic worldview typical of the nineteenth-century radical intelligentsia. In the decade after 1900, he gradually became convinced of the untenability of atheism and of the necessity of adopting what he called a "religious attitude to life" (*Filosofiia* 306), but he continued to harbor a deep distrust of religious organization, religious authority, and formal theology.[1] It was only in 1912, when he was thirty-five, that he received Christian baptism and became a member of the Orthodox Church.

Frank had made his debut as a philosophical writer long before this, in 1903; indeed, by the time he formally converted to Christianity, his philosophical worldview had in many respects already assumed its definitive shape. In 1915 and 1917, he published the first two of the seven major works on which his reputation as a philosopher chiefly rests; in neither book does he make any explicit reference to his new religious allegiance. Not until after 1922, when Frank was expelled from Soviet Russia by the Bolshevik government, did he come forward in his published writings as the defender of an avowedly Christian understanding of human life. (The earliest work in which Frank adopts this role is *The Downfall of the Idols* (*Krushenie kumirov*), published in 1924).

The insights out of which Frank assembled his mature doctrine of Godmanhood first presented themselves to him during the earliest, idealist phase of his philosophical activity, long before he became an adherent of the Christian faith. Their origins lay in the moral universe of German idealism and nineteenth-century liberal humanism, and reflected the influence on Frank of philosophers such as Fichte and Windelband. As late as 1916, when he wrote *Man's Soul* (*Dusha cheloveka*), Frank was able to produce a theory of the human soul's relation to the Absolute that is hardly distinguishable from his later doctrine of "Godmanhood," without making any use of Christian terminology or distinctively Christian concepts, much less ideas proper to the Eastern Church Fathers. When, following his exile from Russia, Frank reformulated his views in "Christian" language, he eagerly sought to reinforce the persuasiveness of his teachings by investing them, where possible, with the authority of the great masters of Christian spirituality. It is in this context that his attempt to appropriate the patristic doctrine of deification should be viewed. Yet Frank's effort to incorporate this doctrine into a preexisting system of concepts of nontheological origin was bound to encounter difficulties. Indeed, he could have fully assimilated the doctrine into his system only at the cost of modifying the latter substantially, and jettisoning some of his oldest and most cherished philosophical convictions.

Frank's relationship to the doctrine of deification typifies his relationship, as a "religious" philosopher, to theology generally. There is no principle to which Frank was more deeply committed than that of the autonomy of philosophy. A philosophy such as he conceived his own to be, one "based upon religious and metaphysical experience" (*Reality* xvii), could not allow itself to be dictated to by theology. On the other hand, the philosopher was bound by no corresponding obligation to keep off the territory that theology assigned to itself. In every culturally fertile era of the European past, the philosopher, Frank affirmed, had enjoyed the acknowledged right "to give a free philosophical interpretation" to questions about life's meaning that "theologians and unreflecting believers" are persuaded only "the authority of the Revelation and traditional church doctrine" can answer (*Reality* xvii). He claimed the same right for himself. Indeed, Frank felt that philosophy, in the present age, must take upon itself the task of illuminating the relevance of Christian truth to the spiritual struggles of modern man, a mission that "abstract dogmatic theology," remote from life and "prone to sinful idle talk," is incapable of discharging (*Light* xix–xxi).

To study the ways in which Frank resisted accepting the full import of the patristic teaching on deification, even as he claimed to be in fullest accord with it, is to place oneself at an ideal vantage point from which to perceive the divergences between the assumptions underlying Frank's philosophical anthropology and the vision of man characteristic of Greek patristic thought. I do not claim that the results of a comparison of the doctrines of Godmanhood and deification provide us with the means to settle once and for all the question of Frank's relationship to Orthodoxy as a body of ideas. But I do think that such a comparison points up some of the difficulties involved in portraying him as a thinker who took a distinctively Orthodox approach to the philosophical interpretation of the world.

The doctrine of Godmanhood that we find in Frank's emigre works has as its basis a conception that played a central role in his thought almost from the start of his career as a philosophical writer: the conception of "spiritual life" (*dukhovnaia zhizn'*).

The two books in which Frank expounds his conception of spiritual life most elaborately are *Man's Soul* (*Dusha cheloveka*, 1917) and *The Unknowable* (1939). Although the first of these books was written before Frank's emergence as a self-declared champion of the Christian view of life, and the second long after it, the two works do not differ in any significant way in their treatment of this topic.

The fundamental thesis of *Man's Soul* is that man's inner world, the sphere of the individual's "psychic life," does not merely open "outward" upon the world of objects revealed to us in conceptual knowledge; it also opens "downward" into the realm of "spiritual life" (282). The existence of this realm is revealed by certain inner experiences, marked by a common feature that distinguishes them from the phenomena of merely "subjective" psychic life. They are all accompanied by a peculiar self-awareness, a consciousness of one's "I" as partaking of "a significance, a value, or an authority" that is "absolute" (251). Frank claims that every human being, however impoverished his inner life, is vouchsafed such "experiences" (252). But not everyone, of course, grasps their "theoretical, objective significance" (256). This significance is, however, self-evident to the person who casts aside the false presuppositions of the "naturalistic world-conception" (256–57) and takes his stand on the firm ground of immediate "intuition" (258). Intuition reveals that, in these experiences, the individual is conscious of his personality as "fused with" or "rooted in" a suprapersonal life that is the "primordial ground of being in general" (258). Ultimately, the human soul must therefore be seen as the "active incarnation [*voploshchenie*] or emanation [*izluchenie*] of absolute reason or spirit" (261). "Consciousness of self and consciousness of God are one and the same: the path to consciousness of God leads through a plunge into one's own depths, through the intuition of the absolute root of our 'I' which is transcendent to our *subjective* 'I' " (260).

These ideas recur again and again in Frank's writings, with some variation in terminology from book to book, but hardly any difference in content. In *Man's Soul*, the term "spiritual life" itself is sometimes

employed "phenomenologically," to designate the mode of inner experience through which is made evident to us the metaphysical fact of our
rootedness in the suprapersonal absolute. But it is also used to designate
the metaphysical fact itself. In his émigré writings, references to spiritual
life as a mode of experience remain plentiful, but the tendency is for the
metaphysical fact to be designated by the term "Godmanhood."

As Frank's reference to the soul as an "incarnation" of the "absolute
spirit" suggests, there is some analogy between Frank's conception
of human personhood and the understanding of the person of Christ
expressed in the patristic theology of the hypostatic union; the term
"Godmanhood" makes the link between these ideas quite explicit. In *The
Unknowable*, the second part of which covers much of the same ground
as *Man's Soul*, the duality of human personhood is given particularly
striking expression. Here Frank argues that "there . . . exists no precise,
univocal boundary between soul and spirit" (169). Hence, "the ultimate,
most intimate, and most 'inner' *depth* of the human soul is located
not *inside* the soul but *outside* it, is a sphere into which we penetrate
only after crossing the bounds of our subjective 'I' as such" (171). We
might say, therefore, that Frank sees the human "person" as "made
known in two natures," the one merely human, the other transhuman, or
"spiritual": "Thus, the element of selfhood essentially always stands on
the threshold between psychic being and spiritual being. It is the place
where the spiritual penetrates into the soul, the place where the spiritual
merges with the psychic into unity. . . . The "person," that which makes
up the ultimate, primordial *unity* of my psychic life, its substantial form
as it were, is given to me only through *duality*" (*Unknowable* 174–75). We
shall discuss the significance of this analogy shortly.

Hitherto I have said nothing about the *content* of the inner experiences
in which the spiritual life of the individual manifests itself. Frank makes
it quite clear, both in *Man's Soul* and in various other works, that this
content is diverse. In a very general sense, all these experiences may be
considered "religious," inasmuch as they all involve an intuition of the
presence, beneath our subjective "I," of a supra-individual "support"
or "ground" (261). But those experiences we ourselves are inclined to
classify as religious are not the only experiences in which spiritual life
can manifest itself; they may just as well be of a sort we would choose
to label ethical, or cognitive, or aesthetic (251). We can be conscious of
the suprapersonal spirit acting in us and through us not only when we
strive to know ourselves, but when we strive to know other selves or
the life and culture of human communities (271, 280–81); when we find
ourselves gripped by an inward moral compulsion to adopt a particular
course of action or a particular calling (204–5, 206); when, as creative

beings, we seek to embody the values of spirit in external reality (274–75); and when we love (273–74).

It is readily apparent, I think, that the "spirit" which, for Frank, manifests itself in spiritual life is, in all essentials, the *Geist* of German idealism. It is that spirit which (the Baden neo-Kantians argued) expresses itself in all our judgments of value. It is that spirit which attains objectification (as Hegel or Dilthey would have put it) in the religious, ethical, artistic, legal, and political forms that constitute the subject matter of the *Geisteswissenschaften*, the sciences of human culture.

It should occasion no surprise, therefore, that the article in which Frank first made use of the term "spiritual life" was written at the period in his life when he was most deeply under the spell of German idealism—the years just prior to the 1905 Revolution. This essay, published late in 1904 under the title "On Critical Idealism" ("O kritich-eskom idealizme"), is one of Frank's earliest philosophical articles. It nonetheless contains, albeit in a rudimentary form, all the elements of his mature conception of spiritual life.

In "On Critical Idealism," Frank discusses a class of inner experiences—which can be ethical, aesthetic, or religious—that he calls "integral experiences of the spirit." These are clearly the same sort of experiences dealt with in *Man's Soul* as manifestations of "spiritual life." Like the latter, they elude "merely rational [*rassudochnoe*] thinking," yet are perfectly accessible to anyone "who takes them as they are given"; like them, these "integral experiences" have their origin in "the inscrutable depths of life" (245–46).

The most plausible construction to be placed on Frank's rather incoherent argument in "On Critical Idealism" is that he conceived these experiences as originating in what he calls the "transcendental self," a supra-individual "consciousness" distinct from the "empirical self" (the conscious "I" of introspection). The critical idealism Frank expounded in his 1904 article was a not fully digested melange of ideas drawn from a variety of German idealist philosophers. At the time, the paramount influence on his thought was the philosophy of Fichte. (In all likelihood, it was from Fichte that Frank borrowed the very phrase "spiritual life.")[2] He was also very much taken with the views of the neo-Kantian philosopher Wilhelm Windelband, whose best-known work, the collection of essays called *Präludien*, he had just finished translating into Russian (Frank, *Biografiia* 35). The idea of distinguishing between the "empirical" and "transcendental" layers in consciousness is one he undoubtedly derived from them. Both philosophers sought to ground the possibility of universally valid knowledge, of ethics, and of religion by positing, behind the empirical subjectivity of the individual, an impersonal, supra-individual consciousness in which the individual in some way "participated." The prototypes of the "transcendental self" of Frank's 1904 article are the "absolute ego" of Fichte and the "normative consciousness" of Windelband (Swoboda 385–87).

In "On Critical Idealism," Frank made no effort to conceal what attracted him about the doctrine of the twofold self. It enabled him, first, to justify a belief in the infinite value of the individual personality. The individual is of infinite worth because he is the point of tangency between the empirical world and the "transcendental self" that is the repository of all value ("O kriticheskom idealizme" 261). But, what was equally important to him, the doctrine exalted the individual precisely as the creator of culture, as the instrument through which "spirit" imposes ideal values on empirical reality (258–61). The doctrine thus gave philosophical sanction to his struggle to redirect the attention of the Russian intelligentsia from political tasks to cultural ones—a struggle that absorbed the greater part of his energies as a publicist from 1903 to at least 1910.

Indeed, Frank never ceased to champion either the principle of individuality or the belief that man's highest calling is cultural creation. In his late writings, he invariably presents the doctrine of Godmanhood as involving an assertion of man's *"eternal aristocratic dignity"* (*Light* 66, emphasis in original; cf. *God with Us* 154–59). And nowhere does he glorify man's creative powers more eloquently than in his last book, *Reality and Man* (153–61). When he states in this volume that "It is as a creator that man is most conscious of himself as 'the image and likeness of God'" (156), he is giving voice to a lifelong conviction.

There are, to be sure, significant differences between the philosophical opinions Frank held in 1904 and those he defended in his mature books. By the time Frank wrote *Man's Soul* and his major émigré treatises, he had come to reject the epistemological presuppositions of post-Kantian idealism in favor of an intuitivist theory of knowledge. Consciousness had ceased to represent for him the ultimate reality; its place was taken by being. This change compelled him to reformulate his view of the twofold inner structure of man's selfhood in ontological terms. "Spiritual life" or "Godmanhood" became a mode of being rather than merely a mode of consciousness. Yet Frank's abandonment of the idealist epistemology did not require him to modify his conception of what it implied, in concrete terms, to define man as the point of juncture between the realm of empirical reality and the realm of spirit.

When Frank, in his late writings, made allusion to the doctrine of deification, it is the doctrine of the Eastern Fathers of the Church, and not anything more recent, that he had in view (see, e.g., *Reality* 141).

He would appear to have owed his knowledge of patristic teaching primarily to the now-classic account of it written by his personal friend Myrrha Lot-Borodine, originally published in 1932–33 as a series of articles in the *Revue d'histoire des religions*.[3] Lot-Borodine quite justly emphasizes the intimate linkage between the Fathers' thinking about deification and their ascetic spirituality; this probably helped encourage Frank to describe the doctrine of deification as a product of "the mysticism of the Eastern Orthodox Church" (*Unknowable* 258; cf. 236), rather than of Orthodox *theology*. But whereas Lot-Borodine takes it for granted that theology and "mysticism" are inseparable facets of a single body of patristic thought, Frank conceives "mysticism" as the "highest potency" of both theology *and philosophy*: "in speculative religious mysticism," he writes, "[the] concrete-positive revelation" that is the object of theology, and the "general, eternal revelation" that is the object of philosophy, "merge into inseparable unity" (*Unknowable* 235–36). The effect of Frank's defining the doctrine of deification as a "mystical" teaching is to lift it out of the sphere proper to mere theology so as to permit him to lay claim, in the name of philosophy, to its "mystical" content, while leaving open to him the option of modifying or rejecting the *theological* content which, in the thought of the Greek Fathers, forms a no less integral part of the doctrine.

The Eastern Fathers conceived man's supreme end as his participation, through grace, in the uncreated "energies" of God. Man is to be deified: without ceasing to be fully human, he is destined to become, in a true though derivative manner, divine. This is an end that accords with the nature of man as God created him; Eastern patristic theology took a very exalted view of man's "natural" constitution, contrasting, in this respect, with most Western theology, which since Augustine has been prone to see eternal beatitude as an end appointed by God for a creature whose nature is not intrinsically oriented to such a fulfillment (Lot-Borodine 50–51). Yet however glorious man's natural potentialities may have been when he was created, the Fall had the effect of incapacitating him from achieving the destiny he had been assigned in the scheme of creation. The purpose of the Incarnation was to restore to man the possibility of realizing his true end. The Incarnation, uniting in a single *hypostasis* the divine nature of the Logos and a full and complete human nature, communicated the properties of the former to the latter, thereby deifying the humanity of Christ. The salvation of man comes about by his sharing, through sacrament and prayer, in the deified humanity of the Incarnate Logos.[4]

Two points stand out in this necessarily superficial summary of the patristic doctrine of deification. The first is the complete logical dependence of this doctrine on the theology of the Incarnation worked out by Athanasius, the Cappadocians, Cyril of Alexandria, and others, and confirmed by the authority of the ecumenical councils, particularly Ephesus and Chalcedon. "For Maximus [the Confessor]," writes Lars Thunberg, speaking of the seventh-century theologian generally agreed to have given the doctrine its classic formulation, "the doctrinal basis of man's deification is clearly to be found in the hypostatic unity between the divine and human nature in Christ" (457). The second is the doctrine's temporal dimension: one cannot summarize the doctrine without relating it to events occurring in time—Creation, Fall, Incarnation.

The relevance of the first of these observations to our current inquiry is obvious: to determine whether or not Frank's conception of Godmanhood is really akin to the patristic doctrine of deification, we must focus on the passages in his writings in which he seeks to relate his view of man as the "incarnation" of absolute "spirit" to the theology of the Incarnation of the Word; in which he discusses the connection between the compresence of divine and human elements in human nature, and the hypostatic union in Christ. Now, in several of these passages, we encounter at least one striking divergence between Frank's ideas and those of the Eastern Fathers. For the latter, it is the Incarnation, and it alone, that makes possible the union of man's nature with God's energies by grace in which deification consists. The logical priority belongs to the hypostatic union. For Frank, however, the relation is reversed. Frank willingly acknowledges that there is something "unique" and "miraculous" about the hypostatic union (*God with Us* 161; *Reality* 139). Yet the latter appears to be nothing but a preeminent exemplar of a union of divine and human being that is characteristic of man's nature as such. Human "Godmanhood," Frank suggests, is logically prior to the union of divine and human natures in Christ. This view is expressed with particular clarity in a passage of *Reality and Man*:

Deeper metaphysical reflection shows that in spite of the immeasurable difference between the average man and the God-man Jesus Christ, something "divinely-human" is inherent in man's being as such; there is potentially present in it a certain divine element as its immanent constitutive principle. Far from conflicting with the Church doctrine of the Incarnation, it is its necessary precondition: awareness of the potential divine-humanity of man as such reveals the metaphysical perspective in which the perfect Incarnation, without ceasing to be miraculous, loses its arbitrary character and fits in with the general meaning of human life and nature. (140–41)

There is a certain sense in which the Eastern Fathers would have agreed with Frank that the Incarnation must be seen in the wider perspective of an anthropology, a general doctrine of man, in order for its "fittingness" and full significance to be grasped. They themselves underscored the complementarity of creation and restoration: in the Incarnation, the Logos came to the rescue of a humanity that he created in his own "image," as "rational" (*logikos*) (Lot-Borodine 41, 44). Yet the materials from which the Fathers built up this anthropological context were the data of scriptural revelation: the first three chapters of Genesis and the commentary on them contained in other books of the Bible. The perspective in which they viewed the Incarnation was, in a word, *theological*, not "metaphysical." What Frank means when he speaks of seeing the Incarnation in a "metaphysical perspective" is clearly something very different: he means viewing it in the context of an anthropology resting on universal human experience. But if universal human experience—which can only be, on a Christian view, the experience of fallen man—reveals that "a divine element" is already "potentially present" in man's being, does this not *magnify* the "arbitrariness" of the Incarnation, by casting doubt on whether the latter was really *necessary*? For the Fathers, there could be no doubt of the "*nécessité absolue du Verbe fait chair et venu à nous* propter nostram salutem" (Lot-Borodine 53–54) precisely because the coming of the Word was a response to the corruption suffered by man's "nature" as a result of the Fall, the effects of which were felt above all by his intellect (*nous*), the very repository of the divine "image" in him (Lot-Borodine 43–44, 47–49).[5]

It is hardly surprising, given Frank's sense of the logical priority of "Godmanhood" to the "God-man," that his disquisitions on the purposes of the Incarnation tend to stress its educative function: Christ manifests, in a superlative degree, what all men are, in order to waken them to knowledge of themselves. This approach is best exemplified in *The Light Shineth in Darkness* (68–70), where it also shapes Frank's presentation of Christianity as "gospel," as the "good news." Frank identifies the fundamental content of the "good news" as something that has reference first of all to us, and only secondarily to the person of Christ. He writes: "The good news is news of *the Godsonhood of man or* (what is the same thing) *of the Divine-human ground of human existence.* We leave aside for the moment the significance of the person of Jesus Christ in this connection; for—in the plane not of theological theory but of our religious experience, our living knowledge—this significance derives from the general meaning of the good news" (*Light* 63; emphasis in original). To be sure, Christ's significance is not, in Frank's view, exhausted by his role as revealer of our potential divinity. On the contrary, he pours out upon us the "spiritual forces" that alone render us capable of actualizing our "Godsonhood" (*Light* 70–71). But if Frank does, both here and elsewhere, acknowledge Christ as the source of a grace indispensable to our salvation, in none of his last four books does he ever explicitly affirm, with the Fathers, that Christ's unique power to help us is the consequence of the union of divine and human natures in his person.[6]

The last passage I will consider illustrates better than any other I have found the gulf between Frank's conception of Godmanhood and the patristic doctrine of deification. Toward the end of *The Unknowable,* Frank writes:

> We already know that the way from me to God passes through spiritual life, through the domain of the spirit. . . . [T]his domain is the "roots" of my self-being, which imperceptibly merge with the "soil" in which they are anchored. . . . But insofar as God appears to me as the end point on the path through the domain of spiritual life and therefore belongs to this domain in some way, it follows that the revelation of God as "Thou" . . . is complemented by another, much more immanent form of being which we can call "God-in-me" or "I-in-God." . . . We have already mentioned that the "Thou art" of God is the foundation of "I am." But this leads us to the fact that God's "art" is in a certain sense already contained in the depths of my own "am," or that my "am" is somehow rooted in the "am" of God Himself. . . . This relationship (at the highest and most explicit level of its revelation) is recognized by the mysticism of the Eastern Orthodox Church as the "deification" of man. In its *general* form this consciousness of the inner unity of man and God can be called the "God-man" being of man. (257–58; emphasis in original)

What is most striking about this passage is Frank's obliviousness of the fact that the patristic term "deification" (*theosis, theopoiesis*) is a verbal noun, and hence descriptive of a process, or of the result of a process, but not of an eternal *relationship*. When the Eastern Fathers discussed the "deification" of man, they started from the premise that man, in his fallen condition, is not inwardly united with God; on the contrary, he is alienated from God, and deprived of the ability to realize his "natural" end, participation in the divine life by grace. For Frank, however, "Godmanhood" is a "given" of human existence as such, an ontological relationship that cannot be canceled by anything man does or fails to do. "Man is a being rooted in superhuman soil. . . . He is this kind of being whether he likes it or not" (*Unknowable* 259). It was impossible for Frank to conceive it otherwise, given his unyielding conviction that man's "rootedness in God" is an ever-present reality, manifesting itself in the whole range of activities that make up human culture.

To assert that every human being, regardless of his character or acts, is grounded in divine reality did not imply, for Frank, a denial of the power of sin in human affairs, or of the possibility that this or that particular individual might never, over the course of an entire lifetime, make contact with the more profound strata of spiritual being. Yet there is a sense in which, for Frank, the divine element in human nature makes itself effective in every human life, however undistinguished that life may appear to be. No human being fails to attain to the dignity of "personhood"; none of us remains wholly submerged in the element of pure potentiality that is the essence of psychic being as such: simply by living and acting in the world, we impose some kind of form on this formless potentiality, and we accomplish this by summoning forth the powers of spirit to penetrate and organize the restless activity of the soul (*Unknowable* 174). The means to the achievement of a sanctifed human life accordingly do not differ in essence from the means by which we achieve a life that is merely human (*Unknowable* 259). The true Christian, the saint, differs from the common man only in the extent to which, in freedom, he opens himself up to the action of the "gracious powers of salvation" (*Light* 121) that emerge from the ultimate depths of his being, from below the threshold of his singular human existence, and allows these forces to direct his thoughts and deeds.

The full actualization of man's potential divine-humanity through the attainment of an existence illuminated by divine truth is thus, like deification, a process involving man's collaboration with divine grace. Yet if, for Frank, the divinization of man is a task to be achieved in each individual self, this achievement takes place within the unchanging framework of man's eternal ontological relationship with the divine. Frank resists the idea that the mighty acts of God in history—above all, the Incarnation of the Word—can alter and have altered the very terms of man's relationship with his creator; that the free act of the Second Person of the Trinity in taking on a perfect and complete human nature has opened up possibilities for man unavailable to him since the Fall. Frank's claim, put forward in the above-cited passage from *The Unknowable*, that the doctrines of deification and Godmanhood are equivalent, can be accepted only if we also accept the view that the historicity of the Christian revelation is wholly incidental to its meaning—a view I find it impossible to ascribe to the Greek Fathers themselves. Yet for Frank to have given full weight to the historical dimension of patristic thought would have entailed his submitting himself, as a philosopher, to the authority of a historical revelation. It would have required him, in other words, to accept the primacy of theology over philosophy. Only by disregarding the theological premises of the patristic doctrine of deification could Frank uphold the pretensions of speculative philosophy to offer an *independent* witness to man's potential for divinization.

Notes

1. See, for example, the articles "O svobodnoi sovesti," "Kul'tura i religiia," "Preodolenie tragedii" (*Filosofiia* 312–20), and "Budushchnost' religii" (*Filosofiia* 321–27).

2. Swoboda 383 n. 129. On the general topic of Fichte's influence on Frank, see Swoboda 246–48, 363–69, 376–77.

3. In a footnote to *The Light Shineth in Darkness* (67), Frank notes that he owes to Lot-Borodine's writings his awareness of the difference between the pessimistic theological anthropology of the Western Church and the anthropology of "the Eastern church, which still remembers the original meaning of the kinship between man and God. " The reference here is almost certainly to her articles of the 1930s, later collected and republished as *La déification de l'homme.*

4. In composing this brief summary of the patristic doctrine of deification, I relied particularly on Meyendorff, *Byzantine Theology* (esp. 163–64, but also chaps. 10–13 passim); Thunberg (454–9), and Lot-Borodine (40–66 and passim). These books, along with those of Pelikan and Burghardt, were also of much assistance to me as I wrote other portions of this chapter.

5. One might also ask whether that aspect of the Incarnation that Frank calls its "arbitrary character" is something against which the intelligence of an Orthodox believer ought necessarily to revolt. Does not the Orthodox Church, in its liturgy, proclaim its own astonishment and that of the entire cosmos in the face of God's appearance in the flesh, exulting in the Incarnation precisely as a manifestation of a gracious loving-kindness wholly surpassing human expectation or desert? See, e.g., *Festal Menaion* 204 (canticle 1), 205 (canticle 3), 208 (canticle 8), 238 (stichera). Many other similar examples might doubtless be found.

6. He comes closest to doing so in *God with Us* (161), where he calls Christ "the new and perfect progenitor of man's true nature." But he seems to me to undercut the force of this when he says, a few sentences later: "The Godmanhood of Christ is the realization of a possibility latent in man's being. It is not an abstract possibility, incapable of concrete realization in anyone else."

Works Cited

Burghardt, Walter J., S.J. *The Image of God in Man According to Cyril of Alexandria.* Woodstock, Md.: Woodstock College Press, 1957.

The Festal Menaion. Trans. Mother Mary and Archimandrite Kallistos Ware. London: Faber & Faber, 1969.

Frank, S. L. *Biografiia P. B. Struve.* New York: Chekhov, 1956.

Frank, S. L. *Dusha cheloveka: Opyt vvedeniia v filosofskuiu psikhologiiu.* 2d ed. Paris: YMCA Press, 1964.

Frank, S. L. *Filosofiia i zhizn': Etiudy i nabroski po filosofii kul'tury.* St. Petersburg: Izdanie D. E. Zhukovskogo, 1910.

Frank, S. L. *God with Us: Three Meditations.* Trans. Natalie Duddington. New Haven: Yale University Press, 1946.

Frank, S. L. *Krushenie kumirov*. Berlin: YMCA Press, 1924.

Frank, S. L. "Kultura i religiia (Po povodu novoi knigi D. S. Merezhkovskogo)." *Poliarnaia zvezda* 12 (March 5, 1906): 46–54.

Frank, S. L. *The Light Shineth in Darkness: An Essay in Christian Ethics and Social Philosophy*. Trans. Boris Jakim. Athens: Ohio University Press, 1989.

Frank, S. L. "O kriticheskom idealizme." *Mir Bozhii* (Dec. 1904): 224–64.

Frank, S. L. "O svobodnoi sovesti." *Poliarnaia zvezda* 6 (Jan. 19, 1906): 413–19.

Frank, S. L. *Predmet znaniia: Ob osnovakh i predelakh otvlechennogo znaniia*. Petrograd, 1915; rpt., Paris: YMCA Press, 1974.

Frank, S. L. *Reality and Man: An Essay in the Metaphysics of Human Nature*. Trans. Natalie Duddington. New York: Taplinger, 1966.

Frank, S. L. *The Unknowable: An Ontological Introduction to the Philosophy of Religion*. Trans. Boris Jakim. Athens: Ohio University Press, 1983.

Lot-Borodine, M[yrrha]. *La déification de l'homme selon la doctrine des Pères grecs*. Paris: Cerf, 1970.

Meyendorff, John. *Byzantine Theology: Historical Trends and Doctrinal Themes*. New York: Fordham University Press, 1979.

Meyendorff, John. *Christ in Eastern Christian Thought*. N.p.: St. Vladimir's Seminary Press, 1975.

Pelikan, Jaroslav. *The Christian Tradition: A History of the Development of Doctrine*, vol 1: *The Emergence of the Catholic Tradition (100–600)*. Chicago: University of Chicago Press, 1971.

Sbornik pamiati Semëna Liudvigovicha Franka. Ed. V. V. Zen'kovskii. Munich: n.p., 1954.

Swoboda, Philip James. "The Philosophical Thought of S. L. Frank, 1902–1915: A Study of the Metaphysical Impulse in Early Twentieth-Century Russia." Ph.D. diss. Columbia University 1992.

Thunberg, Lars. *Microcosm and Mediator: The Theological Anthropology of Maximus the Confessor*. Lund: Gleerup, 1965.

Afterword
Religious Philosophy in Russian Culture Today

James Scanlan

The Russian philosophers of the past whose thought has been examined in this volume do not belong only to the past. Although long dead they are not museum figures, for in the present day they have emerged as living voices in one of the greatest acts of intellectual recovery the modern world has seen—the rebirth of Russia's religious philosophical tradition following the collapse of the Communist system. Not since Europe reclaimed its classical heritage after the Dark Ages has there been so notable a return to an earlier and richer store of philosophical wealth. And never has a philosophical renaissance proceeded with such explosive speed, thanks to modern technologies of publication and communication.

Bulgakov, Florensky, Frank, and Soloviev speak to their countrymen today through reprints of writings that were banned in their homeland during the long darkness of Soviet rule—writings originally published either before the Russian Revolution or outside Russia, mostly in Paris by a press established by the Young Men's Christian Association of North America. (The YMCA Press was an unlikely successor to the Irish monks who kept much classical literature safe for the Renaissance, but it performed a parallel and praiseworthy service.) Their writings are widely available in Russia today, and they find throngs of receptive readers. They also elicit lively response in the form of expositions, appreciations, analyses, critiques, conferences, lectures, symposia, anniversary celebrations, and societies of admirers. The non-Marxist Russian philosophers have come home again, to a public eager to honor them and to hear their message, late though it be.

The return of Russian religious philosophy has brought undoubted benefits to post-Soviet Russian culture. For one thing, it has served simple historical justice by filling a huge gap in Russians' knowledge of their own intellectual history. Under Soviet rule, readers were officially confined to the Marxist-Leninist version of that history, in accordance with which every philosopher who could not be distorted into a materialist precursor of Marx was dismissed as unworthy of serious attention. Soviet citizens (aside from a few trusted "specialists") were given no opportunity to study the ideas of a prerevolutionary thinker as important as Soloviev, perhaps the most talented and stimulating of all Russian philosophers. They did not know that Bulgakov and Frank, along with a great many other non-Marxist Russian thinkers, were forcibly exiled by Lenin in 1922 and prohibited from returning on pain of death; if they saw references to those thinkers, it was only in the context of the "emigration" of certain reactionary and obscurantist enemies of the proletariat. They did not know that Florensky, who stayed behind, had been shot in a prison camp in 1937, or why he had been shot. They did not know in what directions Russian philosophy had been developed in emigration by Berdiaev, Bulgakov, Frank, and others, or even that there had been any such development. The filling of this void marks a great step forward in the ability of Russians to understand their own philosophical past.

In addition to its historical contributions, the reintroduction of non-Marxist Russian philosophy has greatly benefited Russian philosophical culture by providing it with paradigms of excellence—that is, by presenting readers with works of far higher philosophical quality than their standard Soviet fare, quite apart from the question of doctrinal content. When philosophy in Russia was confined to the Marxist canon with Leninist glosses, its vocabulary was impoverished and fixed: a small set of prescribed terms and phrases sufficed to say everything that needed saying, and to say anything more was fraught with danger. The lexicon of Russian religious philosophy, on the other hand—as the reader of this volume will have discovered—is not only different but incomparably richer, opening up far more possibilities for philosophical expression. The same is true of philosophical argumentation. Under Soviet rule, Russian philosophers relied heavily on the argument from authority; hence the prevalence of *tsitatstvo*—citationism, or the marshaling of quotations from Marxist scripture to support one's point. Although the Russian religious philosophers might have been expected to rely at least as much on a canon, typically they did not: their argumentation, like their vocabulary, was diverse and philosophically productive; Bulgakov and Frank, in particular, were dedicated to finding philosophical substantiation of their views independent of scriptural dogma. Perhaps the fundamental stylistic advantage of the religious philosophers stems from the fact that, unlike the Marxist-Leninists, they did not assume that all philosophical truth is already known or that it is the common and transparently clear possession of a particular group of people. For the Marxist-Leninist, individual speculation was as egregious an offense in the philosophical sphere as it was in the economic. The religious philosophers, with their free explorations and imaginative formulations, thus bring to the Russian philosophical world a new model—the philosopher in the original sense of a seeker rather than a mere keeper of truth.

What does the specific content of Russian religious philosophy contribute to Russian culture today? Above all, knowledge of an entire philosophical orientation—in broadest compass, religious idealism—that was systematically rooted out during the decades of Communist domination. In a sense, post-Soviet Russian philosophers are recreating the experience of the late-eighteenth-and early-nineteenth-century founders of Russian philosophy, who were reacting to systems of thought that came to them intact from foreign sources—first French Enlightenment thought, then German Romanticism and idealism, eventually French and German materialism. The comparable process of importation today differs only in that the systems coming to fill the existing philosophical void are no longer "foreign" but a product of Russia's own past—although this past was itself heavily indebted to earlier *Western* philosophical and theological doctrines, from those of the Church Fathers and Christian Gnostics to Schelling and Hegel, as the authors of the essays in this volume have amply demonstrated. In that sense much Western thinking, too, outlawed by Communism, is once again having an impact in Russia, through its reflection in Russian religious philosophies.

These philosophies, moreover, have a uniquely intimate relation to two of the greatest manifestations of the country's culture—Russian literature and the Russian Orthodox faith. No reader of Bulgakov, Florensky, Frank, or Soloviev can fail to see the myriad linkages of their philosophizing and their faith; much of this volume has been devoted to those linkages—above all, to the philosophical aspects of the central Orthodox doctrines of the Incarnation and Deification, but ranging more widely to an understanding of the sources and traits of Orthodox spirituality in general. Moreover, the frequency with which the names of Dostoevsky, Tolstoy, and other Russian writers are found in works by and about these religious philosophers demonstrates the extent to which the latter' s thinking resonated with the concerns and assumptions of Russian literary creativity as well. Although neither Russian literature nor Russian Orthodoxy was suppressed to the full extent that Russian religious philosophy was during the Soviet era, each was compelled to exist in a conceptual vacuum that deprived it of its proper philosophical grounding and implications. The restoration of the philosophical dimension of these cultural enterprises makes possible once more the rich symbiosis that lay at the root of Russia's "Silver Age" before the Bolshevik revolution.

A final and very specific contribution of these Russian religious thinkers to recent Russian intellectual life, though one largely beyond the purview of the present volume, is that they produced trenchant critiques of Marxism and of Bolshevik rule. Some of them (Bulgakov, for one) had been Marxists themselves, but had foreseen early in the twentieth century the dangers inherent in the Bolshevik system. Others, though not so prophetic, were able to follow and critically analyze the unfolding Soviet experience from the outside (but with an insider's sympathies) in a way not possible for those caught up in it. Together, these early and later Russian critics of Soviet Marxism created a literature that could explain to Russian readers of the glasnost era and beyond just what had gone wrong in their society. For interested Soviet readers, the sophisticated critiques of Marxism offered by the religious philosophers were one of the main attractions of their writings. Much of the case against Marxism as it is formulated in Russia today consists of arguments originally advanced by Bulgakov, Berdiaev, and other representatives of Russian religious idealism.

For all its obvious cultural benefits, however, the post-Soviet renaissance of Russian religious philosophy is not without its problems. The welcome accorded the rediscovered idealist thinkers has been accompanied in their homeland by extravagant expectations and dubious claims that reflect some disturbing features of the current Russian philosophical scene. Three such features stand out.

The first is the continuing lure of utopianism. The utopian temptation has a long history in Russia, but one might have thought that the utter failure of the Marxist utopia would put an end at last to this particular species of enchantment. Instead, for many Russians it sparked a search for a new utopia. The visions of the religious philosophers, themselves not immune from Elysian hopes though having so much else to offer, were the obvious candidates, all the more attractive for their native pedigree in contrast to imported Marxism. The initial popularity of the idealist philosophers was heavily fueled by expectations of a magical remaking of Russian life, whereby a figure like Bulgakov or

Florensky would assume the mantle of Marx and Lenin and Russian society would be reorganized on spiritual lines. When society was not immediately transformed, disillusion set in, and ardor for the religious alternative somewhat cooled. Nonetheless there is still a pronounced tendency, particularly among the national-patriotic and other extremist movements, to view the religious philosophies as blueprints for national salvation and to promote them as simple sociocultural panaceas rather than the demanding philosophical and spiritual quests that they are. Accordingly, much of the Russian acquaintance with them today is regrettably superficial, devoid of close or critical study of their actual philosophical content.

A second questionable feature of the current vogue of religious philosophy in Russia is the role played by nostalgia—nostalgia for a Russia that existed before the Revolution, before the terrible deformation of Russian culture by triumphant Bolshevism. There is a longing to return to the condition preceding the Communist "interruption" and reattach oneself to the religious tradition in philosophy that was linked with Russian Orthodoxy. An unspoken argument in much of the current discussion of Russia's philosophical heritage is that because the religious philosophy was an organic product of an earlier Russian Orthodox culture, it is what Russia needs now. How defensible is this argument?

From a logical point of view it is simply a non sequitur. It ignores the malleability of culture and assumes without justification that the future should resemble the past. The argument would carry some weight if Russian culture in the present day were still somehow suffused with Orthodoxy, but that is no longer easy to maintain. Some have questioned whether Russian culture was saturated with the Orthodox spirit even in the nineteenth and early twentieth centuries; be that as it may, there is still less evidence that it is so saturated today. Modernization, industrialization, and urbanization have wrought their familiar work in Russian society, cruelly heightened and accelerated for almost three-quarters of a century by the special circumstances of collectivization as Lenin and Stalin understood it. What once was a predominantly religious culture now looks more like a predominantly secular culture. "Godless Communism" appears to have been replaced in Russia by Godless capitalism, despite the relative revivification of the Orthodox Church and the lively interest in Russian religious philosophy among many intellectuals.

Hence if the cultural significance of philosophy in Russia is examined in the light of its appropriateness to Russian culture today, rather than in the distant past, the fact that Russia has an Orthodox religious philosophical tradition has only limited relevance. The Russia of today is not the Russia of Soloviev and Florensky, much less the Russia of the original Slavophiles. For that reason we may wonder whether a sufficient demographic base exists for a socially significant rebirth of religious spirituality in Russian philosophical thought.

Such doubts would be angrily dismissed by today's zealous Russian champions of the Orthodox religious tradition, who see the cultural changes induced by Communism as challenges to be met rather than as facts demanding acquiescence. This secularization can and should be reversed, they would say, in order to restore the dominance of the religious philosophy that is uniquely suited to Russian history and the Russian national character.

This introduces my third and final misgiving about the present vogue of the Orthodox religious tradition in Russian philosophy: that vogue is rooted at least in part in what I should like to call the myth of "one culture, one philosophy." That is, its extremist proponents assume that for every national culture there exists a distinctive philosophy that is appropriate and adequate to that culture—a coherent set of ideas that uniquely articulates the essence of the culture and nurtures it. Hence they strive to locate in Russia a philosophy that is historically rooted in Russian culture and thus supposedly is best attuned to it. The power of this myth is discernible today in the often-encountered call for something to "fill the philosophical vacuum" left by the demise of Marxism-Leninism, as if some other single outlook must occupy the place of the ideology that held a monopoly before. Indeed, more and more frequently we encounter calls for the establishment of a new official state ideology in Russia.

I refer to the idea of "one culture, one philosophy" as a myth because I see no reason for there to be a single philosophical expression of any culture, and no possibility of establishing one without resorting to an authoritarianism that would end by crippling the culture it was designed to advance. A highly developed human culture such as Russia's, with a complex language, a rich literature, and a long history, is a treasure house that transcends any philosophy. No one "coherent" set of principles and concepts can do justice to the multiform experience of such a culture— religious, scientific, social, artistic, and much more.

The religious philosophical tradition based on Russian Orthodoxy has produced a great many distinguished thinkers, including those considered in the present volume. But to regard it as exhausting Russia's entire philosophical heritage is to leave out an enormous wealth of philosophical creativity that is an integral part of Russia's intellectual history. It omits the Enlightenment thinkers of the time of Catherine the Great, such as Aleksandr Radishchev; it ignores the "Westernizing" philosophers who were the Slavophiles' nineteenth-century opponents, including Aleksandr Herzen and Nikolai Chernyshevsky; it overlooks the Russian neo-Leibnizians Aleksei Kozlov and Lev Lopatin, whose metaphysical and ethical personalism had little in common with Russian Orthodox thinking. It includes only tangentially the towering figure of Lev Tolstoy, whose anti-ecclesiastical Christian anarchism was more Protestant than Orthodox in inspiration (and who was in fact excommunicated by the Russian Orthodox Church). And it largely omits the Russian liberal philosophers whose work on the foundations of constitutionalism and civil society, so needed by Russia today, was not directly connected with their Christian metaphysics. In sum, Russia's philosophical heritage is broader than even the great Orthodox religious tradition within it, and all its diverse elements are integral components of "Russian philosophy."

When calls are made in Russia today for a "national philosophy" that will "satisfy the spiritual requirements of its people," the request is for an impossibility; a philosophy can at best respond to only a fraction of a people's spiritual requirements. If some one set of ideas did effectively "fill the vacuum" left by Marxism-Leninism, no matter how seemingly appropriate to Russian life those ideas might be, we could expect the same unfortunate consequences as when Marxism filled the vacuum created by the destruction of the old order in 1917. The only way in which a philosophy can genuinely and productively be "appropriate" to the spiritual requirements of a great nation (especially a multi-ethnic and multireligious nation like Russia) is by recognizing that it captures a necessarily limited range of that nation's cultural possibilities and must leave room for other philosophies.

The philosophers considered in this volume are not themselves responsible, of course, for the utopian, nostalgic, or exclusivist uses to which they are often put in today's troubled Russian intellectual atmosphere. They offered neither easy salvation nor a return to a Golden Age, and they did not claim to speak for all Russians. They were engaged in exploring philosophical and theological aspects of a great religious tradition, not in rescuing a disoriented post-Soviet society from a crisis of identity. The fact that they are popular in their homeland today partly because of the need of present-day Russians for reconnection with their heritage, and for new guideposts in a time of change, should not impel us to read these philosophers exclusively in that light. The best corrective for the latter impulse is the serious study of their views in the context of their own timeless concerns—not of our topical concerns, Russian or Western, at the end of the twentieth century. Both in Russia and beyond, a genuine understanding of these thinkers in their own terms is the true philosophical benefit to be gained from their rediscovery.

Index

Index

Abelard, Peter, 35
Absolute, the: deification and, 38; antinomy of, 147; Spirit, 149; Subject, 147, 149; Consciousness, 149; mentioned, 32, 225, 237
Achamoth, 59, 61, 65
Actus purissimus, 149
Actus purus, 146–47
Adam: 167; and Eve, 33, 160, 170–71
Aeon, 56–57, 62
Agathon, 72
Akhmatova, Anna, 113
Albert the Great, 126
Aletheia, the, 56
Alexander I, 8
Alexander II, 28
Alexander III, 28
Allen, Paul M., 52
All-unity. *See Vseedinstvo*
Anima Mundi, the, 59, 62. *See also* World Soul, the
Annensky, Innokenty, 112
Anselm, Saint, 35; *Cur Deus Homo?*, 34
Anthropos, 56
Anthroposophy, 53, 63
Antichrist, the, 13, 70, 75, 79, 81, 183–84
Antony, Vladyka, 128
Aquinas, Saint Thomas, 6
Apocalypse: idea of, 13; Soloviev's story of, 69–70
Aristophanes, 72
Aristotle, 6, 8, 119
Arnold, Gottfried: *Geheimnisse der göttlichen Sophia*, 52
Askol'dov, Sergei, 143, 151n7
Athanasius the Great, Saint, 6, 34, 38, 68, 243

Augustine, Saint, 6, 39, 125, 242

Baehr, Stephen, 15, 22, 128, 130n14
Bakhtin, Mikhail, 14, 17, 121, 143, 150–51n8
Bal'mont, Konstantin, 112
Balthasar, Hans Urs von, 12, 45
Baltrushaitis, Iu. K., 112
Bartseva, Tat'iana (wife of S. L. Frank), 196
Bary, Beatrice de, 11–12, 19, 23
Basil the Great, Saint, 6, 34, 143. *See also* Cappadocians, the
Belinsky, Vissarion, 9, 220
Belyi, Andrei (Bugaev, B. N.), 52, 59, 63, 65n6, 70, 91, 97, 113; "Adam," 63; *First Symphony*, 63; *Silver Dove*, 63, 66n11
Berdiaev, Nikolai, 5, 10, 136, 142, 149, 167, 169, 200–201, 214, 228n3, 250, 252; *Meaning of the Creative Act*, 174n9; *Two Types of Worldviews*, 201
Bethea, David M., 15, 21
Bible: as Good News, 6, 244; Proverbs in, 13; Revelations in, 79; as Torah, 82; Philippians in, 95, 103; Genesis in, 100, 169–70, 244
Blavatsky, H. P., 52–53; *Secret Doctrine*, 52
Bloch, Howard R.: *Medieval Misogyny, 171*
Blok, Aleksandr, 59, 63, 65n6, 70, 112, 162; "Beautiful Lady" (*Prekrasnaia dama*), 63; "Ravenna," 128n1; "Stranger, The" (*Neznakomka*), 63
Blok, Liubov' Dmitrievna, 59
Boehme, Jakob, 52, 64, 164, 169, 170
Boff, Leonardo, 150
Bogochelovechestvo (Godmanhood, humanity of God), 11, 13, 17–18, 20, 31, 36, 39, 42, 45–46, 60–61, 64, 68–69, 73, 75,